WICCA
COVENS

WICCA COVENS

~

HOW TO START AND ORGANIZE YOUR OWN

Judy Harrow

A CITADEL PRESS BOOK
Published by Carol Publishing Group

A Citadel Press Book
Published by Carol Publishing Group
Citadel Press is a registered trademark of Carol Communications, Inc.

Editorial, sales and distribution, rights and permissions inquiries should be addressed to Carol Publishing Group, 120 Enterprise Avenue, Secaucus, N.J. 07094

In Canada: Canadian Manda Group, One Atlantic Avenue, Suite 105, Toronto, Ontario M6K 3E7

Carol Publishing books may be purchased in bulk at special discounts for sales promotion, fund-raising, or educational purposes. Special editions can be created to specifications. For details, contact Special Sales Department, 120 Enterprise Avenue, Secaucus, N.J. 07094.

Manufactured in the United States of America
10 9 8 7 6 5 4 3 2 1

Library of Congress Cataloging-in-Publication Data
Harrow, Judy.
    Wicca Covens : how to start and organize your own / Judy Harrow.
       p.   cm.
    "A Citadel Press book."
    Includes bibliographical references and index.
    ISBN 0-8065-2035-3 (pbk.)
    1. Witchcraft.   2. Covens.   I. Title.
BF1572.C68H37   1999
133.4'3--dc21   98-48167
                                                    CIP

On a sunny afternoon, many years ago, we sat and talked about writing the book we wished we had: a handbook for coven leaders. I took notes and even typed up an outline on an old manual typewriter, which was all I had back then. You got the original and I kept the smudgy, tea-stained carbon copy. But back then, we didn't really know enough to write the book—not about coven leadership, and not about writing books, either. Over the years, my carbon copy got so beat up that I photocopied it, smudges, tea stains, and all. And now I've written the book, but you aren't here to read it.

Still, John Patrick McClimans, this is for you!

Contents

Acknowledgments ix

Introduction xi

1. Starting Points 3

2. Basics of Groupwork 13

3. Gathering in Love and Trust: Choosing to Coven 41

4. Parents, Children, and the Coven: Balancing
   the Needs 66

5. We Call Thy Name: Coven as Worshiping Group 86

6. Change in Accordance With Will: Coven
   as Magical Growth and Support Group 109

7. To Learn In Order to Serve: Coven
   as Training Group 139

8. Spirit in the World of Form: Coven as Task Group 170

9. We Choose Each Other: Coven as Second-Chance
   Family 196

10. Soul Friends: Wiccan Working Partnership 210

11. To See It Grow Tomorrow: A New Coven
    Hives Off 244

12. The Nurturant Matrix: The Coven's External
       Support Systems   259

13. And Yet It Moves: Why Us? Why Now?   269

     Appendix A: Glossary   271
     Appendix B: The Charge of the Goddess   279
     Index   281

Acknowledgments

Thanks to Camp Wel-Met, where I spent six childhood summers learning to love the forest.

Thanks to Western College for Women, and especially to Dr. Joseph Backor, who assigned *The Feminine Mystique* as required reading for our European history class in 1963. Dr. Backor understood very quickly how profoundly that book was to change our lives. Rev. Henry Brockmann, campus minister, who introduced me to liberal theology.

Thanks to Dr. Julius Rosen, director of the masters program in counseling at City College of New York. Julie nurtured and confronted us as we learned how to do those things for others.

Thanks to GBG; to the lineage of faithkeepers between us—Monique, Rosemary, Judy, and Claudia—who passed it along; and to my own teachers—Mary Grace, Gerard, Bruce, and—with all my love, gratitude, and loyalty—Margot.

Thanks to my students and their students, all the amazing, proud, creative people of Proteus who keep our minds young with their questions, arguments, insights, and enthusiasm.

Thanks to the Proteus "Class of '97"—Ben, Charlie, Kirsten, Redleaf, and Renee—for bearing with a stressed-out and absentminded Priestess, and thanks to Alice for constancy and loving support.

Thanks to Moose, who nagged me for years to write a book. Hey Moose, it's your turn now!

Thanks to Chas Clifton, who midwifed my transition from amateur to professional writer, and to Richard Smoley for seconding this.

Thanks to my lifemates, Brian and Gwyneth, and to Robert Francoeur, another kind of faithkeeper, role model, and guide. To Maury and Vivian for the rescue I've never forgotten. To Little Judy for a cup of coffee on Fordham Road.

Thanks to Jennie Dunham, my agent, for presenting me with an irresistible opportunity before I was ready, which is the way of growth.

Thanks to Mike Lewis, my editor, for patience and perspective.

And thanks always to the Earth Mother and the Green Man, and to the Stone Lady who bade me write. This is my prayer of dedication: May this work, and all my work, bring good to many, harm to none, and praise to You!

INTRODUCTION

My name is Judy Harrow. I am a Witch. I am a Witch. I am a Witch. I was initiated into Witchcraft in September 1977, and so I have been thinking, meditating, and dreaming about what it means to be a Witch for more than twenty years. I have also been practicing my Craft all these years, learning by doing, succeeding, and failing. For seventeen of these years I have been High Priestess of Proteus Coven (New York). Proteus is my heartspace, my chosen family, the home of my spirit, and the lived experience from which I write this book.

Traditionally, Witches gather in covens. A coven is a mutually committed, closely bonded, small group of Wiccan initiates. We keep covens small by custom and by preference—the traditional upper limit is thirteen members, but most groups are only about half this size. Covens have no back rows. Every face is visible; every member matters.

Covens serve many functions. We worship with our covens, and regard them as our second-chance families. They are support groups for our magical and spiritual development, and training groups for our future clergy. We sometimes also work with our covenmates on group projects intended to serve the Old Gods, the Pagan community and culture, or our Mother the Earth. Each of these functions is nurtured by, and contributes to, all of the others.

It's hard, then, to know where to start. Coven lore is, by nature, neither linear nor sequential. Each chapter in this book is best understood in the light of many of the other chapters. There are a lot of reasons why this chapter might logically precede or follow that one, but the reasons contradict each other. So please read the chapters in the order of your own need or interest, and revisit them occasionally. Or skip around, if you like—I'll be including lots of cross-referencing. You can also pursue the recommended readings to explore a web of knowledge far larger than could be included here.

In the real world of Wiccan practice, like any other human experience, all knowledge is interconnected, and it ramifies like a green and living tree.

The "W-Words:" Witch, Wiccan, Witchcraft, Wicca

I am a Witch. I am Wiccan. Very recently there have been some attempts to retrofit a distinction between these two words. Some say that *Wicca* refers to those magical and spiritual traditions that are native to the British Isles, while *Witchcraft* includes both the British traditions and similar ones from other areas. Others say that a Wiccan is a member of a religious congregation that is led by an initiated Witch. These proposed distinctions may eventually be useful, but they are still very new. No community consensus has yet developed around either one.

The present use of the word *Wicca* was originally a workaround. Twenty years ago, when I first came into contact with Witchcraft, we were thought of as either Devil worshipers or delusional misfits. To avoid these inaccurate and unpleasant connotations, many of us adopted the original Anglo-Saxon spelling, but not the pronunciation or grammar. In Old English, the double *c* is pronounced "ch" as in cherish, so the pronunciation is "witcha." *Wicce* means a female Witch in Old English. *Wicca* means a male Witch (and yes, there certainly are male Witches). *Wiccan* is the plural, Witches, and *wiccian* is the verb.

Most contemporary Witches pronounce the double *c* in Wicca as a hard *k*, "wikka," so it sounds less like Witch. We use *Wicca* as a collective noun, in place of Witchcraft, referring to what we do. *Wiccan* is used as an adjective, and can denote an individual practitioner. So when I say I am Wiccan, it is the same as saying I am a Witch. I use these two words as I learned them, nearly interchangeably. One is just a bit less confrontive than the other. My choice is based on my mood and my perception of my audience.

When I call myself a Witch, what do I mean? I was taught that Wicca is a religion, the Old Religion of pre-Christian Europe. There's an ongoing debate among Witches about whether our religion survived underground during the long centuries of repression or whether what we are practicing is actually a reconstruction of an interrupted tradition. I suspect that the truth is a little of both. Witches seem to thrive on ambiguity. In any case, however Wicca came to us, we know that it works for us, and this is what really matters.

But after twenty years I no longer think of Wicca as a religion, exactly. Our involvement is far more intense than that of the ordinary church or synagogue member. For us, Witchcraft is not an activity that supports the main events of our lives and helps us stay ethically on track. Instead, it is central, one of our primary commitments, our way of making a difference in the world.

Also, there are several different "Traditions" of Wicca. While these are certainly far more similar than they are different, each has its own particular focus, its liturgical style, its characteristic organizational model, and its boundary-maintaining secrets. More about this later, too.

For these reasons I have come to believe that my *religion* is neo-Paganism. Later on in this book (in chapter 5), I'll describe some of the symbolism and thealogy (the study of Goddesses and of Goddess-oriented religion) of this religion. I perceive Wicca as being a cluster of closely related, committed *religious orders* within the neo-Pagan religious world. In other words, being a Witch is more like being a Franciscan or a Maryknoll than it is like simply being a Catholic. The basic beliefs are the same, but the level of focus and intensity are quite different.

Because Witchcraft is more, demands more, and offers more than simple membership in a religion, covens are much more than tiny churches. Understanding this is key to understanding their great importance and their functional complexity.

WICCA
COVENS

1

Starting Points

The Word "Coven"

Folklore has it that the word *coven* (which almost rhymes with *lovin'*) derives from a mispronunciation of *convent*. Maybe so. The famous "Covent Garden" theater in London was once the site of a community of Catholic sisters. Local dialect dropped the first *n* sound.

But let's go back a few more steps. According to the *American Heritage Dictionary*, *convent* is related to *covenant* (a binding agreement, a compact) and to *convene* (to come together, to assemble formally). All of these are derived from the Latin *convenire*, which means "to come together." So the root understanding of the word *coven* has to do with people coming together in a formal, committed way. A coven is not a changeable gathering of people, no matter how fervently they agree. It isn't an open house. You can count on your covenmates to be there for the long haul, and this is very important. Covens nurture the spiritual and magical growth of their members, and this cannot be done in a session or two.

Like Wicca, *coven* is a word in process. For as long as I can remember, coven members have been called *coveners*. It's logical, then, that a covener is a person who covens. So the noun *coven* seems to be evolving into a verb. Usages like "Alice and Charlie are covening together," or "She wants to coven with Proteus," are increasing. Unlike the distinction between Wicca and Witchcraft, this transition is not being debated, simply adopted. This linguistic evolution makes excellent sense to me—coven is something we do, a choice and an activity, not merely something we passively "belong to."

Why Do We Coven?

CAROL   My coven is like a collective best friend that is willing to give me useful feedback.

Most Witches work in covens most of the time. And it is more work. We have to coordinate schedules, accommodate ourselves to other personalities, abide by decisions and rules we did not make and very often had no say in making. We have to meet standards we did not set. Why bother?

- Some of us believe that religion is about relating, about connection. It is not just a personal journey to the Gods but also an interactive community experience.

- In a good coven we learn how to support each others' inner growth and worthy goals. We learn how to blend our energies. This means that a greater pool of energy is available to each of us for our own purposes.

- The magical worldview of our religion perceives that all things are connected. We can more easily explore a world of interconnection while in connection with other people.

- Working with the same people, in a stable group, develops trust. We learn to count on our covenmates for the challenge and support that are needed for deep mutual spiritual exploration.

- A stable group develops its own shared knowledge base and ways of doing things. Each coven member brings her own lifetime's worth of learning and skill. We all benefit from hearing different viewpoints, learning different techniques. This sharing stimulates further exploration that the coven can do as a team, thus continuing to add to our knowledge resources.

- In addition, many covens have access to the accumulated lore of a lineage or a Tradition. Coven members need not start from scratch.

- Beginners benefit from direct contact with elders. There's excellent information available in books, but none of it can substitute for an experienced and compassionate person observing our work and offering specific feedback and suggestions.

- Elders benefit from direct contact with beginners. Beginners' enthusiasm is refreshing for elders who are becoming jaded. Beginners' "naive" questions are a challenge and a gift to elders who have grown too comfortably set in their ways. Sometimes we need to be reminded that the emperor is nude!

- A coven is a context for moving beyond theory or book-learning to experiential learning, a venue for trying out our ideas, a reality check. The presence of experienced elders makes our experimentation much safer.

Are Covens Obsolete?

RONALD   To suggest that group working is obsolete because there are enough books in the shops is rather like suggesting that nobody needs to travel any more because there are such great travelogues on television.

Lately a scattering of Wiccan voices, mostly from the mercantile end of the Craft, has been busily pronouncing the old-fashioned coven structure dead. Instead of organizing ourselves into our traditional small affinity groups, they say we should become a community of individual free agents. Funny, just when many of our neighbors are restructuring their large congregations into cozier forms: house churches, Christian base communities, Jewish *chavurot*. Could it be that our neighbors are coming to value something we have always enjoyed, just when some of us are trying to "outgrow" it? Or perhaps, as Mark Twain once said, the death rumors have been exaggerated.

ALEXEI   One could then say that the congregational aspects of all the more mainstream religions are also obsolete, that people should be content with buying a few good books on Christianity or Judaism or Buddhism and doing it all inside their heads, without necessarily bothering to meet with anyone else on the same path. This is a morbidly left-brained and naive approach. Religion—all religion, regardless of the particulars of theology—is about relating—to the cosmos in general and to other people in particular. A coven is not just a place where one receives formal instruction: it is where one learns to put it into practice by interaction with other people. It also brings home the understanding that people are not interchangeable but complement each other, that the same information may be assimilated and put to use in radically different ways by different people, and that these differences enrich us and actually enhance our effectiveness when they are brought together around a common purpose. Our diversity *is* our strength, but we have to come together to appreciate our diversity.

Rugged individualism is the Big American Lie. The terrible effects of its pervasive acceptance would fill a very different book. This book is about celebrating health, not diagnosing sickness. The reality is that all *healthy* human life is lived within a complex matrix of relationships: marriage, household, family, and community.

Community is not the same thing as mass or mob. It is anything but a featureless aggregate of interchangeable individuals. True community, like all other living things, has a complex and well-articulated internal structure. It consists not of individuals but of families, congregations, ball teams, neighborhoods, unions, garden clubs, choruses—all those many groups into which people coalesce around different kinds of affinities and common interests. We can only know each other, share our lives, a few at a time. It's so easy, otherwise, to get lost in the sauce.

If this matters for a hobby group, its importance multiplies when people are involved in something difficult or risky. For this reason, back in the days of the peace movement, we were advised to come to demonstrations with small "affinity groups" of our friends: hopefully just someone to pass the time of day with, but also—should there be need, tear gas, or just heat-stroke—someone to look out for you, look after you, be sure that you are okay. For this same reason police work with part-ners, firefighters in small squads. Even the homeless who sleep on park benches look out for one another. If they didn't, they'd die. True loners are rare and pitiable.

Firefighters and cops trust their partners to look out for their physical safety and survival, which are not generally at risk in religious activities, at least not in this century and on this con-tinent (we're lucky that way). Still, hearts, minds, and souls are not trivial issues.

Our neighbors are finding that smaller is better even for basic worship purposes. They'd rather pray where they can see each other's faces, know each other's names. Well, so would I. But that's just the start, because Wiccan covens are not simply places of worship. Our working partners and our covenmates are there with and for us as we sometimes dance and some-times struggle through the processes of personal psychospiritual growth. There are a lot of deep emotional and psychological risks involved. We're going to be trusting our covenmates to be present at some of our most vulnerable moments. For this rea-son alone we should be as careful about whom we bring into our covens as we are about whom we invite to share our homes. This selection process will be explored in depth, from both sides, later in this book (see chapters 3 and 11).

To further complicate the matter, a coven serves apparently contradictory functions as church, seminary, and licensing agency. Again, much more on this later. For now let's just recognize that this confusion can make good grapes taste sour. Covens, we are told, are snooty and elitist. Doesn't everyone have the right to worship? Invidious comparisons are made to some of the more commercial mass Pagan organizations. "They," we are told, "are at least welcoming." Well, yes, and well they should be. They welcome people as consumers, as paying customers. Wal-Mart is welcoming toward customers. The Harvard Divinity School is selective about its next incoming class.

Solitary Witches

Contrary to popular belief, you certainly can be a Witch alone. Given the mobility of modern life, many are. Things change. Covens break up. People move across the country for new jobs or new marriages. Many coven-trained Witches find themselves without a coven for some periods of their lives. Some people become interested in the Old Ways while living in rural areas where there are no covens yet, or where the local group is very, very discreet.

The Gods are not limited by human-made rules or institutional structures. They may well choose to accept an individual's self-dedication and provide life experiences that are in some ways parallel to coven initiations. The person may be learning what he needs to know about human bonding and teamwork in some other aspect of his life.

With all respect to my solitary sisters and brothers, I cannot tell their story. My entire experience is as a coven member. The first coven I belonged to did dissolve, but I joined another within a week. The coven experience is all I know of Wicca, all I can write about.

> *It's a bit like singing; solo artists can be wonderful, but there are certain effects which can only be achieved as part of a band, or a choir; and most people would surely understand that.*
>
> —RONALD

Binocular Vision

We see things in depth by looking at them out of both eyes. Though our eyes are close together, that small difference between their viewpoints is what allows our brains to build a three-dimensional image.

Humans tend to gather in many kinds of groups. In this century group process has been extensively studied by psychologists, sociologists, and anthropologists. They've looked at the naturally occurring groups: families, work groups, friendship groups. They've also constructed formal, controlled, field and laboratory experiments to explore how people interact in groups. Meanwhile therapists, counselors, and social workers have developed techniques for creating groups and using these groups to facilitate positive change in people and in organizations. Some of these group workers also write, reporting and reflecting on their working experiences. All this, too, is my heritage.

I hold a master's degree in counseling. I was in graduate school during the same period that I was training as a Witch and Priestess. My own coven was formed just about a year after I received my degree. So it was only natural for me to take a particular interest in group counseling and group dynamics, to follow the literature in this field and to take whatever specialized workshops were available to me.

Covens are groups. The secular literature about group dynamics has a great deal to offer the working coven leader. One of the contributions I hope to make to other Witches is to adapt and import good tools for their use. So I set out to write this book, to share information that I believe will be helpful to our covens.

The fit isn't perfect. The professional literature often sets forth crisp, clear rules, and these are not always perfectly applicable to the way we work in our covens. In the professional world, too, clear distinctions are drawn between different types of groups: growth groups, study groups, task groups, families. The chapters of this book, related to these secular categories, really just describe different aspects, different options, in the complex life of a Wiccan coven. We are not limited by the conventional categories, nor should we be, for we are the Witches. We live in the borderlands, the realms of ambiguity, on the edge of the forest and at the edge of the sea, in the dawn and at twilight, in between.

Good and Getting Better

If covens are groups, Witches in covens are group workers, with lots of good, practical experience. We're obviously doing pretty well already. The rapid and accelerating growth of our religious community demonstrates, among other things, that our covens *as they are right now* are doing an adequate job of nurturing their members' magical and spiritual growth.

What we have is very good, worthy of our devotion and our pride. This doesn't mean we already know it all. No living tradition, no living thing, is ever perfect or complete. Good can get even better. Our predecessors, those who reconstructed or revived our Traditions in the early twentieth century, did not pass their work to us in mummified form. We have as much right as they to be intellectually adventurous and spiritually creative. We have as much potential as they to be in contact with the Ancient Gods. Far from disrespecting their good work, we honor it—and them—best by keeping it growing.

Witches talk a lot about polarity. Some oversimplify it into a code word for differential (and stereotypical) gender roles. Actually, there are many different polarities operating within our work. But just what does *polarity* mean? For some, it's about paired opposite dangers or problems to be avoided, like being between a rock and a hard place. This model has us nervously walking a path as narrow as a tightrope. Sometimes this is the case.

Far more often, if we choose, we can work from a more spacious and generous alternative model, and one that comes naturally to us. The way of the Witch is to refuse false dichotomies. We live at the edges, in the places in between. We seek balance and integration—the "both . . . and" instead of the "either . . . or."

Accordingly, we can interpret the word *polarity* as a description of "any situation involving two things, both of which are good, desirable, even necessary, but that are commonly understood as being opposites or reciprocals." Either without the other is incomplete or out of balance, but their interaction can energize our ongoing work with the power of conjunction. Instead of fearfully avoiding both, then, we should try to embrace both as fully as possible.

In this light any healthy, living tradition needs both continuity and change, in lively and fluent interplay. Unbalanced continuity is stagnation, laziness, the smug and stupid assumption that we have nothing left to learn or discover. Taken to the extreme, it's fundamentalism—a pernicious malady that afflicts every religion. On the other extreme, random and reckless change can cut off our roots, stripping us of identity and meaning. We need both heritage and innovation, in creative interaction. We need not, and should not, choose between them.

No one Witch can presume to speak for all Wiccans. I make no such claim. Contemporary Wicca is multifaceted and diverse. No single viewpoint can adequately represent the whole. To create this book I had the generous assistance of a group of experienced and well-respected coven leaders, from several Traditions and from all over the United States, Canada, and Great Britain. I sent them a variety of questions, mostly by E-mail. They responded with astonishing honesty and openness, often exploring difficult issues. Without them, this book would be nowhere near as rich. Nevertheless, I framed the questions. I chose who to ask, which tales and thoughts to include, and in which order. The finished product, this book, is my work and I take responsibility for it. It is completely shaped by my personal—and perhaps idiosyncratic—perceptions and opinions.

So take this information, these ideas, and weigh them. See how they fit with your religious values and the teachings of your tradition. See how they apply to your coven's life and work.

Use what works for you, and discard the rest, as the wise have always done.

To Learn More

Adler, Margot. *Drawing Down the Moon*. Boston: Beacon, 1987.

Clifton, Chas, ed. *Living Between Two Worlds*. St. Paul, Minn.: Llewellyn, 1996.

_____. *The Modern Craft Movement*. St. Paul, Minn.: Llewellyn, 1992.

_____. *Modern Rites of Passage*. St. Paul, Minn.: Llewellyn, 1993.

_____. *Witchcraft and Shamanism*. St. Paul, Minn.: Llewellyn, 1994.

Hopman, Ellen Evert, and Lawrence Bond, eds. *People of the Earth*. Rochester, Vt.: Destiny, 1996.

Hunter, Jennifer. *21st Century Wicca*. Secaucus, N.J.: Citadel, 1997.

Lewis, James R., ed. *Magical Religion and Modern Witchcraft*. Albany, N.Y.: SUNY Press, 1996.

2

BASICS OF GROUPWORK

I was trained in a lineage-based coven that used a three-degree system. Our High Priestess and High Priest had been similarly trained in another coven, then "hived off" to form ours. The rest of us all started together as a pre-initiate training group. Once our group was under way, it was closed. No new members joined while we were in process. We worked through the degrees together. Shortly after we all were elevated to Third Degree, the coven dissolved. Two of us then started daughter covens. Our mother coven had lasted just a little over three years. It started, functioned, and finished, leaving trained Witches and wonderful memories.

In contrast, both of the daughter covens are still in existence eighteen years later. But here's a revealing detail about my own coven, Proteus. Of the five original members, *I am the only one still here.*

Something like forty people have come and gone. Some reached Third Degree and hived off to create a new generation of daughter covens—by now there are even a few granddaughter covens. Others left before initiation. Some left in anger. Some simply lost interest in Witchcraft. Some left for unrelated reasons, perhaps moving too far away to get to meetings. People join, leave, achieve degrees, hive off, all at their own pace. Most of the time we have had members at all levels, from pre-initiate to Third Degree, working together in our group.

My coven of origin was a closed coven. Closed covens work something like college classes. They have well-defined beginnings and endings, and the population is normally stable throughout the group's life. In contrast, my present coven is an open coven. The population of an open coven changes gradually, allowing the group as a whole to continue, just as it would in an old-fashioned one-room schoolhouse.

In a moment we'll be looking at some commonly accepted ideas about the stages of group life. These stages are easier to perceive in closed covens. Remember, though, that they also operate in the more complex open covens, in which each member progresses through the stages separately.

Another important way that covens differ is that some grow out of a lineage, as Proteus did, while others are self-generated. The typical self-generated coven begins when a group of friends decide to study and practice Witchcraft together. They determine when they feel ready to call their group a coven, when they feel ready to call themselves Witches.

Neither the Goddess nor the magic is the private property of any established group or lineage, nor even of all of them together. Anyone can become a Witch at any moment by saying, wholeheartedly, three times, "I am a Witch," and then by thinking about it, working at it, for years to come. Her success, and her acceptance by other Witches, depends on the quality of her follow-through. The same reality check applies to those who have received formal initiation into well-respected lineages.

Of course a successful self-generated group can be the start of a lineage–that's how all of our Traditions and lineages began. Whether or not this will eventually happen, there are special issues for a self-generated group, and some differences in how the usual stages and processes will manifest.

Stages and Their Issues

Textbooks on groupwork generally describe five typical stages in a group's life: forming, storming, norming, performing, and mourning. But those stages begin with a group's first meeting. Before this meeting can be convened, some other things need to happen. So I'm proposing seven stages, instead of the usual five. Each of these stages presents typical issues, problems, and opportunities. The seven stages are:

- *Gathering:* Open meetings, drop-in groups.
- *Birthing:* Self-definition.
- *Forming:* Getting acquainted, establishing trust.
- *Storming:* Power issues.
- *Norming:* Development of group rules and customs.
- *Performing:* Working toward the group's major goals.
- *Mourning:* Completion, moving on.

This is a model, an abstraction, and models are necessarily simplified. To make a model we use only those details that we think matter. It's easier to understand relationships and processes this way, separated from the complexity and confusion of real life. So we increase usefulness by decreasing accuracy, risking some anticipated complications later on. Still, models provide a useful framework for keeping track of a group's progress. Let's take a closer look at how these stages manifest in Wiccan covens.

Gathering: The "Pre-Phase"

The contemporary neo-Pagan revival is a century or more old. Still, because of a rapid recent increase in our numbers, most of us are first generation. We were not raised in this faith, but came to it as adults. Perhaps we are tentative, experimental, not immediately sure that this is our path. We'd like to learn a bit more before we actually make a commitment.

There wasn't always a way to do this in the past, but now, in many areas, the curious can find open, public rituals at the Sabbats, and sometimes even at the Full Moons. There are also Pagan student groups on many college campuses. These are ways to explore Nature spirituality, discover how it feels to regularly celebrate the solar and lunar cycles, learn some basics, and get to know the local Pagan community.

In secular writing about groupwork, such open gatherings are called "drop-in" groups. As the name implies, drop-in groups have no really clear boundaries or definitions of membership. People come when they feel like it; they stay away when there's something else they'd rather do or they just aren't in the mood. This is an exploratory, low-risk level of involvement, a good place to start exploring Pagan ways.

"Open to beginners," however, also means "limited to beginner-level work." A drop-in group cannot assume that participants have any previous knowledge or experience. Their rituals will be limited to rote repetitions of simple scripts, or at best to theatrical spectacles. Participation will mean joining a chant or dance, not sharing from the deep self. If the membership isn't stable enough to develop a trust-bond, people will be understandably reluctant to expose their wounds, hopes, or dreams in Circle anyhow.

For many people this is just fine. Their primary focus of attention is on some other aspect of their life: a profession or career, artistic self-expression, parenting. All they want is a regular opportunity to connect with Earth's cycles and draw nurturance. "Come-as-you-will" public worship meets these needs. People like this make up the newly emerging "Pagan congregation." For them drop-in participation is not a pre-phase, it's a community and a source of guidance and support for their full and complex lives—just like joining any other church.

Others want a deeper and more intense group religious experience. Some of us find in religion one of the primary focal points of our life, our outlet for creative self-expression, our opportunity to feel that we are making a real contribution. In other faith communities we might feel we had a calling to join the clergy or a religious order. Pagans who feel called to commit themselves to the service of the Ancient Gods may choose to become Witches.

Here's one typical scenario: There's work involved in keeping a drop-in group going. Somebody has to arrange for the space, perhaps put out meeting notices, plan and conduct the rituals, clean up afterward, make sure expenses are covered, facilitate any necessary discussions of the group's business. These responsibilities are typically handled by people who are also motivated to attend fairly regularly.

Often these regulars get to know, like, and trust each other. They will probably come to think of themselves as the "core group." They go out for coffee after meetings, maybe see each other socially in between. Having a mutual interest in Pagan religion, they begin to talk about ideas that intrigue them. Perhaps they loan each other books. Trust grows, and these conversations become increasingly intimate as people share their hurts and hopes. If they feel they're too caught up in the logistics of the public rituals to have a meaningful worship experience there, they may quietly begin to gather for alternative, "just-for-us" rituals.

As the people involved become ready to seek more depth and intensity in their magical and spiritual work, the core group may well evolve into a self-generated coven.

Another possibility: Not everyone who shows up at a drop-in group is a beginner. Public rituals may be offered by established local covens as a community service. Experienced Witches come to visit, network, and check out the new crop of seekers. People who seem particularly interested and helpful may find themselves invited to join a study group or coven.

Birthing a Group: Finding Your Identity and Goal

Groups need some preliminary sense of who they are and what they are about. To convene, to transform from a casual gathering of people into a committed group in the process of becoming a coven, requires some conscious notion of your identity and goal, of who you are and what you propose to do.

The exercise of self-definition is worth some time, care, and thought. Clarity about your starting assumptions may avoid confusion and trouble later. But don't be too rigid, either. Keep your self-description open, growing and changing, consistent with your lived experience, a support for your ongoing growth, not a restraint. Real magical and spiritual development changes people. The group must necessarily change as the members change.

Before any group gets to performing—to actually working toward their goals—they must pass the three thresholds that I have named: forming, storming, and norming. Self-generated groups went through these stages almost imperceptibly in the process of transforming from core group to proto-coven. They can simply settle down to working.

In contrast, people who trained within a lineage and are now preparing to hive off will begin to gather members for a pre-initiatory study group. They may place a notice in a local newsletter or bulletin board or make an announcement at a local open gathering. If some people respond, the group is launched. The typical phases of group life are most easily seen in a group like this: beginners not previously known to each other who are gathering for a common purpose.

Mini-Ritual for the Birth of a Self-Generated Coven

1. Begin with each group member holding a full cup; an empty pitcher rests on the altar.

2. Pass the pitcher around. Each group member expresses a hope or wish for the new group and pours a bit into the pitcher. Continue for as many rounds as needed.

3. Bless and consecrate the pitcher. Raise power by chanting, drumming, or dancing.

4. The pitcher now contains the commingled and empowered hopes of the group. Pour from it into each person's cup. Toast and drink.

Forming: The Issues of Inclusion

It's September, time for beginnings on campus. In the university counseling center a group of freshmen meets to work on relaxing their exam anxiety. Across campus a room fills with volunteers for the campus newspaper. In another building the first session of the graduate seminar on the *Mabinogion* is getting under way. Support group, task group, learning group—we will revisit these terms in more depth in later chapters.

This evening a new Wiccan study group will also hold its first meeting. It will have aspects of the above three groups, and more. Regardless of their major differences in purpose and function, all four of these groups must work through some preliminaries.

The first challenging threshold is entering a room full of strangers. Will you like them? Will they like and accept you? Can you trust them? Can you gain their trust and respect? Will you bond well enough to accomplish the purpose that draws you together? The basic goals and operating procedures—the "bargain"—of each group may be very different, but in all cases, members need to trust one another to hold up their end of that bargain.

New group members typically use social small talk to size each other up. People stick to unimportant or even irrelevant topics—the weather, sports, fashion, the latest television series—until they have begun to build as much of a relationship as is necessary for this group to address the task before it. Early group theorists described such topics as the "goblet issues." This is not a reference to a Witch's ritual goblet—a symbol of unity and transformation—but to a cocktail party, where people look around over the tops of their glasses to see who they might want to approach.

The members of a class or a task force may only need to trust one another to do their share of the work. Covens, however, nurture their members' deep magical and spiritual development. This entails a whole lot more risk. There will almost certainly be moments when our tender old wounds or fragile new hopes are exposed and vulnerable to our covenmates. So a much deeper level of rapport and trust—we call it "perfect trust"—is necessary, and this can't be forced or faked. It takes the time it takes. This may frustrate inexperienced group leaders, who have a carefully thought-out plan and are eager to get going with it.

Our caution about joining a coven, or about admitting new members, is reflected in the traditional minimum requirement of a year and a day of study before initiation. In lineage-based groups, such preparation often happens in a formal pre-initiatory study group, which may be called a *grove* or an *outer court.*

Here's how two eminent elders, Theos and Phoenix, described the activities of a typical pre-initiate training group of twenty years ago. (Note that *pagan* meant "pre-initiate" in the idiom of that time.)

Our pagan training groups were established mainly so that we could observe neophytes over a period of months before deciding whether or not to initiate them. We wanted to evaluate things like the seeker's attitude, degree of interest, dedication, reliability, ability to participate and contribute to the group, relate to others in the group, etc. These circles also provided initiates with a chance to meet these potential coven members, and vice versa.

Because these people were not oathbound and were free to (or might be asked to) leave at any time, we elected not do any significant teaching/training in our pre-initiation groups. We did, however, use the time to teach some preliminaries. Sometimes a neophyte would be assigned to prepare a topic for the following circle's discussion. There was always a lot to do, and there were a million questions to answer. Eventually, we selected those neophytes to be given initiation.

After they were properly oathbound, then a significant training curriculum commenced. We found this approach suited our coven's needs quite well and it was used by many later Gardnerian training groups during the 1970s and early '80s.

Outer court membership serves the same transitional function that working as a core group does for the self-generated covens. Both require far more commitment and far more work than simple participation in a drop-in worship group. The pre-initiatory study group is usually understood as a place to get familiar with basic concepts and skills. Participants also get to know people, to begin building rapport and trust. Elders, in turn, screen seekers, assessing their motivation and reliability over a period of time. Both of these tasks are essential before the deep work can really begin.

The difference is that joining an outer court is a consciously taken step whereas core groups evolve more gradually. In Proteus we mark entry into formal study with a ritual of Dedication, a commitment to abide by our basic ethics and to study and explore Witchcraft as a potential life path. So our Dedicants are in a position similar to that of a Roman Catholic postulant.

In many traditional covens, the working meetings of the coven and outer court are held separately, even if the groups come together to celebrate the Sabbats. I used to think this practice was intolerably elitist. But on reflection it seems sensible to allow the Dedicants a place where they can go about forming, storming, and norming, as they need to, without blocking the initiates from performing their own work.

Storming: Allocating Power

The first threshold question is, "Can I work with these people?" The second, and even more challenging, one is, "Who is in charge here, and how is power shared?" In the storming phase, participants work out their pecking order and determine who is in charge of what aspect of group life.

Issues of interpersonal power are difficult for Witches to think or talk about, since we cherish an image of ourselves as free spirits, guided only by our own individual True Will and perhaps the leadings of the Goddess. Or we may feel that questions of power and authority are essentially political questions—as they are—and that spiritual people should somehow be above all that.

In reality, where there are people, there are politics. Power relationships inevitably exist, born of the need to make strategic decisions and coordinate people's efforts.

Our only choice is whether or not to face the fact that authority, power, and internal politics exist in every coven, just as they do in our various councils and organizations. Those who are willing to look at these processes can keep the inevitable conflicts fair, clean, and within bounds. Denial will not make politics go away, but it will force them underground, out of sight, out of control. So let's think together about power.

Sources of Power

Power is the relative capacity to influence what will happen (the outcome) and how it will happen (the process). *Authority* represents the ways in which this capacity is granted, legitimated, or validated. We can describe several different kinds of power and authority, deriving from different sources, working by different rules, and interacting together in fascinating complexity.

PERSONAL POWER   The capacities that we develop within ourselves may also win for us the respect of others, and with this comes greater influence within the coven and the community.

Expertise   In the elevator of a corporate office building, with everyone else barbered or coiffed, tailored, pressed, and polished, a man with long stringy hair and a rumpled sport shirt rides to the floor that houses data processing. After he leaves, one suit says to another, "I assume he's very, very good." Across town, in the law school, an eminent professor bullies and insults a reciting student to the point of emotional abuse. This professor's knowledge of the law, and of courtroom argumentation, is also excellent. Students sign up for her class, knowing how difficult it will be, because the rumor mill has it that anyone who can get through the semester will really know his stuff. Expertise compels respect, even toward people we otherwise find obnoxious.

Knowledge is power. We defer to people whom we perceive to have extraordinary knowledge or skill. (For more on training—on how covens help members develop expertise—see chapter 7.) The problem is that appearances can be deceptive. A person can be very knowledgeable, very skillful, and yet not have the will or skill to make this widely known. An additional skill—communication—is necessary to transform expertise into leadership.

Also, some areas of knowledge are objective and measurable. If somebody claims to be a toolmaker, or a musician, or an herbalist, we can evaluate the quality of her work. But our religious activity mostly deals with the inner self—with spirituality and with magic. These matters are subtle and subjective, difficult to assess.

Some people are, in all sincerity, deluding themselves and their followers. Others intentionally make false claims. Beware of those who practice the Craft for ulterior motives. Beware of those who foster dependency in others. Beware of anyone who claims to stand between you and the Ancient Gods.

Spirituality   The Goddess has no grandchildren. All of us are Her beloved children, and ultimately equal before Her. Not just all humans, all living things have their own direct connection. Gatekeepers and intercessors are, in all truth, unnecessary and probably detrimental. However, because of old habits and hurts, or bad familial and cultural programming, many of us have lost awareness of our own living link to the Source. The purpose of spiritual practice is to restore, maintain, deepen, and clarify that conscious connection to Deity in each one of us, and to let it guide and empower all aspects of our lives.

Logically, then, some people have been less hurt, less misdirected than others. Some people started sooner, or worked more effectively than others, on the process of restoration. So in the short run some people have a clearer conscious connection to the Gods than others. General recognition of more developed spirituality in someone gives her intrinsic authority in the group.

Caution: It's very easy to fake it, very easy to pose as a mystic. Another caution: It's very easy to fool ourselves. The sincere fanatic is harder to spot than the profit- or power-driven phony. History is strewn with examples of people who honestly believed that their Deity commanded them to commit genocide against the next tribe over.

The corruption of any religion begins when some members claim to be more equal in the sight of the Gods than others. The door of Spirit is always open to all. No human authority figure can place limits on the Gods; neither can we force Their participation.

When people perceive that one of their covenmates does have a better-developed contact with the Old Ones and lives a congruent life, they will want to draw close to her, to take her as a model. Her insightful and thoughtful statements will carry great weight in council. Authentic mysticism, intrinsic power, is a great blessing to any coven. This is the true power-from-within. Gatekeepers are detrimental; guides are helpful.

DESIGNATED LEADERSHIP   This appears when one or more people perceive (whether accurately or not) that a person has effectively developed his personal power, and recognizes this by conferring leadership authority upon him. Leaders get designated by different methods in different types of groups.

Positional Authority   Positional authority is inherent in a role or an office. When the officeholder changes, positional power transfers to the new incumbent. We see this transfer of power when a new mayor is elected, or when a new manager replaces one who has retired or been promoted. Positional power is prototypical power-from-outside, power that we can put on like a piece of jewelry, take off again, and then hand over to the next person.

Formal Authority   In contrast, formal authority belongs to the person rather than the role. The secular parallel is a university degree or a professional license. A person earns this credential by meeting the requirements, satisfying her teachers or elders. Although formal authority can be removed as punishment for malpractice, keeping it does not depend on the person continuing to function in the role. A doctor working as a hospital administrator, seeing no patients, is still a doctor. Similarly, two of my original covenmates did not go on to start groups of their own; they are nonetheless still Third Degrees. Despite eighteen years of inactivity, they have the formal authority within our Tradition to start a coven anytime they want.

When elders confer formal authority, they tell the community that they consider a person to be properly qualified for leadership. Typically, leaders of lineage-based covens have worked through the training system of their Tradition or their coven of origin. Their elders assessed their skills and their personal maturity and wisdom. They have been formally—and most often ritually—empowered to train and initiate others. Even if we don't know them as individuals, we can rely on our knowledge of and trust in their lineage, and of the elders who stand behind them.

This is a hypothesis, a pretty decent one, but not absolute proof. We are a young religion, learning as we go, only just developing our standards. Elders make mistakes about their students' wisdom and maturity. People change after elevation, and not always for the better. So respect your elders, rely on traditional credentials, but also remember that your healthy skepticism is your ultimate quality control.

Emergent Leadership   This develops naturally from within a self-generated group when one member seems to have markedly more talent, knowledge, or skill than the rest. The coven can acknowledge and celebrate the emergence of a leader from within itself. When they do so, the emergent leadership develops into formal authority. Emergent leadership might also be suppressed, stifling the potential leader and robbing the coven of his talents. Or it can continue to operate unacknowledged, under the table, as covert leadership.

The real test of emergent leadership is in performance. If the coven works well and wins the respect of their local community, the leader also acquires another sort of formal authority— other coven leaders have seen her do the job, the surest proof of ability, and begin to treat her as a peer. If she achieved this without formal training and without elders of her own to consult, she did it the hard way. Her authority is fairly earned, and is every bit as valid as the Third Degree my elders conferred on me by their Traditional authority.

Shared, or Decentralized, Leadership   The nonhierarchical collective is an ideal, a dream toward which we may aspire, a golden moment in a coven's life. I believe that all of us can attain it some of the time, but it's as hard to hold as a butterfly.

Here's the lovely ideal: Everyone in the group is of good faith, no ulterior motives or hidden agendas. All have deep personal insight and clear spiritual contact. They have built a solid relationship of love and trust with one another. They are aware of one another's special talents, interests, and resultant areas of expertise. They have the leisure and energy to consider carefully what they do. Within this context, all major decisions are made by full consensus. Within this context, authority moves freely among members, depending on whose special knowledge is applicable to the matter at hand. Trouble is, most of us are only rarely within this context.

Interestingly, self-generated groups start out as nonhierarchical collectives but may soon develop emergent leadership. Lineage-based covens, in contrast, begin with clearly designated leaders, but as they mature they move toward more collective decision making. In terms of power sharing, a coven of elders will look very much like a newly formed, self-generated group. So perhaps the secret is that authority is most easily shared when the members are roughly equal in experience, expertise, and spirituality. When new seekers are admitted to an ongoing group, the elder-to-younger relationship naturally reappears.

Proteus runs by consensus as much as possible, the joke goes, because I happen to like consensus. I believe that participatory decision making is by far the healthiest mode for any group, and I use it as much as possible in my own. But the reality is always more complex than the ideal. I hold formal and positional authority in the group, which means my opinions carry great weight. As discussion leader I summarize and restate the forming consensus. This gives me a disproportionate amount of input. More important, all of us know that in matters of safety or ethics, the buck stops in the High Priestess's lap. It's my job to draw the line when it's absolutely necessary, and people feel more secure knowing that I will.

That's the accepted social contract of a lineage-based group. For other groups, being a nonhierarchical collective is an important part of their self-image. A very few have consistently worked this way over long periods of time. In many other cases, though, this self-image has actually masked the development of covert leadership.

Use of Power: Reward and Punishment

Leadership means motivating people, coordinating their efforts, acting as a role model, sharing knowledge and skills. Most of us leaders are comfortable with all of these. But there's another, far less palatable, aspect to leadership: Leaders are enforcers. Every designated coven leader has the power—and sometimes the daunting responsibility—to reward and punish the behavior of coven members. This capacity can be used well, or poorly, or abdicated altogether. It should not be ignored or denied.

This can often be the scary, bad stuff, "power over," domination. Far too often people use physical strength, force of arms, or sheer wealth to impose their will on others. Those who do so often develop elaborate rationalizations for their greed and cruelty. Because we have seen so much conquest, oppression and abuse in human history, because our own religion has been so brutally persecuted, we associate the capacity to control others with evil.

It's important to remember that might does not ever make right. Coercive power never conveys legitimate authority, which can only come from what some of our ancestors termed "the consent of the governed." Others of our ancestors expressed this a different way: "Those who cannot bear your rule will leave you." The open exit door, the assurance that there will never be material consequences for leaving a coven that fails to meet our needs, is complete protection against any improper use of power.

Given this assurance, we can face the reality that legitimate authority does confer some capacity for control—within carefully established bounds. A coven leader can grant or withhold some rewards, or apply certain sanctions, in an effort to shape the behavior of coven members. So do the oppressors, whomever you think they are, but so also does any classroom teacher.

The only rewards most coven leaders can offer are intangible: acknowledgment of work well done, thanks, praise and, eventually, initiation and elevation. We can be infinitely generous with such rewards. Because there will always be more praise to give, there is no need for envy or competition, no reason for covenmates to tear each other down. In fact cooperation is one of the behaviors we should most strongly reinforce.

More frightening and difficult is the concept of sanctions, of punishment. But what punishments can we administer? We can't imprison covenmates, evict them, deprive them of a livelihood. All we can do is withhold potential rewards or, in very extreme cases, send people away. We can ask someone to leave a coven if he's just not fitting in or working out. In extreme situations, if he is actually doing something dangerous or unethical, after careful explanation and repeated warning we can banish him from our lineage or Tradition. To cast someone out is always difficult and painful for all concerned, but sometimes necessary for the health of the whole. Here are two true stories:

In Coven A, one member is scapegoated. All the problems of the group are projected onto her. The High Priestess ridicules and humiliates her before the others. The favored ones feel smugly superior, and subconsciously afraid that, if they don't join the pack, they'll be next. For eventually, after this one is forced out, the scapegoat role falls on another member. The pattern repeats for years.

Coven B meets on a weekday evening. One member is always an hour or more late. When others speak to him, however gently, about this, he bursts into tears. Calming him would take another hour, so the group is blackmailed into silence. But four other members all have to be at work, alert and energetic, early the next morning. Eventually, all of them leave. The coven dissolves.

We who screen new students sometimes make mistakes, but neither we nor the rest of the coven needs to live with these mistakes once they are recognized. It's unfair to allow one person to spoil the coven experience for all the others. Exclusion can certainly be abusive, a buttress for systemic dysfunction within a group. But it can also be necessary housekeeping. It is a coven leader's responsibility to keep the space safe and supportive to the group's magical and spiritual growth.

By excluding people, a community defines its boundaries, makes clear what behaviors are utterly unacceptable. Banishment is a difficult, painful process. In eighteen years of coven leadership I have only done it once. The person I banished had wantonly violated many people's confidentiality, and showed no remorse at all for having done so. I have received community-wide support for that hard decision, and still I pray that I may never have to face it again.

Here's the mitigation: In reality no single coven leader *can* banish anyone, since we have no way to bar other local covens from inviting that person to join them. The real effect of banishment is to *nominate* someone for exclusion, to let other coven leaders know about our problems and concerns. Community consensus has the final say. Furthermore, a coven leader who uses the power of banishment lightly or capriciously will eventually get a bad reputation—of Coven A, for instance, it was said that no local coven was complete without one of their refugees.

Both reward and punishment, besides being sources of power, are legitimate and necessary parts of the coven leader's duty. How can we avoid abuse and misuse of this dangerous set of tools? Three ways, I think.

First, make sure that coven membership is truly voluntary by letting people know in advance how things work in this group. If they clearly understand that their relationship to the coven leader is that of student to teacher, that advancement is contingent on achievement, and that unethical behavior will lead to banishment—then by joining, they give their consent to these practices.

Second, be fair and even-handed. Don't play favorites. Don't scapegoat. Have the same standards for everyone. Don't take sides in an interpersonal conflict unless ethics or safety are involved. Don't rely on rumor. Don't ever support one side until you've heard both.

Most important: While fairness is essential, it is not the whole answer. We need standards of conduct that are realistic, sensible, and meaningfully related to both the core values of our religion and the coven's identity and purpose. It's a bad idea to initiate someone who merely shows up consistently for a year, even if everyone who attends regularly is initiated. It's a bad idea to banish someone who asks difficult questions, even if everyone who probes deeply is banished.

Problems With Power

CORRUPTION   Power does not inevitably corrupt, but power holders sure get tempted. People in authority can get to thinking that we know it all, or that what's good for us personally is good for the collective.

Holding specifically religious authority, receiving respect and deference from our students, can become a seductive trap for coven leaders. We can develop the fantasy that we are somehow holier than the others. Worse, we can even fall into the pernicious delusion that we have reached some sort of sublime and ultimate spiritual level, that our own personal work is done.

Even leaving aside the reality that stasis soon turns into deterioration, there is always more to learn, always room for improvement, both personally and collectively. Nothing will obstruct our conscious contact with the Old Gods more utterly than our own false belief that we already know it all. This belief also leads to the kind of ego-poisoning that we call "High Priestess's disease," although it is certainly not limited to women.

In earlier Craft generations, and perhaps still in places, some coven leaders fell into an authoritarian, dictatorial style. (This is reflected in some of the older documents.) They censored their students' reading and attempted to control their students' choice of friends. The leaders required their students to do their laundry, clean their houses, wash their cars, and sometimes work in their businesses without pay (all on the pretext of "internship"). In some extreme cases coven leaders commanded their students to participate in unethical practices.

The modern tendency to deny the very existence of leadership may have started as a much-needed rebellion. But overcompensation won't work forever. Covens thrive on love and trust. The teacher-to-student relationship does involve giving direction and sometimes correction. Abuse happens, but only in rare and sad cases. Constant, nervous monitoring of the coven leader's every word and deed erodes a coven's ability to function.

But we still need to be aware when something begins to go wrong. Denial disempowers us. If we can't even admit that there is a leader, how can we notice if the leader is getting off track? How can we talk over our concerns with our covenmates? How can we confront a leader's inappropriate behavior?

In actual practice, covert leadership is structurally equivalent to authoritarian, dictatorial leadership. Both concentrate all power in the leader's hands, leaving none to other coven members. Both are profoundly dysfunctional. How do we distinguish the natural and necessary authority of a good teacher from dictatorial authoritarianism? Easy. Legitimate teaching is like the training wheels on a bicycle: It provides a safe way to start but is intended from the very beginning to disappear when its function is fulfilled.

Because we all bring our old control issues to the Circle, Lady Brigantia, an elder High Priestess, points out that "most leadership issues aren't about honesty and openness, and therefore there is some rot hidden away within nearly every system. Maybe the rot is like sourdough starter, in that it serves as impetus for human-driven inspiration to change the situation?" Just so, Nature religion teaches us to use the life cycle itself as our model for ever-renewing hope. Whatever humans can subvert or corrupt, other humans can reclaim and reform.

CONFLICT The coven is a context in which each Witch discovers and learns to use her own power. Sometimes we do this by emulating the actions of our coven leaders and others we admire and respect. Sometimes we test our power by dispute and differentiation.

At first everybody wants to be the "teacher's pet." We push and shove to get close to the person we think has the answers for us, or the person who has the power to distribute the rewards. We try hard to attract his attention, to impress him. Sometimes we try to make ourselves look better by putting the others down. Not at all pretty, but very, very human.

Then, to confuse matters even further, we get into power struggles with the coven leader, the very person we were trying so hard to get close to. There are some widely recognized reasons for this:

- We Pagans like to think of ourselves as free-spirited rebels who take orders from no one.

- Many of us were hurt by arbitrary and heavy-handed authority in some earlier part of our lives. Some of us were hurt by authority that was actually corrupt or abusive. These hurts breed distrust of people in authority whom we meet later in life. We sometimes play out old scripts and agendas, and this limits our present scope of action. Learning to see the person before us as she or he actually is, with both flaws and virtues, frees us to react appropriately. (For more about replication of old relationships, see chapter 9.)

- Spiritual self-transformation is risky, hard work. There's a part of every one of us that would rather just stay as we are. Our resistance to change can manifest as resistance to the mentor. (For more about willed self-transformation, see chapter 6.)

- And sometimes we have a legitimate grievance with a covenmate or with the coven leader. Sometimes we are perceiving a problem that this person missed.

From the other side of the altar: It's really tough to handle conflict in the coven, and especially difficult to deal with what seem to be attacks on you. These attacks will inevitably come, and they will *hurt*. Here's what will help you get through:

- HALT! Unless there is an immediate risk to safety or ethics, do not respond when you are feeling ḫungry, ạngry, ḻonely, or ṯired. Be kind to yourself, in whatever ways you prefer. Get yourself grounded and centered. (Hint: This is good advice for people on any side of any conflict, in or out of the coven.)

- Take criticism seriously. Yes, it may stem from a person's old issues, but it might also come from her current perceptions. She may not yet know exactly the right way to offer constructive criticism, so don't confuse the manner of her speech with its content. You might have something to learn.

- Talk the issue over with your working partner, if you have one. Compare impressions. You may also want to consult with other coven leaders you respect (your peers) or with your own elders. It's important to sort out whether this attack is a repetition of old patterns, resistance to change, or a perception of real, present problems.

- Don't forget your Witch's toolbox: Divination, meditation, and dreamwork are all applicable to coven problems.

- Remember, magic is the art of shaping consciousness in accordance with will. Specifically, if you can understand that this attack is probably directed toward your *role*, not your *person*, it will hurt a lot less.

- The best way to teach is by demonstration. Conflict happens in every intimate group, every family, every life. If you can respond to an attack with firm compassion, without becoming devastated and without becoming nasty and vengeful, you can show your students what constructive conflict resolution looks like. Sadly, they may not even be aware of the possibility. (For more about conflict resolution and participatory decision making, see chapter 8.)

In the storming phase we come to a preliminary and tentative balance point between abject submission and compulsive rebellion, as we must. Almost all Wiccan development involves a mentoring relationship. If either side of such a relationship is ambivalent about authority, the participants can't get on with the work. However, this resolution cannot be permanent. The balance of the relationship should change as the work progresses. As we negotiate these necessary and developmental shifts in balance, conflict may arise again. Hopefully, through the initial storming phase and subsequent work, we will have learned to deal with one another fairly, kindly, and with appropriate self-assertion.

Norming: Finding Our Own Ways

Norming is the group's final preparatory task, the last threshold any group must pass over before members can begin to perform, to work toward the primary goal for which they have convened.

This threshold is a formidable one for Witches, because "norms" are a lot like "rules." The Wiccan Rede—our own Golden Rule—teaches us that any harmless behavior is acceptable, but arbitrary limits on our freedom are not. We like to think of ourselves as spontaneous, irrepressible free spirits. When we coven together we yield some of that cherished autonomy.

In the literature on groupwork the word *norm* is used to mean group members' mutual expectations about behavior, guidelines about how to behave, and a way of predicting the behavior of others. Every human group has norms; like power relationships, they are inevitable. Like power relationships, they are often invisible. And like power relationships, they can support or impede our work. But no group can survive or function without norms.

There's no particular reason to drive on one side of the road or the other. The choice is completely arbitrary. But if we don't all pick one side and stay there, harmful collisions will happen. Some of a coven's norms are as arbitrary, and as necessary, as that.

Some norms are implicit, silent, perhaps unconscious. Norms can grow organically from the group's experience. But implicit norms may also spring from old assumptions and habits from elsewhere, useless and often obstructive. Implicit norms are difficult for newcomers, too, who can only hope to learn them by observation. Too often people discover implicit norms by transgressing—which can be embarrassing. This keeps the old hands in a constant "one-up" position, not healthy for either side.

Other norms are explicit, consciously chosen, openly known to all. As a coven in formation develops their starter set of norms, they can draw from many sources. Here are some:

- *Our upbringing and cultural background:* We all have some idea of what is polite behavior, appropriate grooming, and so forth. In many secular situations this once was a pretty good starting point. Today, as we try to work with people from diverse cultural backgrounds, hidden assumptions from the dominant culture can act like booby traps.

  More important: Covens are places for willed magical and spiritual self-transformation. We are here in large part because we were not satisfied with the values and practices of conventional society. So letting unquestioned cultural programming shape our group norms seems self-defeating.

- *The outcomes of prior internal conflicts:* During the storming phase there may have been barely acknowledged struggles for control of what gets done and how. The result of such struggles is that we do things however those who emerged as top dogs wanted. Covert norms can be understood as the manifestation of covert leadership. They are both profoundly disempowering to the group.

- *Precedent:* Lineage-based groups inherit a written and oral tradition. Self-generated groups may develop documents and anecdotes of their own, which are presented to later-joining members. These explicitly stated norms are at least clear and fair. At best, they embody what our predecessors learned from their own practice and wise reflection.

  However, they may also be excessively limiting. Precedent should be thoughtfully considered but not enshrined as gospel. In a healthy, living tradition every generation learns, grows, and contributes.

- *The coven leader:* In my discussion of the storming phase earlier in this chapter, I described the multiple sources of a
  coven leader's power. Influence over what gets done and
  how it gets done obviously includes influence over the development of group norms. Since this power cannot be
  avoided, it's best to use it consciously and responsibly.

  The coven leader's influence is naturally multiplied during
  the early days, especially if the group members are relative
  strangers. While the others are still engaged in forming and
  storming, the coven leader may be distributing handouts or
  offering classes on ethics and etiquette. I certainly do. Far
  more important, however, is quietly demonstrating appropriate behavior. What you do in this formative period will
  set the tone for a long time to come, so walk your talk!

- *Inspirations and brainstorms:* Occasionally someone gets a flash
  of insight. This may come in a dream, during a formal divination session, or at any other time. It may come to the
  coven leader or to any member. Much of our work, after all,
  is preparing ourselves to receive such gifts. (For more on
  opening to the Divine, see chapter 5.) Like precedent (or like
  the information in books such as this, for that matter), such
  information should be respectfully considered but not absolutely followed. None of us is a perfect channel. Instead
  we are collectively responsible for interpreting, weighing,
  and integrating inspirational information—just as we do information from any other source.

Just as they arise from a variety of sources, group norms
apply to several different facets of group life. Here are some
types of norms:

- *Procedural norms* define how things are done in a group. This
  ranges from administrivia to core ethics. Are guests welcome, and under what circumstances? How do we manage
  the group's expenses? What should a member who has to
  miss a meeting do? How do we make decisions and resolve
  conflicts? What are our standards of confidentiality? Do we

sit on the floor or in chairs? Does our cup hold fruit juice or wine? Do we want to admit new members after the group is under way? Do we use recorded music in rituals?

- *Communication norms* are about both the style and the content of our interactions. Communication style is an important part of identifying where we are. Mycota Coven, for example, uses only highly stylized, formal language during their rituals. To make this possible they thoroughly discuss whatever work they intend to do in a preritual briefing. They also hold their classes outside of Circle to encourage questions and discussion. In Proteus, in contrast, we discuss coven business and do all teaching within Circle. We use ordinary language for such discussions. This means that, for us, language style is not an indicator of whether we're in Circle. Neither of these approaches is right or wrong, and a member of either group can easily adapt when visiting the other.

  Content is even more important. Any group will have norms governing appropriate levels of self-disclosure under different circumstances. Consider, under normal social circumstances, when people ask "how are you?" in greeting, whether they really want to know your diagnosis. Unusual amounts of self-disclosure are necessary for the coven to function as a support group for inner growth (for more on this, see chapter 6), and this in turn requires correspondingly high concern for confidentiality.

  Deviation from group expectations concerning self-disclosure is far more disconcerting than stylistic difference. Once, years ago, at a Hunter's Moon ritual, we were each asked to talk about a time that we experienced ourselves as either hunter or prey. All but one of us did. That person recited a poem about the hunt instead. The poem was beautiful and beautifully recited, but still not her own. By acting as a voyeur rather than a participant, one person shattered the trusting atmosphere for all present, deadening the remainder of the rite.

- *Achievement norms* are a coven's understanding of what success means. This will vary, depending on their self-defined goals. For a training group, the requirements for initiation and elevations are achievement norms. For a coven that has undertaken to publish a magazine, it might be meeting deadlines.

Covens nurture members' growth. As people change, their relationships necessarily change. So it's not at all surprising that our basic operating procedures, our norms, will also evolve. Neither is it surprising that, as our insight deepens with growth, we might come to understand that some of our initial, implicit norms are working against our goals. To keep the coven vibrant and creative we have the right and responsibility to clarify, adapt, or outright change our norms.

Stages or Cycles?

Small decisions, early in any journey, make large differences in the direction we go. But the choices we make at the beginning of coven life are neither perfect nor permanent—simply good enough for the group to get started. Old issues will come up again over time. We will handle them next year in the light of all we will have learned from now till then.

The answers may or may not still be the same. Witches are used to thinking in terms of cycles and in spirals. Each time we celebrate one of the seasonal festivals, we understand it more deeply because we have made another trip around the Wheel since the last time.

This is the case even in secular groupwork. In an often-quoted illustration William Schutz, a major encounter group leader, discussed, "The tire changing model. When a mechanic changes a tire, and replaces the wheel, first each bolt is tightened just enough to keep the wheel in place. Then the bolts are tightened further, usually in the same sequence, until the wheel is firmly in place. Finally, each bolt is gone over separately to secure it fast. Like these bolts, the need areas are worked on until they have been resolved sufficiently to allow the group to continue with the work at hand. Later, the need

areas are returned to and worked on till they are more satis-
factorily resolved. If one bolt was not tightened well in the first
cycle, during the next cycle it will receive more attention."*

In open-ended groups, which occasionally admit new members, all newcomers will have to work through the three
thresholds of entrance into the group. Watching them do so
will bring things up for the others, new insights on old issues,
and so it grows.

Learning, growing, and changing will keep our minds young.

Performing: Doing Our Things

Contemporary secular scholars of groupwork tend to divide
groups according to their primary purpose, including support,
education, and work. Covens span these divisions and add
more: worship, family of choice. For more about what covens
do and how they do it, read the rest of this book.

Mourning: Partings and Endings

As Samhain follows Beltane, whatever begins will eventually
end. Sometimes individual people leave the group. Sometimes
the group itself comes to an end.

Some of those endings have the bittersweet feel of completion, like the graduation ceremony bravely called commencement. Members have learned as much as they can in this
coven, grown as far as they can. Now it's time to move on.
Some will hive off to form new covens of their own (for more
on hiving, see chapter 11).

Some endings leave sad loose ends. A cherished member
moves far away. We promise to keep in touch, but drift apart.
Sometimes the grapes become sour. As they get ready to go
members may tell themselves that it's not such a big deal,
that this coven wasn't all that wonderful anyhow. If they can

---

*Schutz, William, *Elements of Encounter* (Big Sur, Calif.: Joy Press, 1973):
55–56.

convince themselves that they won't miss it so very much, then leaving won't hurt so bad.

As we age, some of us become ill. Some die. Even if the coven admits new members, nobody will ever replace old ones.

Some endings are abrupt, chaotic, angry. Some leave hurts that last for years. Some who leave will try afterward to hurt you, perhaps by malicious gossip. The pain they can cause you mirrors the intensity of the bond that once was. And some of these so-called exit fights are not necessary. It was simply time for a person to move on, but he needed to create a more compelling reason.

Draw closure when you can. Have an "exit interview." Resolve as many issues as possible. Have a farewell ritual for the one who is moving away. Have a coven blessing for the new hive.

In time most departed members will reestablish communication. Most will be back for the periodic visit. And far more meaningful than all the silver buckles on your garter is this measure of their trust: the midnight crisis calls that will come at rare and random intervals for the rest of your life. Covening together, your coven made a home for their spirit.

To Learn More

Conyne, Robert K., F. Robert Wilson, and Donald E. Ward. *Comprehensive Group Work: What It Means and How to Teach It.* Alexandria, Va.: American Counseling Association, 1997.

Engleberg, Isa N., and Dianna R. Wynn. *Working in Groups: Communication Principles and Strategies.* Boston: Houghton Mifflin, 1997.

Wilson, Gerald L. *Groups in Context: Leadership and Participation in Small Groups*, 4th ed. New York: McGraw-Hill, 1996.

3

GATHERING IN LOVE
AND TRUST

CHOOSING TO COVEN

This chapter is for seekers, both those who are thinking about whether they want to join a coven at all and those who are deciding which coven to join. The choices you make now will affect the quality of your Craft experience for some time to come. Go slow. Look deep. Think and dream. Take care.

By now you've done some reading about Witchcraft. Probably you've also tried some private rituals. What you've experienced so far feels right. You want to learn and do more, and that's fine. Every experienced Witch once stood where you stand now. Remember that becoming a Witch means committing your life to the service of the Ancient Gods and of our generous Mother Earth. This service can take many forms, in and out of covens.

A good way to start is with a simple self-dedication. Go outdoors if possible. Find a favorite place, as private as possible, where you feel safe and strong. Rest there till you feel calm and relaxed. Then tell the Lady that you want to become Her Priest/ess, and why. Ask Her to guide your preparation for Her service, your growth in knowledge, wisdom, and skill.

You may want to dedicate a small object, something you could carry in your pocket or purse, or perhaps an unobtrusive piece of jewelry. Keep this with you all the time, at least until you know clearly the direction of your growth path.

Start a journal with your description of this ritual and your reactions. If you know how to meditate, do so more regularly. If not, learn how. Pay attention to your dreams. And watch for learning opportunities of all kinds. You have asked for Her guidance. She may or may not send you to a coven.

The First Decision: Choosing Coven Work

What can an aspiring Witch reasonably expect from the coven experience? Here's how a group of experienced coven leaders answered this question:

SUSAN Puns and headaches. Clergy training. Some reading. Some education in comparative religions. Learning to write and conduct rituals. Learning trancework. Funny smells. Make-believe. Truthfulness. A fair amount of fuss and bother. To identify and honor the Goddess within yourself; and to listen to your own intuition.

WEYLAND Covens range over a wide spectrum of dynamics, from something fairly impersonal and businesslike to a surrogate family. Almost anything seems to work given the right mix of members. There are closely bonded groups, magical practitioners who gather to experiment, gurus-and-seekers, associations of equals, "Party Pagans," and political groups with a Craft veneer. The reasonable expectations within the group will vary with each type of group. What *must* exist is an honest compatibility of goals and needs.

KATHY Extremes aside, you can expect to find fellow travelers to walk the Path with, to whom you may turn for assistance in the learning of the material, and who may in turn ask for assistance along the way.

The "normal" midrange in my experience is a group of people who work together for a time, learning from each other, refining both the individual skills and the group synchronization. (We frequently use the analogy of a band or orchestra. All the players are maestros in their own right, and it still takes practice and frequently a conductor to make the best music.) It is also common, but not universal, for a coven to eventually disperse. Covens have a life span. As people grow and change, the group will also change. The life span is determined by how well the coven serves the coveners. The precise nature of the experience varies and is dependent upon the coven's dynamic structure; the expectations of the seeker; and the match between the coven and the seeker.

ALICE   On the spiritual level, the coven worships and celebrates together, combining their individual energies into unique collective expressions of devotion to the Ancient Ones; each coven has a characteristic "group mind," which in turn is strengthened by working together in magic and worship. Because of the intensity of the shared spiritual work, as well as the small group size, the coven experience can be (should be?) much more intimate and intense than a "congregation."

CAROL   Ideally, seekers should expect a coven that is supportive and friendly and offers an atmosphere that is conducive to the sort of growth and fellowship that they need.

Some come looking for the coven to be a surrogate family, the family they would have chosen given the choice. That sort of coven is the kind that helps the widowed member into her flannel nightgown after the wake and sings her to sleep, the kind that turns the big deep bathtub into a candlelit wishing well where the pregnant member who is due to give birth that week floats amidst fragrant blossoms while the coveners drop in good luck coins for her and the baby.

Others are looking for a more distanced approach, a place where they can worship with others without needing intimacy, or a place where they can study and learn what they need and then move on. We all have differing needs at different times in our lives, and if we can find the right coven that can accommodate these changes we are lucky.

However, given the demographic realities of the Craft, seekers may not always find a coven in their area that offers the tradition that they would prefer to be involved with, or be able to find a group whose personal chemistry works for them. Sometimes the group in which they might do best is a closed one that is not accepting new members. There may be personal conflicts or stylistic mismatches. Seekers should be aware that just because they haven't found the coven that suits them best, it is not necessarily a reflection upon them or upon the covens. Chemistry is an elusive thing.

MAGENTA   At the very least, [covens comprise] people who are willing to be honest and open, and who want to learn and grow. Hopefully, coven members will become friends, even surrogate family—that is what *my* coven is. Personally, I don't know what to make of covens that meet once a month, and the people never see each other in between, never socialize, never do anything together except in Circle. We've gone to pick-your-own apple orchards most years, we go to festivals together, we baby-sit our coven kids, et cetera.

MARGARIAN   I asked my own students. They said "family" and "community within sacred space—and a closer sort of community than you'll find at the open circles."

I agree with both of these, but with a caveat: Families come in many flavors. Some are very close and nurturing, some comfortable but distant. Some spend a lot of social time together; others have members with wildly differing hobbies and lifestyles, and only get together for Sabbats and Esbats. Most have a skeleton or two in the family closet. Some are downright dysfunctional.

Ideally, a coven is a group of Witches with sufficiently similar attitudes and priorities about religion. They are comfortable with one another's ethics and ritual choices, and with sufficient mutual trust, they are comfortable letting down their barriers with each other. Whether they spend a lot of social time together or only a little, they like each other well enough to enjoy that time. They put one another high enough in their priorities that they'll be there for each other when there's trouble—and with substantially more of their time and effort than a Priest/ess would give, anyway, for anyone in need. Realistically, this doesn't mean mortgaging your house to bail out the happy-go-lucky covener who has gotten fired from yet another job, nor lending your car to the covener who's always having fender-benders. Neither does it mean struggling to listen appreciatively to a coven sister's treasured disco music collection, or fry your tongue at her favorite hot-curry restaurant.

It does, sometimes, mean getting out of bed at 3:00 A.M. and driving across town in a snowstorm to sit with a covener who just got word of his father's death, or arranging your schedule to drive a covener to and from the hospital for chemotherapy sessions—and putting that disco cassette in the car stereo while you drive her home.

PATRICK   Many of us in our group feel that the coven experience is one in which we get to create the trusting family environment that we've never been able to achieve in the secular world. And like any family, we fight, scream, tell each other to get lost. . . . But we also know that these people are the people we can go to with our concerns, hangups, hopes, dreams, fears, and know that they will support us in our search in a loving environment. I hesitate to use the word *safe,* only because it is never fully safe when you start working through your stuff. It's scary as hell. But a well-organized coven with a good rapport can provide as safe an environment as we can reasonably hope to achieve.

GAWAINE   I'd say that under the best circumstances, you can expect to be a part of a dedicated working group all focused on a shared goal. The benefits of this are an excellent opportunity for spiritual and "technical" growth (as in magical and ritual techniques); the opportunity to share knowledge, learning what works for others; and a very real sense of family. You should also expect to have to work hard to gain those things. As with most other things in life, what you put in determines what you get out. You should not expect a coven to be a therapy group. As a type of family, certainly a coven can provide emotional support during crises, but that should not be the primary thing a coven member expects from it. And of course, coven membership can lead to close and lasting friendships.

Good passage

IONTAS   A person should expect a coven to provide a safe and nurturing environment for personal growth along with an environment of challenge. (It's not all warm fuzzies here.) This is first and foremost; for, when it comes right down to it, the focus of Wicca (or many other religions for that matter) is on personal growth and development. Yes, we worship our Gods, but to best do that and to best serve the large community, we must grow personally first. We must stretch beyond the boundaries we come into the coven with and move past our old selves into new selves. I see each initiation, elevation, or dedication almost as a shedding of a skin or the emergence from a cocoon after a period of study and gestation. The coven provides that safe space to "gestate."

A coven should also challenge the seeker or initiate. It should provide intellectual stimulation and new ways of looking at old problems, fears, hurts, et cetera. This can be accomplished by means of stories, actual rituals, lecture-type teachings, hands-on learning, service projects, et cetera, et cetera. Only your imagination limits the ways in which you can teach students.

CHUCK   The function of a coven should be more than just the dissemination of knowledge and lore. It should be a place where people are encouraged to practice rather than just read, share information from different traditions, challenge traditional beliefs with new experimentation, and build a family or community type of atmosphere where we can support each other through hard times and celebrate the good times.

ALEXEI   A person seeking to join a coven is presumably someone who has already developed a spiritual link with the Goddess and is convinced that with the help of ritual and controlled imagination, one's will can become sufficiently focused to affect the course of events. In a coven one will find people who share these (nonmainstream) views and who will reinforce them by regularly putting them into practice. More importantly, a coven will provide a reserve of energy for such operations that would not be available to an individual working alone. And even more importantly, it will expose one to the experience of others who have been on the path for a longer time, and facilitate an inner growth process that could otherwise take longer and be more painful. In time, one will be able to provide guidance for others less experienced.

Because of the "perfect love and perfect trust" vow, a coven should also be expected to provide emotional reassurance to its members in times of stress. It is *not*, however, a place where one should expect immediate approval of all one's opinions and tastes. Learning to function within a coven involves learning all the lessons in interpersonal communication one has to learn in the outside world, and should lead to an understanding that one is enriched rather than challenged by others' differences. A coven where all the members had similar personalities and agreed on everything would probably raise little magical energy.

DEVYN   I think being able to work, learn, experience, discuss, and share with others has to be the primary reason why people join covens.

Also, membership in a coven will give the opportunity to learn and practice the Craft. Members would participate in rituals and learn magic. Coven members may expect to discover new features of their own selves, experience trance states, and sometimes have profound and sublime spiritual visions.

The coven experience may result in developing significantly new perspectives toward existence. It is, in my opinion, the essence of Mystery traditions to shake the foundations of previous perception as a means toward initiating (!) growth and development, and so the coven experience can and will directly affect the member's daily life in a lasting way. It is the work of the coven to build leaders.

People may not enter covens expecting to learn leadership skills . . . but without them, how else may we best wield the other gifts that the Gods may bestow us with?

RHEA   To be at times intensely engaged. Sometimes emotionally, sometimes psychologically, sometimes spiritually. This engagement will be at various times with individuals in the group, with the group at large, with various elemental, spiritual, or divine beings. You will change in manners predictable and manners surprising.

The decision before you can be stated very simply: Do you feel the next phase of your learning and growth will be best aided by a solitary or a group experience? You can change your mind later. A solitary can decide to seek coven training and membership at any time. It's more emotionally difficult, but still possible, to leave a coven and return to solitary practice.

Group membership always requires a sacrifice of autonomy—you will have to accommodate at least your schedule, and probably your working style, to those of other members, and usually also to the group's established ways. If you're indecisive about joining a group, it's probably best to stay solitary until you feel quite sure.

You don't need other people to worship the Gods. You can study many Craft-related topics by hitting the library, or by taking many classes and workshops that don't call for complicated and long-term commitment. There are many valid contributions you can make to the community by yourself.

However, the skills of groupwork can obviously only be learned in a group. Beyond this the complex, multiple inputs and interactions of a group can accelerate your growth and amplify your effectiveness. Only you can decide what you need right now.

The Second Decision: Choosing a Coven

There are a lot more Witches, a lot more covens than there used to be. In most well-populated areas today seekers have far more freedom of choice than we had a decade or two ago. What we call "coven shopping" is a new and very healthy development, allowing people to find not just any coven but a sound one that fits them well. First, have clear answers to these two basic questions:

What do I hope to get from coven participation?

What can I contribute to a coven?

Next, you want a competent, functional, healthy coven. The coven leaders suggested some things to look for.

Green Lights

ALICE People who are like-minded enough to accept the seeker, but different-minded enough to be interesting.

ALEXEI A healthy-looking coven is one that obviously embraces a wide variety of personality types and lifestyle choices, without any one being obviously singled out for approval or attention. Another sign of health is people being willing to talk openly about the life of the coven, what they like about it and what potential problems they see. Coven leaders who project a sense of competence but don't constantly occupy center stage are also a good sign.

GAWAINE Good leadership. Not autocracy, but leadership that provides guidance, seeks input from coven members, builds consensus, and is willing to make hard choices when they are called for. I've been in a coven where this is lacking and it makes it bloody painful for everyone.

A willingness to share knowledge and foster growth in the members. An openness to new ideas.

IONTAS   First, the ability of the coven's leaders to say, "I don't know"! After that. . . .

- Experience doing training. Ask to see training materials and a reading list. This will tell you a lot about what these folks are teaching and how organized they are.
- Stability, especially in the coven leaders themselves. If they can't handle their own secular lives, how in the world are they going to handle a coven?
- Caring and gentleness along with an "up-front" attitude from the coven leaders. They're going to treat you with respect and dignity, but they're not going to take any crap or stand any political infighting in their coven or with any other covens outside their own.
- The ability to listen along with the ability to teach.

RHOMYLLY   A sense of welcome that does not cross the line into recruitment pressure. Many levels of experience and initiates, signifying the leader's willingness to let people grow. Polite inquiries into the seeker's special needs (vegetarianism, alcohol avoidance, et cetera).

WEYLAND   The ability for members to trust the coven with their naked selves. I think I've been hit on by about half of the female First Degree students I've had. This usually happens early in their training. I think they're trying to figure out how to relate to the power that they perceive their teacher holds.

Our coven (including any Second Degree students learning to teach) has a strict rule that playing with the students before they're ripe enough to have earned at least a First Degree is child abuse. The students are in a vulnerable position here and should be able to trust the teacher to say no even when they don't yet know enough to do so themselves.

KATHY   Ask questions. How freely do the answers come? How much of your time are you expected to commit? Is this reasonable in the context of your life? Can/will you meet this commitment? What are the "rules," how consistent are they, and can you live with them?

RHEA   Do you want to hang out with these people? Can you get along with these people when the going gets rough? Do you *like* at least some of them? Do they seem like sensible sane people (eccentric, silly, and surreal are fine; totally irrational and crazy are not)?

Is their idea of freedom of expression similar to yours? For example, if you want to be able to write rituals from the ground up and they use a set formula, you are badly matched.

What are the rules? Can you live with them? Our coven suffered drama and strife (and lost a member) because rules had not been clearly elucidated and were then elucidated most ungraciously.

Try to find a coven in which at least one person is good at processing, fighting, therapeutic speech, however you want to put it. What I mean is, you want someone who is gracious, listens, and speaks clearly, using the word *I* a lot.

DEVYN   I think seekers should look for people with whom they can be friends first. I've found that it can really take away from the coven experience if the participants have little or no relationship with each other. This is especially true for the new seeker, who is probably so stressed out over the newness of "being a Witch" that every single experience can make or break confidence and self-esteem.

If the coven has a central leadership core, people of patience and nurturance are best, of course. While I respect and value the outward customs relating to hierarchy, I also think that it's important to remember that you are seeking a coven to learn and grow rather than kowtow. This is a point that I am astonished to often see forgotten among my own peers in Craft leadership.

MARGARIAN   People you like, or think you will like once you get to know them.

People who visibly like, and care about, one another.

People who seem trustworthy, and who visibly honor and live the values they say they espouse.

A coven whose members visibly continue to learn and grow, both in the Craft and in their personal lives.

Red Lights

The coven leaders also shared some things to look out for.

ALICE   Heavy internal politicking, divisiveness and conflict, "soap-opera" personal dramas played out against the group dynamic.

ALEXEI   Avoid covens that focus entirely on one charismatic person to the point that the other coven members are always in that person's shadow. Such covens usually have a host of codependency problems that are bound to manifest in a variety of unhealthy ways.

GAWAINE   Covens that are run for the benefit of their leaders rather than for the welfare of all the members. Covens that exploit members, violate member boundaries, or try to control the personal lives of the members.

HOLLY   I would caution anyone looking for a group to look very carefully at how rigid or controlling a coven is. For example, some teachers try to censor their students' reading. I suggest to my students that they should read and study as much as possible, from many sources. Some will be garbage, probably; some will be great. But I don't think a student can learn to discriminate between garbage and great without exposure to both.

I would also tell them to avoid any group that violates their boundaries (sexual or otherwise), or that tries to control their personal life.

IONTAS   A seeker should avoid:

All those who call themselves "Lord" or "Lady" anything outside of Circle!

Statements like, "I have secret knowledge no one else has." Signs of mental illness.

Asking for money for training . . . yes, I know this can be hotly debated, but I firmly believe that one does *not* sell the Craft . . . *especially* training. Meeting anyone who charges for classes should send up a red flag.

Infighting in the coven or between the leaders. It can only get worse than it already is.

People who see "psychic attacks" everywhere and are constantly fighting off these supposed attacks.

Dictatorial coven leaders. This is not to say they should be spineless . . . but if you walk in and the High Priestess starts with a speech that runs something like, "I'm a bitch and you just better get used to it," RUN!

Coven leaders who can't keep their mundane lives in order—hold a job, keep a reasonably clean house, pay their bills, et cetera; things most of us take for granted. If they can't run their own lives, how are they going to run a coven?

MAGENTA   If someone says she is the only person around who can really initiate, or is the only real Witch, et cetera, avoid her like a cliché! Even fairly small towns have more than one coven or group these days. There are exploitive leaders. Anyone who says you have to study with him or you aren't a real Witch, or you have to have sex with her to be initiated, is someone to shun.

RHOMYLLY   Groups that ask for money. Groups where the leader does all the talking, even in a group situation.

WEYLAND   I'd worry about a teacher who wanted money beyond that which would cover the expenses of the class. I'd *really* worry about a teacher who tried to restrict my contact with other Pagans or with family and friends outside the Craft, or who tried to limit my access to any particular book, movie, or person. I'd run away from a teacher who told me I wasn't free to leave the group at any time.

VESTO   Watch out for covens containing people who frighten you. Get to meet the whole group on several different occasions, and talk to everyone at some point, not just the leaders or your "favorite person," so you will have a chance to feel everyone out. Also, look out for covens that pressure you to join right away and, of course, covens that pressure you to do anything you aren't comfortable doing (sex, drugs, hurting yourself or others, doing baneful magic, recruiting).

RHEA Avoid people who are engaging in dangerous practices (addictions, unsafe sex, et cetera); they will not consider your safety either.

Don't even try to coven with people you have an unpleasant past with. Minimize the potential for soap-opera-like drama.

Avoid power-hungry manipulators, people who treat you like an imbecile, who treat you like a member of some inferior group (that is, bigots), who treat you as a slave or prey, and who don't listen. Simple rule: Don't coven with assholes.

MARGARIAN Avoid the following: a coven with an ill reputation in the community; a visibly dysfunctional coven; a coven with one or more members who gossip about private coven business; a coercive coven—for instance, one where all members are expected or required to participate in a group marriage, or to use drugs or alcohol, or to live a particular lifestyle; a coven that asks for money beyond reasonable operating expenses; a coven that asks for a firm commitment before you've had a chance to try one another out; a coven that tries to isolate you—from non-Craft friends and family, or from the rest of the Craft community (but it *is* reasonable to be asked to belong to only one coven at a time, or study with only one Craft teacher at a time); a coven that places a "glass ceiling" over members' growth and learning—though this is *not* the same thing as asking a student to wait a reasonable length of time for some kinds of learning; and a coven in which you sense hidden hostilities among members, or where there seem to be a lot of power games.

As a final caution, and by Isaac Bonewits's gracious permission, I include here his Cult Danger Evaluation Frame. First written in 1979, and since revised, this is the single best framework for making sure your religious exploration, in or out of the Craft, takes you only to safe and sane places.

~~~~~~

The Advanced Bonewits Cult Danger Evaluation Frame

by Isaac Bonewits

Copyright 1979, 1996 C.E., Isaac Bonewits

Introduction

Events in the last few decades have clearly indicated just how dangerous some religious and secular groups (usually called "cults" by those opposed to them) can be to their own members as well as to anyone else whom they can influence. "Brainwashing," beatings, child abuse, rapes, murders, mass suicides, military drilling and gunrunning, meddling in civil governments, international terrorism, and other crimes have been charged against leaders and members of many groups, and in far too many cases those accusations have been correct. None of this has been very surprising to historians of religion or to other scholars of what are usually labeled "new" religions (no matter how old they may be in their cultures of origin). Minority groups, especially religious ones, are often accused of crimes by members of the current majority. In many ways, for example, the "Mormons" were the "Moonies" of the 19th century—at least in terms of being an unusual minority belief system that many found "shocking" at the time—and the members of the Unification Church could be just as "respectable" a hundred years from now as the Latter-Day Saints are today.

Nonetheless, despite all the historical and philosophical caveats that could be issued, ordinary people faced with friends or loved ones joining an "unusual" group, or perhaps contemplating joining it themselves, need a relatively simple way to evaluate just how dangerous or harmless a given group is liable to be, without either subjecting themselves to its power or judging it solely on theological or ideological grounds (the usual method used by anti-cult groups).

In 1979 I constructed an evaluation tool which I now call the "Advanced Bonewits Cult Danger Evaluation Frame," or the "ABCDEF," a copy of which was included in that year's revised edition of my book, *Real Magic* (Samuel Weiser Pub., 1989). I realize its shortcomings, but feel that it can be effectively used to separate harmless groups from the merely unusual-to-the-observer ones. Feedback from those attempting to use the system has always been appreciated. Indirect feedback, in terms of the number of places on and off the Net this ABCDEF has shown up, has been mostly favorable. For example, it was chosen by and is now displayed on the website of the Institute for Social Inventions, who paraphrased it for their "Best Ideas—A compendium of social innovations."

The purpose of this evaluation tool is to help both amateur and professional observers—including current or would-be members—of various organizations (including religious, occult, psychological, or political groups) to determine just how dangerous a given group is liable to be, in comparison with other groups, to the physical and mental health of its members and of other people subject to its influence. It cannot speak to the spiritual "dangers," if any, that might be involved, for the simple reason that one person's path to enlightenment or "salvation" is often viewed by another as a path to ignorance or "damnation."

As a general rule, the higher the numerical total scored by a given group (the further to the right of the scale), the more dangerous it is likely to be. Though it is obvious that many of the scales in the frame are subjective, it is still possible to make practical judgments using it, at least of the "is this group more dangerous than that one?" sort. This is *if* all numerical assignments are based on accurate and unbiased observation of *actual behavior* by the groups and their top levels of leadership (as distinct from official pronouncements). This means that you need to pay attention to what the secondary and tertiary leaders are saying and doing, as much (or more so) than the central leadership—after all, "plausible deniability" is not a recent historical invention.

This tool can be used by parents, reporters, law enforcement agents, social scientists, and others interested in evaluating the actual dangers presented by a given group or movement. Obviously, different observers will achieve differing degrees of precision, depending upon the sophistication of their numerical assignments on each scale. However, if the same observers use the same methods of scoring and weighting each scale, their comparisons of relative danger or harmlessness between groups will be reasonably valid, at least for their own purposes. People who cannot, on the other hand, view competing belief systems as ever having possible spiritual value to anyone, will find the ABCDEF annoyingly useless for promoting their theocratic agendas. Worse, these members of the "Religious Reich" will find that their own organizations (and quite a few large mainstream churches) are far more "cult-like" than the minority belief systems they so bitterly oppose.

It should be pointed out that the ABCDEF is founded upon both modern psychological theories about mental health and personal growth, and my many years of participant observation and historical research into minority belief systems. Those who believe that relativism and anarchy are as dangerous to mental health as absolutism and authoritarianism could (I suppose) count groups with total scores nearing either extreme (high or low) as being equally hazardous. As far as dangers to physical well-being are concerned, however, both historical records and current events clearly indicate the direction in which the greatest threats lie. This is especially so since the low-scoring groups usually seem to have survival and growth rates so small that they seldom develop the abilities to commit large-scale atrocities even had they the philosophical or political inclinations to do so.

The Advanced Bonewits Cult Danger Evaluation Frame
(version 2.0)

Factors: Low   1   2   3   4   5   6   7   8   9   10   High

1. INTERNAL CONTROL: Amount of internal political
   power exercised by leader(s) over members   _____

2. WISDOM CLAIMED by leader(s): Amount of
   infallibility declared or implied about decisions or
   doctrinal/scriptural interpretations   _____

3. WISDOM CREDITED to leader(s) by members:
   Amount of trust in decisions or doctrinal/scriptural
   interpretations made by leader(s)   _____

4. DOGMA: Rigidity of reality concepts taught; amount
   of doctrinal inflexibility or "fundamentalism"   _____

5. RECRUITING: Emphasis put on attracting new
   members; amount of proselytizing   _____

6. FRONT GROUPS: Number of subsidiary groups using
   different names from that of main group   _____

7. WEALTH: Amount of money and/or property desired
   or obtained by group; emphasis on members'
   donations; economic lifestyle of leader(s) compared to
   ordinary members   _____

8. POLITICAL POWER: Amount of external political
   influence desired or obtained; emphasis on directing
   members' secular votes   _____

9. SEXUAL MANIPULATION of members by leader(s):
   Amount of control exercised over sexuality of
   members; advancement dependent upon sexual favors
   or specific lifestyle   _____

10. CENSORSHIP: Amount of control over members'
    access to outside opinions on group, its doctrines,
    or leader(s)   _____

11. DROPOUT CONTROL: Intensity of efforts directed at preventing or returning dropouts _____

12. VIOLENCE: Amount of approval when used by or for the group, its doctrines, or leader(s) _____

13. PARANOIA: Amount of fear concerning real or imagined enemies; perceived power of opponents; prevalence of conspiracy theories _____

14. GRIMNESS: Amount of disapproval concerning jokes about the group, its doctrines, or its leader(s) _____

15. SURRENDER OF WILL: Amount of emphasis on members not having to be responsible for personal decisions; degree of individual disempowerment created by the group, its doctrines, or its leader(s) _____

16. HYPOCRISY: Amount of approval for other actions (not included above) which the group officially considers immoral or unethical, when done by or for the group, its doctrines or its leader(s); willingness to violate group's declared principles for political, psychological, economic, or other gain _____

Right for You?

There is a lot of variation among competent, functional, healthy covens. The next set of issues to consider in your search are those concerning "goodness of fit." You'll sometimes hear it said that a particular seeker is "good for the Craft, but not for this coven." This can work both ways. A perfectly good coven may still not be the right one for you.

For this reason it's important to clarify your own needs and desires. Try this: In a relaxed and unhurried moment, imagine your ideal coven as vividly as you can. Then make a list of whatever you noticed about this coven, in the order of importance to you. Note whether each item is essential, important, or just nice. Here are some of the things you might notice about your dream coven:

- *Mixed gender or all female or male?* You may be more comfortable with your own gender, or feel you need to work on particular gender-related issues. Alternatively, you may feel that the best context for Nature religion is an inclusive group that reflects the wholeness of nature.

- *Size:* The traditional maximum is thirteen. Beyond this, quieter members tend to fade into oblivion. The average size of a coven is more like five or six.

- *Ritual style:* Can range from highly ceremonial to free-form "shamanic."

- *Formal, structured curriculum or student-directed learning?* If there is a formal curriculum, what subjects do you most want to learn? (For more on curriculum, see chapter 7)

- *Decision-making style:* This can range from consensus through authoritarian hierarchy. (For more on decision making, see chapter 8.)

- *Time demands:* Obviously, more thorough training requires more contact time. But how much time and energy can you realistically give while staying in balance with your other responsibilities and having time enough for rest, fun, other close relationships?

- *Theological emphasis or focus:* Goddess only, Goddess and God in balance, or full polytheism? Any particular pantheon or historical or cultural emphasis?

- *Programmatic emphasis or focus:* Some covens have a specialty, others do not. Specialties can range from performing arts to astrology, interfaith education, or whatever engages the group's energies.

- *Perspectives and practices concerning magic.*

- *Social contact:* Do you want your coven to also be a major part of your social life, or would you prefer to keep social life and coven life mostly separate?
- *Relationship (if any) with other groups:* Lineage, tradition, national organizations, local networking. (For more on community, see chapter 12.) Do such linkages matter to you?

These are only some of the possibilities for you to consider when you construct your own wish list. The more of the list that comes from inside you, that reflects your own values and desires, the better the list will serve you as a decision-making tool.

The next step in your search is to get to know as many local covens as you can. Some will want you to write a letter of self-introduction or even fill out a questionnaire before they will meet with you. Almost all will want to interview you in a restaurant or other safe public space before they invite you to their home. Most will want to evaluate your prior training and experience. Many will invite you to visit and get to know all the members before they make a final decision. The process will take time. Don't be offended if they screen very cautiously. They are deciding whether to make themselves vulnerable to you in many ways. You will be taking similar risks, and should be exercising exactly the same caution.

With patience and perseverance you will find a group of people whom you trust, and whom you feel you will in time come to love. You feel at home with them. They know something you want to learn, and are willing to teach it to you. Within their Circle you can begin to work toward initiation into Witchcraft.

Joining a Study Group or Grove: Beginning to Begin

Just like starting any other serious professional training program, this decision will immediately change your life. You are taking on a major responsibility, that will make claims on your time and energy. The self-exploration that is inherent to any spiritual path will bring you to difficult, frightening, and even painful moments, as well as times of great joy. As the growth process changes your character, some of your relationships may change. In short, as you progress changes will evoke other changes throughout your entire life. And it's a risk. Just as students entering medical school or law school can't be sure they will graduate or become licensed to practice, you may discover that you were not suited for initiation after all.

The point at which a person decides and formally begins to study for the priesthood is another important life passage and one that should surely be celebrated! Also, many teachers will want your formal commitment to confidentiality and to ethical use of what you will learn. So more than ten years ago my coven instituted a ritual of dedication, to mark the beginning of serious preparation for initiation. I offer it here simply as an example. Use it if you find it inspiring, or adapt it to your own principles and aesthetics.

Pre-Initiatory Dedication Ritual as Used in Proteus Coven

Before the ritual, the candidate should choose a mentor from among the elders of the coven. S/he is also given a list of the questions s/he will be asked, so that the candidate can ponder his/her response. Candidates should bring to the ritual a small physical object, such as a piece of jewelry, that represents their personal power.

Make Circle as usual, with the entire coven present.

ELDER: [candidate's name], what do you seek?

CANDIDATE: I seek to study Witchcraft. I ask you to teach me.

[The Candidate now responds to each of the Elder's questions.]

ELDER: Do you understand that Witchcraft is the priesthood of the Old Gods and Old Ways of Nature, and that every Witch is a priestess or priest?

ELDER: Do you understand that initiation into that priesthood will change your life forever, in ways that no one here can now foresee?

ELDER: Do you understand what priesthood requires: that, if you become a Witch, you serve the Lady and the Lord by serving Their People, to the fullest of your ability?

ELDER: Knowing these things, do you want to study Witchcraft and its related arts until you know enough to decide whether this is truly your Path?

ELDER: Do you understand that Witchcraft is one of many means to serve the Old Gods and awaken the Old Ways, and that even if this is not your way after all, you may learn and grow while you are here? Can you accept that the answer may be no?

ELDER: Teaching what I love is a great joy. But I can only teach in joy if I know that what I love will be used and shared with care and honor. Before I am willing to teach you, there are three things and a fourth that you must promise to me:

Will you respect and protect the right of all those you meet in the Circle and any who seek our aid to choose when, how, and by whom they will be known, calling them as *they* choose to be called and revealing their participation to no one except by their explicit permission?

ELDER: Will you practice and teach the Craft for love alone, using this knowledge or teaching it only as a free gift, as I give it now to you, never accepting payment for it in money or goods or labor?

ELDER: Will you promise never to use what I teach you to direct any magic toward any other person, avoiding not only baneful magic but all well-intentioned meddling, unless you have that person's explicit permission?

ELDER: And if time brings fullness, as all here hope and expect it will, when you teach new students of your own in this tradition, will you require these three pledges of them, along with their pledge to similarly bind their own students, so that all who spring from this line may be so pledged?

ELDER: [Only proceeding if all responses have been affirmative]: This being so, I consent to teach you. This is how I value my labor—that I will plant only good seed in good soil, to become fruit both sound and sweet. I will teach you, I will learn from you, I will learn with you. So we begin by exchanging our pledges. Place your hand on this token of your power and repeat after me: I, [candidate's name], here and now pledge to you [mentor's name], to the Gods, to all in this Circle and, most truly, to myself, that I will explore the path called Witchcraft, its lore and its symbols; its rituals and its deeper meanings, sharing with you my joy in discovery and all my doubts and qualms. I pledge to explore all questions with open mind and heart until I know surely whether or not I am for the priesthood and Witchcraft is for me. In token of this pledge I swear to devote myself, from this moment on, to learning the ways of Witchcraft.

ELDER: [Covering candidate's hand on talisman with own hand]: And I make this pledge to you in return: For the lesser knowledge, which can be taught, I will be your teacher. For the greater knowledge, which must be discovered, I will be your guide and your friend. For the questions and perplexities of the path, I will be your companion, to answer when I may, or simply to be silent as you seek your own answers. And when the time comes to choose whether you will enter the priesthood, I will share with you all I have observed and thought; and may the Gods prosper our work together.

Know that although I am your primary teacher, the Circle is not made of the two of us alone. All here are dedicated to the Old Ways and each has unique knowledge. All of us learn from and with each other. You, too, bring the learning of a lifetime and the fresh insight of a beginner's questions. Together we are more than the simple sum of each of us alone. Go around the Circle, now, and accept each person's greetings.

COVENERS: [Embracing the candidate in turn]: I am _____ . I am your friend. In time, I may be your sister [brother].

[The candidate responds with the same statement.]

ELDER [Blessing the talisman that the candidate brought into Circle]: I return this token to you with my blessing. Accept it, as I have accepted your pledge. Use it now, as your first ritual act.

CANDIDATE [Goes to each Quarter and salutes in any way s/he knows]: Powers of the [South, West, North] I, [candidate's name], call on you to witness my pledge and ask you to bless my time of exploration. [Silent salute in East.]

ELDER: [Candidate's name], be welcome in the Circle!

[Embrace, almost certain to be followed by group hug.]

ALL: SO MOTE IT BE!

4

Parents, Children, and the Coven

BALANCING THE NEEDS

Debbi, a mother of three and a High Priestess, writes: "Kids are a part of life and as such, are welcome in our Circle. Yeah, it sometimes gets a little disruptive, but we try to cope with it. I will agree that there are a very few times the kids should not be there. Having the kids sit outside when we raise power is probably a good idea. We have coloring books and small toys just outside the Circle to keep the kids in sight.

"But at purely worship Circles, the kids just become a part of the group. Strangely, the most profound wisdom has often come from the smallest child, and laughter and a bit of chaos add to the feeling of the presence of the Gods in our midst. I have nursed my babies in Circle and they have learned much of love and joy there. How could I deny them that?"

And how can we deny ourselves the presence of the babies? Ours is a Nature religion, perhaps even a fertility religion. What kind of Nature religion would not welcome the young? Excluding our children is like excluding the life force itself!

But what are we doing here? A coven is a small group of people gathered to support each other in our magical and spiritual growth. At our meetings our focus is on intense inner exploration and transformation. Our work demands more than just an adults-only environment, but one limited to others of like commitment. It demands focus, discretion, wisdom. That's why our working Circles are for initiates (and perhaps dedicants) only.

Just as children don't belong at an orchestra rehearsal or an editorial conference, they do not belong in a working Circle. Little ones are not mature enough to understand what we do. Their attention spans are too short to participate. Also, they have every right to parental attention. Their presence, no blame to them, is a demanding distraction to their parents and to the whole group.

Both opinions are valid. How can they be reconciled?

Maybe we do the important things in life sequentially, so we can fully concentrate on each in its turn. Many religious traditions teach that mysticism belongs in the second half of life. Nurturing children is worthy, holy work, nothing less than the shaping of the human future. Infancy and early childhood, the times when children need constant attention, take just a few years. Perhaps for this short time mysticism can wait. Parents of toddlers can take leaves of absence from their covens. When the kids are big enough to quietly amuse themselves in another room, the parents will be welcomed back.

RHEA The Buddhists believe that you should spend your young adulthood in the raising of a family, of course following various precepts of how to live properly, and then, when the kids are grown, go follow a spiritual path. I can't say that I disagree with them entirely.

MARJORIE Parenthood sometimes means putting some things on hold for a while. Magical workings can be one of those things. I haven't done certain rituals since Ellen was born, but may again soon. But having children in Circles to celebrate the holidays and the seasons is part of raising a Pagan child.

THEOS Your children come first. Children always have to come first. If a parent can't find proper child care, her place is with her child. Remember, Craft is a lifetime commitment. At times, when other responsibilities took precedence, I couldn't participate. That doesn't mean that you leave it. It's part of you. It's inside you. You come back at a later time. If a parent is committed and if it's really within her, she'll come back to it.

But here's another consideration: Spiritual practice is not just a chore, not just one more competing demand that we can and should set aside for the more urgent responsibilities of parenthood. Spiritual practice, contact with the Sacred, with the Ancient Gods, is a source of sustenance.

Parenthood is indeed holy work. It was always hard and exacting work, and these days it's work made far more difficult by the loss of customary support systems. Many marriages dissolve. Even intact households need two incomes. Adult siblings live too far apart to help each other. Stressed and exhausted, parents live at the edge of burnout. They need and deserve a place to refresh, renew, tap into the source. Coven is an oasis for them.

The primary purpose of any coven is to support the ongoing spiritual growth of its members. That means the adults: the initiates and those preparing for initiation. Many coven members are parents. Some are parents of little ones. Covens serve the children indirectly by serving their parents.

How can covens serve the special needs of young parents? First, the children need to be safe and well cared for. Without this assurance no parent can or should relax and concentrate on what's happening in Circle. Covens that are able to assist with child care should certainly do so. If a coven can also offer members' children some elementary religious education, this is a wonderful extra.

Children can be cared for, or even included in many ways. There are several relevant factors to consider when planning for the children. Vesto's story highlights some of these considerations:

We've had two coveners with small children. Both were also in stable partnerships and had extended family or regular baby-sitter(s) nearby. One woman raised two sons from baby age while she was with our coven. Later, another woman was in the coven between her daughter's ages of five and nine. Both women have since hived off to form groups of their own.

The mothers' attitudes were that they were in the coven to study, so the kids didn't generally come along with them on Circle night. One did bring her children to Circle while they were still "babes in arms." We didn't think it odd to have a baby in a working Circle—it got to feel quite natural, even though most members of the group are hard-core childless-by-choice people! Under toddler age, the babies were not usually any bother in Circle, and could be nursed generally as needed. A lot of the time they were sound asleep. As soon as they became big enough to be awake at that hour and try to knock over altars, they were left home, away from working Circles.

Their mother would not have had them there at all if, 1) she'd thought it was harmful to them, or 2) she felt that they wouldn't be under enough control, that she would have to limit her magical participation. She didn't feel it was right to have us watch the kids, even though I think most of us would have been generally okay with it now and then.

From the coven leader's perspective, our basic requirement was that coveners showed up regularly enough for training that they were able to form a magical bond with the rest of the group, and that they arrange their lives so that they could achieve their goal of magical training in a reasonable amount of time, thus helping them to feel that they had an attainable goal. Perhaps our requirements are skewed more toward childless people who make up the bulk of our experience, but these particular parents were able to make it work.

In fact, we questioned one of the mothers about whether it was the proper time for her to start coven work or whether she should wait a little. When she first considered dedicating, she had just borne her first child. He had a medical problem that took him in and out of the hospital numerous times during his first year. When he finally seemed stable, we all decided it was a good time for her to dedicate. Her stay with us went smoothly from that point.

We also had children at our open Sabbats, when the ritual is usually lively enough to interest or amuse the kids (far more so than our working Circles). Even then, the mothers would tend to pack a snack and a quiet toy into Circle for the child to play with if s/he got bored.

One woman's non-Pagan husband often came for Sabbats. If the kids suddenly turned fussy or sleepy, he usually didn't mind staying out of Circle (elsewhere in the house) with them, even though he would otherwise take part in the ritual. Having children is fraught with a lot of emotional baggage; it may be that these parents argued occasionally about whether the way the kids were going to be dealt with that evening was the best way.

We didn't tend to change our Sabbat rituals to make them more interesting to the older kids in general, although we did often accommodate their individual needs if they were taking part actively (by circle dancing at a speed kids can keep up with, just as we would for an adult with mobility problems, or by explaining who was behind the mask to one child who was rather frightened by masks).

If there were more children in the situation, or if we'd had single parents who had nowhere to leave the kids, this whole scene would probably be different. I figured I'd better just tell you what worked for us, rather than speculate on what these other contingencies might be like.

The original outline for this book made no reference to children. Part of my reason for this was simple denial. I didn't want to remember how poorly my own coven had handled a child-care crisis. We had a single mother with two children, the firstborn a special-needs child. We also had an aggressively childless-by-choice couple. The little boy was completely out of control and horribly disruptive. We could neither tolerate him in Circle nor develop good alternative child-care arrangements. The situation eventually blew up, and nearly killed the coven. All of the contenders left, including the mother, who had been a long-term and highly valued member. I still have no idea what, in practical terms, we could have done differently.

The other reason for my reluctance is that I don't feel qualified. I'm not a parent. I'm completely bewildered about how to do right by coveners who are parents, and by their children. So I'm building this chapter around what parents have told me, instead of my own opinions.

I've been able to think of four basic ways that a coven might handle child care. I asked my peers for their reactions to each one:

Decentralized Child Care

Parents arrange for the care of their own children elsewhere, and come to coven without them.

HAWK   For groups that contain few children, or small groups (four coveners or so), this is the best solution, to my mind. It allows for each child to be cared for in accordance with the desires of the parent(s) while not placing the burden for that child's care on any other person. The downside is that interaction with the other coveners and their families is reduced or removed. It also reduces the child's contact with the religion, and this may be undesirable. [Hawk is a father.]

RHEA   Decentralized child care? Not a bad idea, when it can be done. One advantage is that it helps support women's insistence that their partners spend equal time caring for the children. This is a lesson that not all women know, and I have seen them learn it from coven. However, in reality, a lot of women don't have partners or other helpful family members. [Rhea is not a parent.]

GAWAINE   This option will create the least problem for the coven as a whole. While things might have been different in another era, in the age of the nuclear family, parents are responsible for the care of their children. That might sound a little harsh, but I can foresee coven problems if childless members of the coven are expected to help foot baby-sitting costs for those with children. [Gawaine is a father.]

PATRICK   I do not feel that it is appropriate for children to be taking part in the day-to-day workings of a Circle. Children should be being children—playing, watching TV, whatever—and shouldn't necessarily be involved in the Craft. The parents' religion should not be imposed on the children. [Patrick is not a parent.]

Collective Child Care

In this option, children are cared for as a group in a separate room of the covenstead, or even in another house. Questions immediately arise: Do all coven members take turns caring for the children, or just the parents? If an outside sitter is hired, do all coven members or just the parents share the cost? Is it a good idea to try to provide some age-appropriate religious education, or not?

HAWK   With larger groups, I'd favor this. At our coven's Samhain rites in 1994, we had child care at the covenstead while the adults performed the ritual. The baby-sitter was the daughter of a coven member.

As to the "Moonday School" idea, it works well (in my opinion) only if there is a sufficiently organized group. The demands of even a modest religious-education program are significant, and are usually beyond the average-size coven.

GAWAINE   The idea of a kid nursery during Circle is handy if you have the space, but it also runs the risk of Circle being disrupted for minor emergencies. And those emergencies will arise if the children and the baby-sitter know that the parents are in another room.

I think it's up to the particular coven, and the baby-sitter, whether to try to make child care a "Pagan" event. I would point out a potential problem: Kids talk, and they talk about things that are private to people you might rather not have them mentioned to. This could be a problem for people who feel a strong need to stay in the "broom closet."

THEOS   I wouldn't allow parents to bring their children to coven meetings, not unless the children were very young infants, and then only until the new parent had found a decent baby-sitter. Parents in my group found baby-sitters at home. They'd leave the child with Grandma, or they'd have somebody come in.

You can't turn children into another room and expect them to behave. They're going to act up in unfamiliar surroundings. It's not fair to the child. Children need their own surroundings. They need their own bed.

Another room in the same house isn't going to do it. You can't be in another room and not hear the chanting, and not feel the dancing, and not sense the power and not smell the incense. Children are very good at picking up on that stuff. The power's there. They feel it. They sense it. They know it. It may be upsetting to them. [Theos is a mother and grandmother.]

RHEA   Child care at the covenstead sounds incredibly disruptive. Our old coven once tried this. The kids did go to the next room, but we set an eleven-year-old to watch the five-year-olds. Then we kept hearing cries of "Mommy!" If you are going to keep the kids around, you had better have them under the care of someone they trust to deal with cut knees and juice and the other crises of childhood. That means someone they know well. The odds are that one coven member gets stuck being parent instead of getting to participate in the ritual.

If you insist on trying it, whoever feels like it might pay. How could a coven that insists that teaching be done free have the nerve to ask people to pay for baby-sitting other

people's kids? Will you all help pay garage fees for one
member's car? Who buys the candles?

PATRICK   In our group, we do our best to assist each other in
all aspects of everyday life. So if the parent needed help with
child care, we would probably loan money or have one of
our own family members keep an eye on the kids. However,
it would not be in the same place as the Circle, for no other
reason than if the parent could hear them, even the sim-
plest, faintest cry could be enough to "snap them back to
reality"—their focus shifting to the children rather than
to the work at hand.

Include the Children in Adult Rituals

MAGENTA   I think it is unfair to both the kids and adults to expect kids to sit quietly during Circle. If you have a ritual
planned that would be compatible with kids, fine, but I
know of few worse interruptions to a solemn ritual than
a baby crying or a toddler squirming and whimpering. [Ma-
genta is not a parent.]

HAWK   Unlikely, unless the children are of sufficient maturity
level. My daughter (currently age four with a slightly older
maturity level) could not be expected to sit politely through
a rite of any serious length.

GAWAINE   Bringing children into Circle raises several issues:
Are the coveners planning on keeping all conversations in
the coven child-appropriate? This will limit the issues you
can work on.

Can children sit in Circle and not be disruptive? This depends on the age and the child, but the odds are against it.
It's not the fault of the child, but none of mine would have
been able to do so, and they're pretty good kids.

Is Circle a place for children? If you're doing a working
that raises any kind of strong energy, I would question the
wisdom of having children present, both because they could

be disruptive and, more importantly, because it might not be that good for them. Does that mean you should never have children in Circle? Of course not, but the ritual should be one tailored for child participation. If every Circle were like that, it might get boring for the adults.

RHEA   Treat them like adults? Fine with older kids. You can't expect anyone under thirteen to manage it, though. Also, even that thirteen-year-old must have had some prior experience with ritual. And you had best make real sure that the kids want to be there. Make sure they know how dull it all is. Oh, and you do need to consider if the ritual is age-appropriate. I mean, some of what I've done has been pretty graphic. Also, how comfortable will parents be doing real work with baby watching?

RHOMYLLY   The only child I have ever had to deal with in Circle was a six-year-old girl. Our rituals tended to be very activity-oriented, so they needed very little modification for her to be able to fully participate. Because of various members' twelve-step needs, we also didn't use wine as a ritual beverage, so that was never a problem. The only thing we had to be mindful of was her bedtime.

She behaved better in Circle than some of the adults, very attentive, sensitive, and aware. She even called Quarters and invoked Deity on more than one occasion, and better than some of the adults! Of course, she'd been raised Pagan since birth, and her parents had had her in ritual since day one. It astonishes me to realize, as I write this, that although I am not usually fond of children, I miss her very much. [Rhomylly is not a parent.]

Adapt Your Rituals for Children

RHEA   If you have kids of a reasonable age (over three years) this is a splendid idea! I heartily recommend doing a Kids' Circle a few times a year. It will prepare the kids for participating as adults. It will help the parents integrate their religious lives into their family life. It will give everyone an excuse for a really playful ritual.

It may annoy the hopelessly intellectual overly grown-up types. Tough! People who have forgotten how to do rituals appropriate for four-year-olds probably need to relearn that lesson as part of their spiritual growth.

Some guiding principles are:

Remember, the most sacred magical tool really is a toy. If you don't want it broken, don't put it on the altar.

Keep it real short; make a lot of noise, make a lot of mess, perhaps by playing with ritual face paint, or by doing crafty things; move around a lot; have something to eat and drink.

Remember, kids scare easy.

Remember to ground, ground, ground!

Don't try to do more than one ritual at once, or in sequence. Set up the ritual for the youngest of the lot of you, tell everyone else that you are doing so, and just do it. Don't then go on and try to do a ritual for another age group. It is too confusing and tiring.

HAWK   Unsatisfying for many adults. In our coven, we periodically explore the generative and procreative sides of the Gods and of Wicca—subject matter that is inappropriate for most minors. But these topics are appropriate for adults in our religion, and the constant presence of children would stifle these and other subjects.

MAGENTA   Sometimes it is good to have child-friendly rituals, especially outdoor ones where the kids can run around a bit. But I don't think a coven should try to tailor *all* their rituals to kids, unless the group really is of one mind that they want to.

STARSPAWN   Remember, it's not OUR religion immutable to the end, but one that changes with the times and with those who attend. Having kids in a Circle where they are welcome is an entirely new Circle of joy and light. [Starspawn is not a parent.]

Success Stories

Here are reports from two covens that worked well with their children.

MAGENTA   Our group has a coven kid—Kay's son, Robin. We have been very lucky. He has always been part of our rituals, right from a few weeks old. When he was a baby, he would sleep right through rituals. (His mother is also a Morris dancer, and he slept through music and dancing too.)

When he was a toddler, it sometimes took the whole coven to keep an eye on him. We coped, or he was left with his father, who was very good about sharing child-care duties. However, this reinforces our decision not to have both members of a couple in the core coven. On holidays, when his father was invited, we all coped with Robin as best we could.

Now that Robin is seven, our care is beginning to pay off. He is an active participant in many rituals, and an excellent drummer.

I think each coven has to work matters out differently, depending on the number of kids, the number of adults, and the sort of rituals performed.

We have not had Robin at our Samhain ritual yet, and probably won't for a few more years. Kay manages to find someone to watch him. Actually, finding or starting a baby-sitting co-op that includes non-Pagans might be the best solution. "I'll take care of your kids on Yom Kippur if you'll take care of mine on Samhain."

JIM   Our coven was very child-oriented at one period. Six children were considered coven members, including our son. We had a wide age range—from six months to eleven years old—which made things more interesting. One advantage to having some older kids was that we could have them sort of supervising play and reporting to the adults if there was a problem. We had to be accepting about important interruptions during the rituals, and so we set them up accordingly.

We didn't see incorporating the kids in our activities as a problem. It just seemed like a natural thing to do. Wicca is a life-affirming religion. Few things are more life-oriented than growing children. Also, we were, and are, a teaching coven. Teaching the next generation about the Earth and our religion seemed imperative.

We took care of the kids in a variety of ways. Sometimes all the parents pitched in for a baby-sitter, or someone had a family member who was willing to sit. Sometimes we just waited until 9:00 P.M. or so, bedded the kids down where we were having the ritual (usually the house of a parent), and had the ritual after they were asleep. Samhain was usually one of these.

Sometimes we had a "preritual" or a two-part ritual that had a kid-oriented beginning. Then they went to bed, or perhaps one covenmate (not always a parent) took them off for a separate program while the rest of us continued with the ritual. Beltane was often done like this.

We often would include the kids in celebratory rituals like Ostara. When the kids were included, we would tailor the ritual to appeal to both kids and adults. Where appropriate, we involved the kids in ritual planning. Our son was the primary facilitator for a wonderful Discordian Ostara ritual at age thirteen!

Moonday School?

This book is about covens. This chapter is about how covens work with members who are parents, and how various covens deal with the presence of members' children. The religious education of these children has not been our primary focus. Yet even though it is tangential to our main topic, I don't think we can completely ignore children's religious training. It is too important to those of us who are parents, and too central to the future survival of our religion. I was fortunate to be able to interview someone who is a real grandmother in both senses of the word.

Mini-Ritual for a Baby Blessing

1. Cast Circle or otherwise create sacred space.

2. Statements on the nature and value of life from respected elders; could indicate *brief* relevant readings or appropriate music.

3. Asperge, anoint, and cense child (taking care to use materials that will not irritate a baby's skin or lungs).

4. Present the child to the Guardians of the Quarters and to the Deities (if the child has a secret name, this can be whispered).

5. Parent(s) state their wishes, hopes, intentions, and commitments toward this child.

6. Older siblings (if any) state their wishes, hopes, intentions, and commitments toward this child. Anyone else who will be living in the same household with this baby should also be included.

7. Godparents or sponsors state their wishes, hopes, intentions, and commitments toward this child.

8. Grandparents (if present) state their wishes, hopes, intentions, and commitments toward this child.

9. Present the child to all present—representatives of the community—using the child's public name.

10. Invite all present to offer a blessing to or wish for this child. (Optional: Guests can be asked in advance to bring tiny symbolic gifts to make a "magic bag" for the baby.)

For thirteen years Lady Theos served as High Priestess of one of the earliest North American covens. During the same period she raised eight children. So she ran Children's Circles, for her own kids and the children of other local Wiccan families. More than thirty children participated in these groups over time. Both the kids and the adults involved thoroughly enjoyed the experience. And yet, on reflection, Theos feels what they did was a mistake. Here, excerpted from the tape of our interview, is what she said:

> I remember the children doing their own rituals. I remember they were very strong. They were very powerful. They were very good. I remember children forcing themselves to learn to read so that they could know the rituals, and write their own rituals. They had a lot of fun at it. They learned the songs. They learned the dancing.
>
> Still, if I had it to do over again, I wouldn't run Children's Circles the same way. I don't think it was beneficial to the majority of the children, including some of my own. That's not to say that they couldn't be taught Pagan concepts and Pagan philosophies. It's a way of life, a way of looking at things.

Lady Theos on parental commitment and stability:

> Children need stability. If you're telling them something is real and something is good and something is beautiful, you can't play with it for a while, get all turned on with it yourself, drag your kids into it, and then leave.
>
> Over the years, there've been very few people who have brought their children in who were themselves truly committed to a Pagan way of life. They thought they were. They were in it for a few years. They dragged their kids in. And then they left for one reason or another.
>
> This is very bad on the kids. This is terrible. I felt a lot of pain for the children who were pulled out of groups over the years.

Lady Theos on secrecy or openness:

> The need for secrecy was very strong. The children had to be cautioned about not saying anything to anybody. They were all very good at that. But is that really what you want to teach your child about a way of life that's very beautiful: that you need to hide? I don't think that was good. You teach children about Judaism, about Christian-

ity, to stand up and proudly announce their faith. A child should be proud and secure.

I asked her whether it would be better and easier for children if their families were open about their religion, so there was no issue of a "family secret" and the double message that this gives. She laughed.

Look at children. Children have to be the same. Children dress the same. If one kid gets an earring in the nose, they all want an earring in the nose. One wears jeans with holes in the knees, do you remember that era? They all wore that. Children, in their fight to be nonconformists, are the greatest conformists that ever were. They all mimic one another.

Now, [by openness] you set children up as separate things, is that good for them? You're setting them apart. You're making them outcasts. You're making others become afraid of them. The Christian world is still saying, "Witches are bad. You're Satanists. You hate our God. You worship the Devil." Others just don't understand. I don't know that that's good for our children. Children don't like to be separate. They want to be part of their peer group.

Lady Theos on age-appropriate instruction:

Children are very clever. They'll use the tricks they're taught. They're very good magically, especially during puberty. The magic and the belief all comes natural to them. I've had kids go to school and sell "pass your test" oil, and "get out of detention" and "get off the hook with your homework" spells. All of these worked.

But I don't know that it was such a good idea to teach the children the magic at those ages, before they had the wisdom to know when to use it and when not to use it. They would use it for any trick that seemed suitable to them. From what I know now, what they really learned was that they could use magic to manipulate their surroundings. And they did it continuously.

On unforeseen emotional or psychological consequences:

One of the children I taught had a kitten, and wanted to make it her familiar. I let her do it. I never realized what a mistake that would be. And then the cat was hit by a car and killed. You don't know what a job it did on that kid! Children have kittens and they lose pets, but not like this. This was above and beyond. She was emotionally, psychically, and magically tied to that cat, and so she was devastated! I would never let a child do that again.

In conclusion:

It's really hard to tell. I don't know if there was any harm done to any of the children. They seem to be functioning okay in their lives. I don't know that it served any purpose in their lives to bring them in. I'm not sure if it gave them anything that couldn't have been given them if the parents were able to just live the philosophy—and that would've been enough. If I had it to do over again, I wouldn't bring them in.

After I had transcribed the tape and slept on it, I had some additional thoughts, which led to some further conversation with Theos. Since our first interview she had had the opportunity to speak with one of the children—now an adult— who'd participated in the Children's Circles, and with one of the other parents. Both agreed that, although everyone enjoyed those Circles at the time and no one was harmed, it was not a good idea.

But that's an unacceptable paradox. What kind of religion fails to provide religious education for its young? What religious parent doesn't want to pass her faith, her source of divine contact and nurturance, to her children?

The logic of the situation leads once again to the conclusion that Witchcraft is not a religion, but a committed religious order. Our religion is Paganism. When someone is initiated as a Priest/ess, this is not into some vague "priesthood of all believers." That concept actually dissolves the notion of priesthood into meaninglessness. Our initiation brings a person into the dedicated clergy of our religion. Candidates should be reasonably sure that they have this calling, and a lifelong commitment to fulfill it, before they accept initiation.

Covens are not tiny congregations; they are more like non-residential monasteries. The training appropriate for entering a religious order is given at maturity, and only to those who have a specific calling. Seminary is not the same thing as Sunday School.

Pagan kids certainly should get a religious education, but the teaching should be both age-appropriate and oriented toward intelligent participation as Pagan laity. They should learn about the Goddess and the God, the Sabbats and the Quarters. They should learn the songs, stories, chants, and dances. They should learn Pagan philosophy and a Nature-friendly way of life.

When they reach young adulthood, and only if they have a specific calling to the priesthood, the rest will follow.

Conclusions

- Know your limits. Preverbal toddlers and children with special needs are nearly impossible to have in any sort of Circle. When our special-needs child got into tantrum mode, his mother would take him out of Circle. But his screams from the next room prevented the rest of us from concentrating anyhow. This is the Crone's hard truth: Even if the problem is not his "fault," you should not let one person spoil it for everybody.

- Circles that are suitable for children are always suitable for adults. Just about any adult will benefit from lightening up and playing sometimes. Playful, noisy, messy, high-energy activities can certainly be magically transformative, especially for those of us who overintellectualize or otherwise take ourselves too seriously.

- Not all Circles that are suitable for adults are suitable for children. Long periods of sitting still, as for a meditation, are beyond most children's attention span. Adult-level classes are boring. Some topics are frightening or otherwise inappropriate. Some rituals are for initiates only. Children who don't yet know how to ground should not be shown how to raise power.

- Your coven exists to serve the adult members. The adults in your coven are entitled to a preponderance of *adult-level* programming!

- You can't just designate a ritual as okay for kids. What is appropriate for any particular child depends on her age, maturity level, prior experience, interest, and so on. Parents know their own children best. If you let parents know in advance what is actually being planned, they can decide whether to bring their kids.

- Remember that children often regress when confronted with something unfamiliar. A different house, different people around, even their own house set up differently, as for a ritual, may cause a usually placid child to become upset and overactive.

- Boundary maintenance is a coven leader's job. If a parent makes repeated bad decisions about whether to bring a child, the coven leader needs to intervene. If a child is too disruptive to be there at all, and the parent can't or won't see it, the coven leader needs to draw the line. This is extremely hard to do, but still necessary.

- While it's regrettable to deprive a parent of all coven participation, it may be necessary to ask him to stay away from adult-level activities unless he has somewhere to leave his child.

- We should find other, creative ways to support the ongoing spiritual development of parents of toddlers: perhaps private rituals that are not timebound, or buddy systems, or . . . ?

- What seems to work best is a mixture of approaches, balancing the needs of children, parents, and the coven as a whole.

To Learn More

McArthur, Margie. *Wiccacraft for Families*. Custer, Wash.: Phoenix, 1994.

O'Gaea, Ashleen. *The Family Wicca Book*. St. Paul, Minn: Llewellyn, 1994.

Serith, Ceiswir. *The Pagan Family*. St. Paul, Minn: Llewellyn, 1994.

Starhawk, Anne Hill, and Diane Baker. *Circle Around: Raising Children in Goddess Traditions*. New York: Bantam, 1998.

5

WE CALL THY NAME

COVEN AS WORSHIPING GROUP

*The purpose of a religion is to put us in touch with the Divine and to receive what is sometimes called **grace**. I define this word to mean the inner wisdom and harmony we obtain when we are in touch with the divine spirit. Knowing who and what we are, and understanding the beauty and wonder of that self, is what our rituals are about. When I do a ritual to worship the Gods, I am attempting to strengthen my connection with the divine spirit.*

—BLACKSUN, *The Spell of Making* (1995)

In our covens we come together to encounter the Ancient Gods. Together we open our hearts and minds to sacred wisdom and power. Together we seek sacred guidance for all our doings. Covens nurture the development of Wiccan spirituality.

What on earth does that mean?

We are just learning—or reconstructing—the long-suppressed ways of European Pagan Nature mysticism, building our thealogy from the ruins, often from the bare ground up. In fact, up to now we've been so taken up with reconstructing our ritual practices that we've had scant time and energy to reflect on what we do. We barely know how to talk about our religious activity, even with one another. This lack of language isolates us, preventing us from sharing our discoveries and insights.

Here are the definitions I use, derived from my own experience rather than from any dictionary. I hope they can help us think and talk together.

Spirituality: 1) Conscious contact with the Sacred, however you conceptualize or understand the Sacred. 2) Any activities, personal or collective, formal or informal, intended to create, maintain, clarify, deepen, or increase conscious contact with the Sacred.

Religion: 1) Activities intended to create, maintain, and strengthen the connection between spiritual experience and everyday behavior. 2) Organized, institutional support system for these activities, and for spiritual and ethical development in general. (Twelve-steppers will recognize that these definitions are based on steps eleven and twelve, respectively.)

Religion and spirituality are not antagonistic or even mutually exclusive. Their meanings overlap. Spirituality certainly can include organized collective worship, but it is not limited to this. Someone meditating under a tree, all alone, can be in deep contact with the Sacred.

The word *religion* is derived from the Latin *ligere*, which means "to connect" and is also the root for our words *ligament* and *link*. Religion connects inner, spiritual experience with outer, worldly activities. Spirituality is part, but only part, of religion. *Religion* has also come to mean connection with fellow believers, church participation, while spirituality is more private and inward.

Through both spiritual and religious activity we work toward clarifying our understanding of the Sacred, developing conscious contact, and letting that contact shine through all our affairs.

Contact with whom? We are not just generically religious, we are Witches. What does it mean to create and deepen conscious contact specifically with Mother Earth and the Ancient

Gods, and to live our lives in accord with Their ways? Just as with any other religion, answering *that* question is the work of a lifetime.

Explaining ourselves clearly to others is a great way to learn about ourselves. The effort requires us to think through assumptions that we might otherwise leave unexamined. Witches had one such opportunity in 1993, in Chicago, at the Parliament of the World's Religions. I was privileged to be there.

Everyone at the parliament was trying very hard to be respectful and inclusive. The opening ceremony featured brief greetings from many major leaders of the world's "great" religions. Almost all of them said the same polite thing, in very nearly the same words: "We all worship the same *one God*, although we call *Him* by many different names" (emphasis mine). Oh, really?

Four times as many people came to the parliament as had been expected, so there was no way all of us could fit into the main assembly hall. The ceremony was carried throughout the hotel on closed-circuit television. Many of the Wiccans present gathered in the Covenant of the Goddess hospitality suite to watch the ceremony. As each leader repeated the key statement, we winced and groaned.

We were visibly present at a major interfaith gathering for the first time, and were not at all sure of our welcome. We certainly didn't, and still don't, want to make unnecessary waves. But our faith is not just another variant of male monotheism. To honestly gain a seat at the table, we will have to make this understood.

Some of us think we follow a new religion. Others believe our religion is ancient, although newly emerged from centuries underground. Either way, only a very few of us were raised in this faith. It is new in *our* lives. We are, overwhelmingly, a first-generation religion. We do not have centuries worth of unbroken tradition to draw on. Very few of us have any formal training in theological analysis or jargon. I know I felt unprepared, ill equipped, and frightened. Whatever impression we made would reflect on all Witches.

~~~~~~

Mini-Ritual for Casting a Circle

Between the worlds this Circle stands
A ring of light, a ring of clasping hands
Here incense sweet and bitter brine
Shall bless each thing, empower, and make divine.

(from Black Lotus)

~~~~~~

How could we make ourselves understood? Later in the week we conducted a public Full Moon ritual in a park near the hotel, and invited everyone from the parliament. Several hundred came. Afterward one of them told me he was glad to have been at our "coming-out party!" Showing is often easier and sometimes more effective than telling.

In the long run, though, we will need both demonstration and explanation. Our neighbors are naturally curious, and sometimes suspicious, about what we believe and do. We need to learn how to tell our own story in ways that they can understand, but also in our own terms.

At the Pan-Pagan gathering in Indiana in 1980, a respected elder called Brother Cyprian gave a workshop intended to teach people how to explain our faith in terms of standard theology. The problem is that most theology, in the English-speaking world, rests on the Bible.

I still have his workshop handout. There's one page for each of the usual Christian theological pigeonholes, such as theodicy, eschatology, and salvation. It fits us and our beliefs about as well as the bed of Procrustes. We are more different than this—different way down to the roots. Yet the questions that open-minded neighbors ask me are most often guided by these familiar, inapplicable categories.

I think real communication has to start with something as rudimentary as our understanding of the word *religion* itself. Dr. Leonard Swidler, who is a professor of Catholic thought and interreligious dialogue at Temple University in Philadephia and one of the fathers of interfaith dialogue, suggests that religions normally contain four components—creed, cult, code, and community—which he calls the "four c's." These categories are neutral enough that most faiths, ours included, will fit them.

No single Witch can presume to speak for all Witches. From the perspective of my personal experience and that of Proteus Coven, then, this is a description of Wicca in terms of the four c's.

Creed

Creed refers to a religion's belief system or what Swidler calls the "cognitive aspect"—a religion's concepts of the Sacred, its values, its general worldview. For me this would also include the stories, symbols, myths, and metaphors used to convey this understanding.

Ours is not a religion of the Book. No single sacred Scripture defines Witchcraft or neo-Paganism. Instead, we are free to choose among a kaleidoscopic array of poetry, story, and symbol. More important, we are taught that we must ultimately find what we seek within ourselves. Lived experience is the base upon which our inherited structure of written and oral traditions is built, and the standard against which these teachings are continually tested.

I'd rather speak tentatively about the Sacred, since I believe this reality to be far beyond any human comprehension. However, like most Witches, I understand and relate to the Sacred primarily as immanent rather than transcendent. If the concept of transcendence means anything to me, it is that the whole is greater than the sum of all the parts.

Beyond the personal unconscious lies the collective wisdom of humankind, called the transpersonal or the collective unconscious. Beyond, and far greater than this, is the wisdom of the Whole, of the Gods, all that we sometimes loosely call the Otherworld. Although we sometimes conceive of the Otherworld as radically different, it includes all that is familiar and very, very much more. On flat paper we might depict this as a series of concentric circles, but really it's more like concentric spheres. There is no trade-off between depth and breadth. As the radius of inclusion grows, the spheres become both wider and deeper, eventually reaching to the very ground of our being and to our highest ideals.

I am part of this, and so are you. All that lives, and much more, is part of this. But I can no more define it than the wave can define the ocean or the leaf can define the tree. All I can do is describe my own experience and what I know of how others have reported theirs. On the basis of our experiences and perceptions, we guess.

From the perspective of immanence, I experience the Sacred as a very present Source, the life within my every living moment, rather than as a long-ago and far-away Creator or a Holy Wholly Other. I recognize no division between the Creator and Creation. Instead, my quest is to open my awareness to the power and beauty, meaning and value within the everyday and the ordinary—in this body, on this Earth, here and now.

I am also a polytheist. Again, I do not presume to define the Sacred as either plural or singular. However, I do have some observations about how the human religious imagination operates.

Real monotheism is all-inclusive. Since it leaves no one out, it does not oppress anyone. However, history shows that only a few gifted individuals have ever truly been able to sustain this pure consciousness of an abstract all-pervasive Divinity. Most of us, in order to relate to the Sacred, in order to pray at all, need to stick a face onto God.

Once we do so the one all-inclusive God usually devolves into one face, one model. Whichever face you choose—stern white-bearded Father, loving giving Mother, or any other—most of us are left out. Whoever does not resemble the model becomes lesser, or even other—someone it's okay to oppress. Still, to this day some groups refuse to ordain gifted and dedicated women to their clergy because the women do not resemble their male image of Deity. While theoretical monotheism need not lead to oppression, applied monotheism often does.

Instead, Pagan tradition honors the diversity of Divinity and the divinity of diversity. Our many Gods, or, if you prefer, many models of the Sacred, show us an inclusive holiness that crosses all lines: gender, age, occupation, whatever. Balance and integration are also important to us, so we often model the reconciliation of apparent opposites through marriage myths.

Our multivalent model of Divinity is utterly different from simplistic dualism. Dualism views good and evil as an absolute dichotomy without shading or nuance, and personifies them accordingly. The Devil, an evil counterpart to the good God, is only conceivable within a dualistic worldview. Despite centuries of slander, Witches are not Devil worshipers. How could we be? We are polytheists, not dualists.

We do not even acknowledge a God of absolute evil, let alone worship one. We do not invert the values and symbols of biblical religion; nor is our primary religious motivation rebellion against the traditions into which most of us were born. We do not understand or define ourselves in contradistinction to any other faith. Instead we reach back to older and simpler forms, those we believe to be the ancient shamanic ways of tribal Europe, rooted in the living Earth.

I worship the Goddess. Generally, Wiccans offer their primary devotion to the Earth Mother. This is not in any way to deny the existence or power of other deities, and in fact we address Them when we feel the need. But we are born of Mother Earth, nourished throughout our lives from Her bosom, and return to Her in death just as the leaves return to the forest floor. Embracing Her as our primary contact with the Sacred emphasizes the interpenetration of Deity with this ordinary and everyday life that we are living.

Some Witches worship the Goddess exclusively; most also worship Her consort, the wild, free God of animal life, perhaps most widely known in Euro-American culture as Pan. Some covens and groups of covens concentrate on a particular ethnic pantheon: Celtic, Greek, Egyptian, or whatever. Others, like my own, are more broadly eclectic in their practice. Still, it's fair to describe Wiccans as immanence-based polytheists who offer primary devotion to the Goddess, Mother Earth.

In addition to our understanding of Deity, most Wiccan covens use two major symbolic systems to represent the wholeness of life. These are the Quartered Circle and the Wheel of the Year.

The Quartered Circle: The Spatial Metaphor

Our rites almost always begin with casting a Circle and calling the Quarters. Similar symbols, such as mandalas and Medicine Wheels, show up around the Earth. The two central ideas represented by the Quartered Circle are so nearly ubiquitous that they might actually transcend culture.

ORIENTATION IN SPACE The traditional Navajo home is built so the first rays of the rising sun enter the door. Muslims face Mecca to pray. We call the Quarters. All of these are variations on a theme. There are some very different mythological explanations given for some remarkably similar ritual practices. The actual source of this behavior may be observation of the way the sun travels across the sky, and the way the sun's path changes as the seasons change. Or it may be even more basic than our humanity: a subtle, "wired-in" sensitivity to polar magnetism, the same awareness that guides migratory birds.

THE MODEL OF WHOLENESS The qualities or energies any group attributes to the Quarter points will be the ones that this particular group most prizes. The Quartered Circle is a way of making sure everything really important is honored for itself *and* brought into a balanced relationship with everything else that is really important. Its meta-message is the fundamental polarity between unity and diversity.

Witches love to draw correspondences. We map all kinds of things onto the basic glyph of the Quartered Circle: seasons, colors, altar tools, Tarot suits. . . . Some of these make more sense than others. Some are highly debatable. Some actually vary from one group to the next. In the fact that these attributions are not immediately obvious and are not universally held lies a very important lesson: ***Our symbol systems are human-created vocabularies: models, not facts.***

Confusing model with fact, "the map with the territory," is a terrible blunder. First, we might be mistaken. At best our comprehension is necessarily partial. If we let our understanding of the Gods, or of appropriate behavior, become static and reified, we kill all possibilities of further learning and growth. Also, history warns us that people who felt they had a monopoly on truth often took that as a mandate to impose their beliefs and practices on others. By crusade and bloody inquisition, we have caused each other unspeakable suffering. If we hold our metaphors lightly, we can avoid both of these dangers. Instead, we keep alive the potentials for lifelong personal growth and continuing development of our traditions across the generations.

That being said, here are the most widespread Wiccan Quarter attributions:

EAST   East is the place of beginnings, associated with the element Air. This is the quarter of intellect: of research, logic, critical thinking. Contrary to popular notion, we neither reject nor disrespect science—we only seem to do so because we hold it in balance while the culture around us grants it supremacy. You will also find the East associated with spring, dawn, childhood, and the color yellow.

SOUTH   This is the place of peaking, associated with the element Fire. This is the quarter of passion: of courage, will, lust, drive, desire, action. In older texts the word *emotion* is placed in the South. This is confusing, because some emotions are more watery, others fiery. Instead, I use the word *passion*, as a clearer, more specific term for the powers of the South. Energy, in the physical sense, belongs to the South. Other associations include summer, high noon, adolescence, and the color red.

WEST   The West is the place of deepening, associated with the element Water. This is the quarter of wisdom: of compassion, intuition, and insight. Dreamwork is here, and divination, and many other spiritual practices and the insights they bring us, balancing the intellect of the East, each essential to inform and correct the other. West is associated with autumn, dusk, maturity, and the color blue.

NORTH This is the place of transformation, of death and birth and the nothingness in between, associated with the element Earth. This is the quarter of the body: of skilled work and the pleasures of the senses. The form of the North balances the force of the South. North is also traditionally the quarter of silence, balancing with its stillness the South's high energy. North is associated with winter, midnight, both elderhood and infancy, and the color green.

Although we do not usually formally invoke the vertical dimension, we should be aware of it. Many indigenous and shamanic peoples envision some sort of world axis—our Maypole is likely an echo of these—and a three-level universe.

These levels do not correspond to Heaven, Earth, and Hell. Heaven and Hell are later accretions. Witches do not conflate higher with better or lower with worse. Instead, in a Pagan worldview down and up are both good and both necessary, although different enough to look like opposites; nature and culture are another polarity. Life-giving power flows in both directions, spiraling like the Maypole's ribbons, which wind in both directions just like the double helix of life.

What lies below us are sheer natural forces and capacities, which may be conceptualized as power animals. This includes internal qualities like speed, cunning, and strength, as well as such external natural forces as mountain, ocean, hurricane, sun, moon. Some cultures represent these as a separate family of Gods, such as the Titans, who are more ancient than the others. These powers are the foundation of our lives and of all life. The color of Below is black, the nurturing soil, the darkness within the womb.

What lies above us are the great ideals, which may differ from culture to culture. This is why the Gods of one culture never correspond precisely to those of another—different cultures and subcultures uphold different core values. Also, there are a lot more ways than one to categorize reality. Cultural ideals may include love, courage, wisdom, generosity, firmness. Cultural groups create stories and symbols to transmit these values and to inspire people to live by them. The color of Above is gold.

Recently some groups, including mine, have been calling an additional Direction:

CENTER   The Center is the place of magic: of balance and integration, of choice and responsibility, of consummation and wholeness, the place where we stand and to which we draw the powers and qualities of the four Quarters in accord with our needs and desires of that moment. All things come together at Center, and from Center the Mystery emanates outward to fill all the worlds. Center is iridescent, like the shining rainbow of an abalone shell. There, in beauty and wonder, we place ourselves.

The Wheel of the Year: The Temporal Metaphor

The eight-spoked Wheel of the Year represents wholeness in terms of time—the interacting cycles of Earth and Sun, which produce the seasons of the land, the basis for our Wiccan ritual calendar. We celebrate eight festivals, called Sabbats. The Equinoxes and Solstices represent the cycles of the Sun. The four cross-Quarter days of Samhain, Brigit, Beltane, and Lunasa, which marked major turning points in the old British agricultural calendar, are more closely Earth-related.

Like the Directions each Sabbat is a multivocal symbol,* and so is the Wheel of the Year taken as a whole (a multivocal meta-symbol?). Multivocal symbols mean many things—there is no one right and true interpretation—but normally the set of meanings is interrelated, a cluster of associations branching from some common point. The Wheel of the Year, as we celebrate it, has associations both with the seasonal cycle of Nature

---

*Sometimes you'll see the word *symbol* used to mean by definition a multivocal statement, as contrasted with *sign*—a word, phrase, or picture that has one simple and commonly understood meaning.

and the normal developmental phases of human life. Thus it connects them.

Modern technology mediates and cushions the impact of Nature's cycles on our lives. Most of us are warm in winter and cool in summer; we have steady and reliable access to light and food. We are safer and far more comfortable than our ancestors, but this safety and comfort distances us from Nature. We need to compensate for this separation by conscious effort.

Although awareness of Her is no longer inherent in our lives, our lives are still wholly contingent on Hers. People and institutions that have forgotten this dependency are daily putting Her life and ours at significant risk. Using religion as a reminder may sound very modern, even politically correct. In fact part of the most ancient Celtic understanding of religion's purpose was to negotiate and maintain a right relationship between land and tribe.

The Sabbats, as multivocal symbols, are not *only* about the Earth's seasonal cycle. There are similar cycles and changes within human lives. We celebrate "passage rituals" to mark, honor, and integrate individual changes as they happen: a baby-blessing, a coming of age, a handfasting. The actual human life cycle takes much longer than a year. By mapping it onto the Wheel we go through it in microcosm each year.

Doing so allows each of us to revisit the stages we've passed with new understandings and to prepare for the stages yet to come. Celebrating the Wheel of the Year also reminds us that others experience very similar passages, and so strengthens our sense of human connection and community. It also relates our life cycle to Earth's seasonal round.

The Wheel is our metaphor for the endless rhythm of dreaming, doing, harvesting, and letting go that moves through the great and small changes of our lives, and for the greater cycle of the human life stages: birth, adolescence, marriage, death, and so on. This is the pulse of day and night, summer and winter, life and death. We aspire to dance gracefully within this natural rhythm.

~~~~~~

Mini-Ritual to Bless Food and Drink

Blessed be this food.
Blessed be the land that nurtured it,
   and the Sun that gave it power.
And blessed be all hands, seen and unseen,
   that have brought this food to us.

(from Proteus Coven)

~~~~~~

Witches also celebrate the rhythms of the Moon, Earth's lovely daughter, bringer of dreams and poetic inspiration. Traditionally, the solar and terrestrial Sabbats are times for communitywide celebration and attunement with natural cycles, the exoteric aspects of our religion, while the Moons are reserved for more intensive personal and small-group focus on inner spiritual development (for more on this, see chapter 6).

Cult

The word *cult* only recently took on a pejorative meaning. In older and more scholarly usage it simply means "a system or community of religious worship and ritual." *Worship* is defined as "the reverent love and allegiance accorded a deity, idol, or sacred object" and "a set of ceremonies, prayers, or other religious forms by which this love is expressed." Our cult is our worship, the expression of our reverent love for the Ancient Gods, our spiritual practices, prayers, ceremonies, rituals—all our patterned religious activity.

Wiccan rituals come in all sizes. We do ritual alone, or with just our partners. We do open Sabbats for our local communities, and rites at large gatherings that can involve hundreds of people. Central to all of this are the rites we do in our small, intensely bonded, spiritual support groups, our covens.

First, what is ritual?

Ritual action, the dramatization of a significant event, is a major means of social integration. At its most fundamental level, ritual is the enactment of myth. In the past, religious and political myths gave the members of a community a sense of their origins and destiny. In our present technological society, churches and synagogues often provide this kind of attunement to communal principles. For those who genuinely participate, the rituals offer occasions for identity and renewal. Through song, dance, and storytelling, people identify with their society. They gain a greater understanding of the whole of which each is a part. Although the mythic and aesthetic forms of ritual differ from culture to culture, its function remains the same—to provide an immediate, direct sense of involvement with the sacred, confirming the worldview, indeed the very being, of the participant. . . .

In the ritual play of traditional religion, persons seek communion with transcendent being; the myths that are enacted point to the beginning and the beyond. Through faith, the participants perceive dimensions of space, time, and destiny beyond finite experience—an "assurance of things hoped for and the conviction of things not seen."*

Ritual is an art form, a kind of multimedia performance art. Theater is the daughter of ritual. The larger the group participating in a ritual, the more important the theatrical aspect becomes, for this is what keeps participants focused and coordinated.

Ritual is also a set of powerful intervention techniques used to promote psychospiritual growth, a craft that carries us to encounter with the Sacred and personal transformation. In coven we are committed to working together consistently and over a long term. We have established firm trust and deep rapport. From this secure base we can explore deep within and far beyond ourselves. We explore Sacred Immanence.

*Goethals, Gregor T., "Ritual: Ceremony and Super-Sunday," in *Readings in Ritual Studies*, Ronald L. Grimes, ed. (Upper Saddle River, N.J.: Prentice-Hall, 1996): 257–258.

Mini-Ritual for a Morning Blessing of the Day's Work

Stand in the center of the room, facing East, and say,
  "Guardians of the East, may I work today with knowledge."

Take a deep, slow breath, turn South, and say,
  "Guardians of the South, may I work today with passion."

Take a deep, slow breath, turn West, and say,
  "Guardians of the West, may I work today with wisdom."

Take a deep, slow breath, turn North, and say,
  "Guardians of the North, may I work today with skill."

Take a deep, slow breath, turn East, and blow a kiss.
Take three deep, slow breaths and go about your day.

A coven is a group of individuals gathered for a common spiritual purpose. Yet each individual coven member functions differently. It's important for anyone creating a ritual to understand that some of us understand the world primarily through seeing, others through hearing, and still others through touch. (Quick test: When a ritual object is "charged," do you experience it as glowing, humming, or vibrating? If the charged object seems to glow, the person is primarily visual. If it hums, audial. If it vibrates or gets warm, tactile.) To help the group work together, a good ritual will engage as many of the senses as possible, along with the mind. Doing this also enhances the effect for each individual, since engaging secondary sensory channels reinforces the effect on the primary.

Here are some of the possibilities:

- *Words* engage the mind. Prayer and invocation are the most familiar uses of words in ritual, but not the only possibilities. Participants can share their thoughts and feelings through formal "rounds" or open discussion. Affirmations and statements of intention, commitment, or desire reach and root deeper when we speak or hear them in sacred space. Our myths can be told as stories, incorporated in poetry or song lyrics (meter and rhyme make things much easier to remember), or enacted as mystery plays (which adds a dramatic visual dimension to the words).

- *Music, rhythm, and sounds* can be used to relax people or to arouse them. Some possibilities: drums, bells and chimes, instrumental music, the human voice, chanting, speaking, or singing (but remember, there's a big difference between the experience of listening and that of participation).

- *Visuals* create a focus: Altar images and decorations can be varied with the season or with the theme or purpose of the ritual. Robes, masks, ritual jewelry, and even stage makeup can help Priest/esses to represent the Gods in the rites. (From the wearer's perspective, robes and masks are also tactile inputs.) Ritual postures, gestures, and dance, when we watch others do them, are visual inputs.

- *Kinetic and tactile input:* Tactile input comes through our skin, as when we join hands around the Circle, exchange ritual kisses, and the like. Kinetic input is the internal sense of balance and movement, and of how our muscles feel, as in ritual postures, gestures, and dance, when we perform or participate in them.

- *Smell:* Incense and oils. The sense of smell reaches the oldest and most primal part of the brain and makes very long-lasting memories. Nevertheless, go light on the incense if anyone in the group has asthma or other respiratory problems.

- *Taste:* Food and drink. Sharing of food is an ancient and transtraditional symbol for bonding among people ("break bread together"). Eating and drinking something that has been ritually prepared, charged, or blessed symbolizes taking the energy or intention into yourself. *Beware of allergies*, strong aversions, and traumatic psychological associations.

These are just a few of the possibilities. The only limitations are your imagination and the available resources. One of the most important facets of a Witch's training is learning how to plan and conduct rituals. The best way to learn is to do, and then to critique. Here are some things to think about when planning or evaluating a ritual:

• Is the main theme of this Circle in accord with your religion's teachings?

• Is each component part of the Circle in accord with other components, the overall theme, and your core values?

• Is everybody present involved? Is an atmosphere or mood created? Is focus maintained?

• Does the Circle appeal to as many perceptual channels as possible?

• Is the Circle as beautiful as you can make it, to give honor to your Gods, your ways, and yourselves? Is the style consistent with the theme?

• Is the pacing quick enough to hold interest? Is it slow enough for the ideas to take root? Are there moments of meditative silence? Is this ritual design realistic about people's time constraints and attention spans?

• How do you get from one ritual component to the next? Are the transitions integral parts of the ritual? Is there a sense of overall flow?

• Is there an appropriate balance of the familiar and the surprising? Familiar parts remind us we are in sacred space, and so make the ritual stronger. Surprising parts often are those that accomplish any particular ritual's purpose.

• Is there an appropriate balance of the cognitive, the passionate, the intuitive, and the sensual?

• Is the ritual within the group's physical comfort level? Be aware of things like sitting still too long, struggling from floor to feet too often, room temperature, hunger, and thirst.

The differences between our ritual practice—our cult—and those of more familiar religious groups should be clear by now. Like them we have familiar, beloved bits of ritual poetry and action that we like to use a lot. Unlike them our emphasis is on creating the rituals we need, new each time, based on our best current understandings and aesthetic preferences. Most Witches understand that religion is like bread: tastier and more nutritious when homemade.

How does this work out in practice? In Proteus Coven we consider initiation to be ordination into the first level of our priesthood. One of the key skills of priesthood is creating and presenting ritual. Accordingly, we ask all candidates for initiation to conduct a Sabbat rite as a demonstration of their competence. Here's one of the best examples in our archives:

The Brigit Sabbat (February 1) is a celebration of the Irish Goddess Brigit, who empowers poetry, smithcraft, and healing. The candidates, a married couple, had focused on the smithcraft aspect, taking as their theme the idea that transformation requires real effort. After the Circle was cast each participant was given a small plastic container with a snap-on lid. In each container was some sweet cream and a marble. We were asked to stand up and chant while shaking these containers, using a high-energy, fast-tempo chant. We danced, chanted, waved our arms around, got pretty aroused. After a while, the cream was transformed into butter. Then they passed around a basket of rolls and some butter spreaders. As we ate the delicious buttered rolls, we took the energy of the working into ourselves.

Here's another example: My friend's brother died suddenly, thousands of miles away. My friend needed a ritual to resolve some of his shock and grief. I invited him to a Circle. On the altar was an empty goblet made of clear glass, and two pitchers. The gray pitcher held pomegranate juice, while the green pitcher held apple juice. I asked him to share memories of his brother. For each sad memory he poured a bit of pomegranate juice into the goblet. For each happy memory he added some apple juice. When the cup was filled we blessed it, and he drank it down as I bore witness. The memories of his brother are part of him forever.

Examples could multiply, but these will suffice. There are several good books of Pagan rituals available now, if you want more examples in order to get started. As you read, please remember that the best rituals will always be the ones that spring from sacred inspiration and your own caring heart and creative mind.

Mini-Ritual for an Evening Blessing of the Night's Dreams

Stand in the center of the room, facing West, and say,
"Guardians of the West, may I gain wisdom from my
dreams tonight."

Take a deep, slow breath, turn North, and say,
"Guardians of the North, may my dreams bring me
strength."

Take a deep, slow breath, turn East, and say,
"Guardians of the East, may I learn from my dreams
tonight."

Take a deep, slow breath, turn South, and say,
"Guardians of the South, may my dreams tonight
release my passions."

Take a deep, slow breath, turn West and blow a kiss.
Take three deep, slow breaths and go to bed.

(Morning and evening blessings
are both adapted from a ritual by Tigress)

Code

The essential religious question is, "What does it mean to live
by this?" *Code* means the behavioral guidance that all religions
provide, both ethics and etiquette. The central purpose of religion is to sustain, amplify, and clarify the connection between
our values and the way we live our lives, to actualize our
conscious contact with the Sacred. Lacking a concern for
ethics, ritual observance becomes at best a feel-good exercise,
a cheap, safe, and legal high—or at worst an excuse for blas-
phemous hypocrisy.

Typically, religions each have a core ethical statement, some
Golden Rule that summarizes our sense of what conduct is appropriate. Wicca is no exception. We call ours the Wiccan

Rede.* It states, "Eight words the Wiccan Rede fulfill: An it harm none, do what you will!"

This is a simple, powerful statement of situational ethics and radical freedom. Witches accept no arbitrary restraints on our freedom of choice. We have no universally applicable set of "thou shalts" and "thou shalt nots." Any harmless behavior is permissible to us. For us the term *victimless crime* is an offensive oxymoron. Neither does our religion seek to regulate the minutiae of our daily lives in order to maintain our collective sense of identity. We follow a "high-choice" ethic.

This may seem like laxity or permissiveness, but in fact our way is far more demanding than the most stringent set of commandments. Without rules, the burden falls on each of us to avoid or minimize any harm that may come from our actions. Without any absolute standard of good and evil, we are each required to think and feel our way through all the complexities, weigh all the probable results and implications of our choices. In the crises and choice points of our personal lives and in our responses to community and social issues, no authority figure directs us. We are on our own.

We have no "orthodox" rulings on marriage, sexuality, divorce, military service or its avoidance, assisted suicide, and the like, although certainly we think and talk about such subjects. When I, as a Priestess, am asked for counsel, my proper role is to make sure that the inquirer has explored the issue in full depth, considered many perspectives, used both her mind and her heart in coming to a conscientious choice. I do not tell her what to do. She chooses and she accepts responsibility for her choice.

Some of us believe that cause and effect, which we call "karma," can play out over many lifetimes. Others understand reincarnation as a metaphor for all the cycles and changes

---

*Rede is an archaic word, derived from the Middle English *reden*, which means "to guide" or "to direct." *An* is an archaic equivalent of "if." So the modern English equivalent is, "If it harms no one, do what you will!"

within this life, each felt as a little death or a small rebirth. We are also taught the principle of "threefold return." Some of us take the quantity literally; others understand this as a metaphor pointing to the reality that whatever goes around comes around *amplified*, and in utterly unpredictable ways. These differences of detail aside, Wiccans understand that we ourselves will reap the rewards, and bear the consequences, of both our actions and our omissions. In a world of cause and effect there is no need for contrived retribution.

The Rede is basic, a common starting point. First, do no harm. Second, tolerate no restrictions unless the behavior they seek to proscribe is demonstrably harmful. Third, when you see harm done, take what action you can to protect and heal, while respecting the free will of those you would aid. These good rules afford us maximal freedom and full responsibility, but little guidance for personal growth and development.

And here is where polytheism gets really interesting. Each of us is a unique individual with a special set of potentials to develop, gifts from the God/dess for us to bring to the community and the world. We also go through some very different developmental phases during our lives.

We typically work with one, or a very few, God/desses at a time, those whose energies, stories, and symbols seem related to the current stretch of our growth path. We seek Their guidance through ritual invocation and apply it in our daily lives. We would naturally expect to see some very different behaviors from Priestesses of Athena, Aphrodite, and Hestia. This might very well extend to symbolic trivia like our choices in clothing or food. Wearing a particular color or eating a particular food might serve to remind us of the changes we are trying to make in ourselves. None of these choices is seen as holier or more ethical than the other, simply different in useful ways. Through all our stages and phases we live by the Rede.

Our code is clearly not the same as some others, but we have a code. Live in accord with your own core values. Be careful about what energies you call into your life. Take heed of the voices on the wind. An it harm none, do what you will!

Community

Swidler's fourth c, community, refers to the whole web of human relationships that support, challenge, and nurture us—large and small, intimate and extended, formal and informal, all the ways in which we connect with people of like mind and common interest. Here I am specifically discussing religious community, the human context for each person's spiritual growth. Witches find this context in our covens. This book is a description of these covens and how they work.

These are the four c's: creed, cult, code, and community, all clearly present in the ways of Witches. They manifest among us according to who we are and Whom we worship, just as they do among all other religious groups. Our ways may seem unusual, but underlying them is the same basic desire—to bring our lives into alignment with our Gods. Although perfection may be forever beyond us, deepening understanding and developing wisdom is a normal expectation. Our religious beliefs and practices link our contact with the Sacred and our ordinary behavior in a double spiral of intertwining growth.

To Learn More

Myth and Theology

Anderson, William. *Green Man: The Archetype of Our Oneness With the Earth*. New York: HarperCollins, 1990.

Christ, Carol. *Laughter of Aphrodite*. New York: Harper & Row, 1987. (Contains her essay "Why Women Need the Goddess," which is one of the foundations of contemporary feminist theology.)

Cowan, Tom. *Fire in the Head: Shamanism and the Celtic Spirit*. New York: HarperSanFrancisco, 1993.

Downing, Christine. *The Goddess: Mythological Images of the Feminine.* New York: Crossroad, 1984. (Also see her many other books.)

Maslow, Abraham. *Religions, Values and Peak Experiences.* New York: Viking, 1970.

Starhawk. *The Spiral Dance.* New York: HarperCollins, 1989.

Ritual

Bell, Catherine. *Ritual Theory, Ritual Practice.* New York: Oxford University Press, 1992.

Driver, Tom. *The Magic of Ritual.* New York: HarperCollins, 1991.

Grimes, Ronald L. *Readings in Ritual Studies.* Upper Saddle River, N.J.: Prentice-Hall, 1996.

Kondratiev, Alexei. *The Apple Branch: A Path to Celtic Ritual.* Cork, Ireland: Collins Press, 1998.

6

Change in Accordance With Will

COVEN AS MAGICAL GROWTH
AND SUPPORT GROUP

You can find a shelfload of books arguing that religion and magic are separate, even antagonistic. Religion, they will tell you, is about celebrating or propitiating Deity, while magic is about controlling our environments, or natural forces, or even the Gods Themselves. However, *our* religion is sometimes referred to as "magical religion," and it operates from an entirely different set of premises:

- Religiously mature people live integrated lives in which their everyday, secular activities are in accord with their core values, their spiritual experience, and their best understanding of the Sacred. This is an ideal never perfectly achieved, but still we walk our talk as best we can.

- Religion is a set of activities, personal and institutional, that help us create, maintain, and strengthen that integral link between belief and behavior.

- *Magic* is customarily defined as either "the art of creating change in accordance with will" or "the art of changing consciousness in accordance with will." Either definition will work for the purpose of this chapter, although I generally prefer the second. The essence of a magical worldview is the perception that everything is connected, so change of consciousness catalyzes change in the world around us.

- Therefore, religiously based magic is willed change that is congruent with spiritual values.

- The word *craft*, when used as the suffix of *Witchcraft*, means exactly what it means elsewhere: "skill in doing or making something, as in the arts; proficiency."* Witches are proficient at bringing about willed change congruent with values. Like other shamanic practitioners around the world, we are technicians of the Sacred.

By our Craft, we make conscious contact with the Ancient Gods. Under Their tutelage, we weigh various aspects of our lives, and consider new choices. Covenmates bear witness, share stories, challenge outworn habits of thought and behavior, give advice, and celebrate success. As a support group we help each other work through the problems and perplexities that are part of every life. As a growth group we help each other work toward fulfilling our best potentials, in service to the Gods, the community, and the Earth.

Know Your Limits: Support Is Not Therapy

A coven is not and should not try to be a therapy group. Several of the coven leaders who offered advice to seekers (reported in chapter 3) were very explicit about this caution. Covens are clearly growth and support groups, among other things. Growth and support groups might be confused with therapy groups, but they are not at all the same. The Associ-

---

*American Heritage Dictionary, 3d ed. (electronic format).

ation for Specialists in Group Work makes this distinction very clear in their professional training standards:

> The group worker who specializes in counseling/interpersonal problem-solving seeks to help group participants to resolve the usual, yet often difficult, problems of living through interpersonal support and problem-solving. ... Nonsevere career, educational, personal, social, and developmental concerns are frequently addressed.
>
> The group worker who specializes in psychotherapy/personality reconstructions seeks to help individual group members to remedy their in-depth psychological problems.*

Covens do everything mentioned in the first definition, and much more. The second definition is far beyond the competence of most coven leaders. Even those few who do have secular, professional training in clinical psychology would not attempt to do in-depth psychotherapy in the context of a coven meeting.

Here's a simple way to understand the distinction. Psychotherapy is about sickness and healing. Growth and support groups are about health and growth. Only those who are mentally healthy should attempt intense spiritual practice or magical training. Exploration of the deep self and the Otherworld may unbalance those who are not. Many of the world's spiritual traditions advise their adherents to save mysticism for the second half of life, after fulfilling a "householder" phase. Celtic lore warns us that those who sleep through a full night on the fairy mound will awaken as either poets or lunatics.

This distinction is almost accurate, but is not absolute. Perfect mental health, like perfect physical health or perfect spiritual congruence, is an ideal never fully achieved. Furthermore, the line between health and sickness is a fuzzy and very permeable boundary. Essentially healthy people still sometimes need healing, for we all have our bad days. Upsetting things

---

*Association for Specialists in Group Work, "Professional Standards for the Training of Group Workers," in Conyne, Robert K., F. Robert Wilson, and Donald E. Ward, *Comprehensive Group Work: What It Means and How to Teach It* (Alexandria, Va.: American Counseling Association, 1997): 247.

happen—unemployment, illness, divorce, bereavement—and people in pain regress. Inner exploration wakes old demons—wounds, scars, traumatic memories. Covens are not therapy groups, but any decent coven would stand by a member who is in situational, temporary emotional distress. (Note to coven leaders: Occasionally a covener will ask you if he can talk something over with you. His concern may or may not be related to Wicca or the coven, but probably will be emotionally loaded either way. When a person who is not trained in counseling needs to help another deal with the emotional aspects of something they are doing together, this is called ancillary counseling. For example, a doctor who might give a patient a frightening diagnosis would then need to help that patient evaluate treatment options while dealing with shock and fear. Clergy members, such as coven leaders, are frequently called upon for ancillary counseling because people prefer to explore their problems with someone who shares their core values and worldview. When a clergy member engages in ancillary counseling with a congregant, this is called pastoral counseling.

Please remember that you cannot and should not try to solve this person's problem for her. Trust that she will find what she needs within herself, just as the Goddess promises. By giving people who come to you your time and attention, by open and active listening, and by empathy, you can help them with this process. It's a great idea to get some training in active listening; look for peer counseling programs or other volunteer opportunities in your area.)

Still, most of the issues people bring to the Circle will be those of health and growth. What will come up most frequently? One of the great founders of psychotherapy, Sigmund Freud, said that the two great concerns of adult human life are love and work. (*Love*: warm, caring human relationships of all kinds. *Work*: the opportunity to exercise skill, feel competent, and know that we have made a contribution.) A well-lived life still rests upon these two.

A generation later Abraham Maslow described a more detailed hierarchy of human needs. His theory is that each level has to be satisfied before the next can be approached, and that people's focus moves up and down the hierarchy depending on their immediate life circumstances. This is Maslow's hierarchy:

1. *Survival needs*: food, shelter, et cetera.

2. *Safety needs:* the reasonable assurance that survival needs will be met tomorrow.

3. *Love and affiliation*: mutually supportive, caring relationships.

4. *Self-esteem*: a sense of personal worthiness and competence. This is closely related to Freud's notion of "work."

5. *Self-actualization*: growing into our talents, fulfilling our potential, living creatively and in accord with our values.

For covens, which are growth and support groups, working primarily with development rather than deficiency, Maslow's framework is truly useful. The main point is that sound development is sequential, as the spiritual traditions have always taught. Our bodies' needs come first. The core human psychological concerns of love and work are next, leading to the actualization of human potential.

Then we add a sixth item: spirituality, contact with the Sacred. Healthy spiritual development rests on healthy human development. If this base becomes compromised we need to repair it before attempting further esoteric explorations.

Remember, people can move up and down this hierarchy. Someone who is homeless or hungry is more concerned with obtaining the next meal than finding meaningful work in which he can develop his talents. Someone who just lost her job or whose mate just left her may be too distraught to meditate.

Realistically, the secular issues people bring to the Circle are likely to be those of the middle tier: love, family, career, creative work, self-esteem—and these are also the areas where our magic works best. What we do in coven is interrelated with the rest of our lives. How could it not be? "As within, so without" works both ways.

~~~~~~

Mini-Ritual for Healing

This is an invocation for physical healing:

> Flesh and bone be sound as stone
> Cleansed by the healing sea
> All made right by warm sunlight
> And fresh wind blowing free
> Spirit heal, with kiss to seal
> 'Tis well, so mote it be!

(from Alice)

~~~~~~

What Makes a Group Supportive?

In a religiously based growth and support group, such as a coven, people examine their lives in the light of their beliefs, rethink old ideas and behaviors, make new decisions, and find support for living by the insights they have gained and the choices they have made. Inner exploration in the presence of others entails revealing vulnerable parts of ourselves, old hurts, things that are embarrassing and even shameful, fragile new dreams. Self-disclosure is a serious emotional risk. It's easier when people are confident that what they share will not be used to hurt or exploit them, that the facilitator is perceptive, strong, and skilled enough to maintain appropriate standards. Keeping the space safe is the inescapable responsibility of every coven leader.

Safety is absolutely necessary for self-disclosure, but not sufficient to facilitate self-directed change. If I pour out my heart in an empty room, heard only by the Gods, I am completely safe. What I say will not become common gossip, and will not be used against me. But I may not be able to hear Their wise answer, except through caring human voices. What can we do to actively help each other heal, change, and grow?

The secular counseling profession generally recognizes five necessary and sufficient conditions for personal change. These are the attitudes and behaviors with which counselors conduct helping relationships with clients. Since there are five, I call them the counselor's pentacle. In any growth and support group all members should deal with each other by these principles. Part of the facilitator's proper role is to teach this, both by explanation and example. Teaching these ways of interaction is even more essential in a coven because, unlike in secular growth groups, many members will eventually become coven leaders themselves. The five points of the counselor's pentacle are:

- *Empathy:* The ability to perceive the world from the other person's viewpoint and to feel into his emotional responses.
- *Warmth:* Accepting the other person as she is. Caring about her without the need to fix or change her. Emotional support.
- *Respect:* A belief that the other person can make and implement appropriate decisions in his life.
- *Congruence:* Saying what we believe, acting on what we say. Integrity.
- *Confidentiality:* Keeping those secrets with which others have entrusted us.

There's more to say about this last point, confidentiality. Because we have a long history of persecution and discrimination, and in many places still have good reason to fear, many Witches keep their religious affiliation secret. There is near-universal agreement among us that "outing" is intolerable. Mostly it is.

But the secular counseling profession, which takes confidentiality as seriously as we do, recognizes one very important exception. Witches need to know this story. In the early 1970s, Tatiana Tarasoff was a student at the University of California, Berkeley. Another student, obsessed with thoughts of murdering her, sought help at the university counseling center. The counselor kept silence. Tatiana, unwarned, was murdered. Her parents won a wrongful death suit. The California Supreme

Court upheld the decision on appeal* and so established a legal "duty to warn" in situations of imminent, serious danger to self or others.

As clergy, when matters of religious conscience and secular law come into conflict we must follow our consciences and accept the consequences. It's arguable that confidentiality, which is a matter of oath for most of us, supersedes any legally mandated duty to warn, just as it does for Catholic priests who are bound by the seal of the confessional. The other side of the argument rests on the Wiccan Rede, which directs us to avoid harm. We should never break confidence lightly, but in those rare and terrible situations where we believe there is imminent and serious danger . . . ?

Coven leaders and those preparing to become coven leaders should think about this very seriously. By the principle of congruence, let your conclusion be known. People who know your limits are free to choose how much information they want to share.

The five points of the counselor's pentacle are attitudes rather than skills, nexus points between belief and behavior. Over time they root deep in our personalities, becoming part of our basic way of being. They need not be restricted to Circle. In fact they are good ways to interact with anyone we love and trust: family members, close friends, lovers, et cetera.

Typically, in Proteus Coven, we meet for worship or teaching. When the planned ritual or lesson is completed, but still within Circle, I will ask whether anyone has anything they want to work on. If anyone does, the coven has segued into our growth and support group function and I have segued into the facilitator role. This role requires some additional and very specific skills. Again, by practicing these skills, the coven leader models them. I recommend also that they be specifically taught to elders who are preparing to form covens of their own. Some of the facilitative group leadership skills are:

---

*Tarasoff v. Regents of the University of California, 1976.

- *Showing attention:* Open and active listening is essential, but not sufficient. People need not just to be heard but to *feel* heard. "Attending behavior" includes eye contact, posture, little encouraging phrases like "uh huh," and so on. Be aware, however, that many of these signals are culturally defined. In some groups, for example, eye contact denotes insolence rather than candor.

- *Balancing participation:* Gently draw out quieter members. Be aware of strong nonverbal reactions. Work with those who are overbearing or disruptive to make sure that they do not monopolize the group's time and energy.

- *Summarizing and clarifying group members' statements:* Link and bridge statements (explain how one member's statement is related to another's).

- *Pacing:* Know how much people can handle. Watch for emotional or informational overload. Be sensitive to people's attention spans. Even more important, stay aware of where each member and the group as a whole are in their development, and which issues they are ready to work on at this point.

- *Recognizing critical incidents and intervening appropriately to make the most of growth opportunities and to keep the group safe and on track.*

- *Helping group members translate belief into behavior:* Suggest things they can try outside meetings that would be small, manageable steps toward the desired change. Recognize self-defeating behaviors and give gentle and appropriate feedback to the person concerned.

- *Helping group members understand and assimilate the meaning of their group (and other spiritual) experience.*

Those are all things we do to help our covenmates grow. But we are also there for ourselves, for our own growth. What's the receptive aspect of group participation? As you might expect, what we do to receive help from the group is the converse of what we do to help.

Be willing to receive from your covenmates the same gifts that you offer to them. Bring up your own concerns as soon as you feel ready to deal with them. Listen deeply and speak truthfully. If you make new choices, try them here first. Within this safe and sacred space, be and behave as you would hope to be and behave in all places. Seek feedback from your covenmates and from the Gods. Stay open to the process of growth and change. Stay open.

Willed Change: The Spiral

One way to understand the process of change is as an ongoing spiral. Like all models, this is simplified, but the simplification helps us understand a very complex process. On the flat page of a book it looks like a closed cycle, a pattern of repetition. In reality, when we go around the cycle we reach each point changed by all that has happened since we last were there. Also, of course, no one single spiral can describe a human life. Every human being has many facets. We can grow at a different rate (or even regress) in each facet, in different periods of our lives. Here, in simplified form, are the steps involved in conscious, willed change.

Identify the Goal

It's important to describe the change you want in terms of a goal, rather than a problem or a deficiency. Start a sentence with the words "I want . . ." and continue it with "so that. . . ." Be as clear and precise as you can, always in positive terms, about your goal, but not its specific manifestation. Always leave some scope for the Goddess's wonderful surprises. She may know of an even better job, or home, or lover, than the one you had in mind. A well-formulated goal is:

- *Positive:* Describe what you want rather than what you want to fix or change.
- *Possible:* Magic extends the sphere of possibility, but there are still limits. Alas, one cannot teleport between Calgary and New York!

- *Ethical:* Your magic is either self-directed or directed toward a person who is willing to receive it. It is invasive to work your will on another person without her consent. Such workings are also a lot harder to do and far more likely to backfire.
- *Ecological:* Your goal is in harmony with your values and with your other needs and desires.
- *Observable:* You will have a way of knowing when this goal is achieved.

Gather Information

Before you act you need to know as much as possible about the situation and your feasible options within it. For example, if you want a new home you should have a good idea of your budget, research current mortgage rates and possibilities, check out neighborhoods, learn how to recognize basic structural soundness, look at real estate ads, ask around to see if anyone knows of available places, et cetera. If you want a career change look into job market prospects, places where your current skills would be welcomed, available training programs, and possibilities for financial aid. This kind of very normal, secular information gathering comes first. Group participation gives you some additional sources.

If your situation is difficult, you may feel isolated. Just discussing your perplexity in group can remind you that you are not alone. Others have stood where you now stand, and worked their way through to success. Your covenmates may have had similar experiences themselves, or know others who had. They can tell you what seemed to help, or where you can go to learn more or to find various kinds of assistance. Even if they haven't been in this specific situation, friends who care can brainstorm possibilities and help you extrapolate their probable results, so you have a better basis for your decisions. All growth and support groups do these things.

The "Johari Window," an important conceptual model for groupwork, can help us understand how personal information is shared.

The Johari Window

	KNOWN TO SELF	UNKNOWN TO SELF

KNOWN TO OTHERS	*quadrant 1*—open space

quadrant 3—the outside view

KNOWN TO OTHERS

quadrant 1—open space

Consciousness offers the most freedom of choice and of movement. We can enlarge this area by acts of will.

The more trust, the greater intimacy, the larger this space gets. As we feel ready we share (from quad 2) and receive the perceptions of others (from quad 3).

Extending this open space is the essence of any growth group's work.

quadrant 3—the outside view

Sometimes others notice things about us that we don't, including unacknowledged feelings and behavioral inconsistencies. Sharing these perceptions with us is called confrontation. Appropriate and caring confrontation is an act of grace. Those who confront risk anger, rejection, and ridicule.

Accepting confrontation openly, though it can be very uncomfortable, is an act of trust. If we know how we come across to others, we have a better basis for choosing what about ourselves, if anything, we want to change.

Oh, would some power the giftie gie us to see ourselves as others see us.

UNKNOWN TO OTHERS

quadrant 2—private space, personal secrets

Quad 2 material moved into quad 1 is friendship, intimacy, trust, love. All such sharing must be voluntary. Forced entry into someone's private thoughts and feelings is like rape, or like coercive magic.

But if you are not feeling safe enough to share your inner self with your coven, it might be best to look for a different group.

quadrant 4—the unconscious

This quad holds:
1. the shadow (guardian)
2. personal creativity
3. Sacred contact

Techniques such as meditation, divination, and dreamwork increase our conscious access to our deep selves and to the Otherworld.

Quad 4 material moved into quad 2 is insight and mysticism; when it moves on to quad 1 it is art or priesthood.

It's important to get feedback from trusted friends. It's equally important to reach within, to perceptions and emotional responses that have not come to consciousness.

Feelings count, because whatever does not ultimately feel good will not be sustainable. Of course people can work through temporary unpleasantness to advance a long-range goal. For example, learning a new skill can be tedious, even painful (I recall blistered fingertips that eventually turned into a guitar player's calluses). What makes the process worthwhile is a personally satisfying goal, not just something you think you should want or should do. The truth of this, too, lies deep within you.

We help each other discover this truth with "additive empathy." Sometimes a person is telling you how it is with him the very best he can, and yet his body seems to contradict his words. Voice, posture, facial expression, and the general feelings you are getting from him all point to emotions that he is keeping inside, possibly so deep inside that even he is not consciously aware of these feelings. If you have established a trusting relationship, and you feel the person is ready to take another step in self-understanding, you might choose to tell him what you've noticed and what you think it might mean. If you offer additive empathy, remember to be sure to own your inferences, present them tentatively, and gracefully accept correction. When the other person tells you, "No, it's not really this, it's that," he may be hearing and realizing it himself for the first time in the course of clarifying it for you. Your role is to invite self-exploration, not to compel it.

People know far more than they realize. The amount of sheer sensory data that pours in on us is more than we can consciously notice or integrate, but we store it all. Our unconscious minds notice patterns and relationships that our conscious minds might miss. And of course we have emotional responses that we never bring to the surface. In short, our conscious minds may be intelligent, but our unconscious minds are very much wiser. And beyond even this is the wisdom of the Gods.

Seek Inner (and Otherworld) Wisdom

We are Witches, proficient in the arts of willed change. Our toolbox includes some techniques of *receptive magic*, ways to reach deep within and beyond ourselves for guidance. Here are the three I consider most important.

DIVINATION   There are a host of divinatory methods, such as Tarot, Runes, the I Ching, scrying, et cetera. Use whichever you like. There are good books, classes, and workshops available for most of them. The most important thing to remember is that divination extrapolates, it does not predict. Prediction implies a fixed future, but if the future were actually fixed divination would be useless. Extrapolation simply examines trends. At any given moment there are probabilities, paths leading into the future. If we understand these trends we can make choices about whether we want to continue as we are or to make changes.

Also bear in mind that the power is not in the oracle, but in the reader's mind. The oracle is just a focus that helps readers access unconscious perceptions, integrations, and wisdom.

DREAMWORK   Traditions of dreamwork are as ancient as recorded history and as modern as contemporary psychology. To prepare for dreamwork, get plenty of rest. We remember our dreams best when we sleep lightly. Have a notebook and pen or a simple tape recorder by your bed. When you wake record your impressions in the first person, present tense. If you wake with a feeling, but no story, stay with the feeling and make up a story. Then, as you interpret the dream, do not impose any preset definitions on the dream images; just see where your own associations take you. Follow through on dreamwork by making any art that the dream suggests: Write the poem, draw the picture, and so on. Keep the artwork near you; further associations may come up.

MEDITATION   This is the purest, most accessible, and yet most difficult method of all. Just sit and let your mind go where it will. Don't try to structure or follow your thoughts, just watch them. One method is to imagine that each thought or image is a flower floating down a stream. Just watch them as they go. Eventually, you will realize both deep insight and inner peace. When you are confused or stressed, meditation may seem to be procrastination, or plain laziness. And yet people rise from sitting with a much clearer sense of direction.

Finally, does what you are considering harmonize well with your religious values? Is it in keeping with the Wiccan Rede? With the specific ethical teachings of your Tradition? With the great myths that you have found inspiring over the years? If you or your Tradition have a particular tutelary deity, is what you are planning congruent with the spirit and energy of this deity?

Decide

When you have gathered all the information you can from all possible sources, put the whole matter on hold. Give your decision as much time as you can to gestate. A day is good, a week is better. When you have the luxury, a full lunar cycle is optimal. By then you will probably know your desire. For a final check, sit quietly and just ask inside yourself if any part of you has any problem with this decision. Then place yourself at Center and ask for guidance from the Guardians of the Directions, like this:

- *East:* Do I have all the information I need? Does this make sense?
- *South:* Do I have the energy to carry this through? Do I feel enthusiastic, even passionate, about my plan?
- *West:* Is my plan wise? Is it compassionate and loving to myself and to others it will affect?
- *North:* Do I have the material resources to carry out my plan? Do I have the skill? Do I have a way to obtain whatever I still need?
- *Below:* Am I capable of doing what I plan? Do I have the requisite talents and temperaments?
- *Above:* Is my plan in keeping with my ideals and values?

You can do this alone, but it's much better done in Circle, while your covenmates support and bear witness to your exploration.

Empower Your Decision

Witches are proficient at bringing about willed change in accord with our spiritual values. *Projective magic* refers to that set of skills by which we project our will out into the world to empower change.

Most likely your covenmates have been with you through all the steps of goal setting, information gathering, and decision making. If not, tell them what you want, and seek their input. If all agree that your goal is a good one that they can wholeheartedly support, it's time to raise power.

RAISE POWER   Write or choose a simple chant that is related to your goal. Stand in the center of the Circle, or kneel at the altar if that's your style. Ask your covenmates to chant what you have chosen. They might also use drums or rattles. If space permits they might even dance around you.

While they do this, you imagine that your goal is already accomplished. Imagine this as actively and as specifically as possible. What do you see from your new living room window? How does it feel to be riding a horse again with your arm fully healed?

If you've ever rooted for an athletic team, you know what your covenmates are doing. They are putting their own energy, will, and enthusiasm into your project. Let it in. Let it energize the image you have created. Let it energize you. Remember this, and draw on the memory as you work toward your goal.

STORE POWER   Find a small object that reminds you of your goal, something small enough to fit in your pocket or purse, or even an unobtrusive piece of jewelry. Consecrate it to your goal. Place it on the altar while your covenmates are raising power for you. Then keep it with you at all times until your goal is achieved. When you get tired or discouraged—and we all have such moments—this talisman will help you remember

Mini-Ritual for Goal Setting

This is an invocation to use for goals involving inner transformation:

Spirits of change, come to me
Spirits of life and change
Help me become who I would be
Help me to rearrange
Renew my heart in wisdom, and in truth my power renew.
Help me become a seed of change in service unto you.

that your sisters and brothers stand behind you. Hold it and re-peat the chant that was used when the object was charged. It will bring you back, in memory, to that place of power and to what you felt at that moment.

Another technique is to bring a candle in a color that seems related to your goal.* Place it on the altar while your coven raises power for you. Then take the candle home. Burn it for a few minutes when you feel you can use an energy boost—for example, right before going out for a job interview or a medical treatment. This releases the energy stored in the candle.

In your Tradition's lore and your coven's collective experi-ence, you will probably find lots of ways to raise power, carry the energy home with you, reinforce it with your own personal workings, and draw on it as you work toward your goal. It's equally valid to create your own methods. You know best what symbolic acts will speak to your own deep mind. The message is, "You are supported. You are empowered. You are loved."

---

*Color associations are personal or cultural. They are vocabularies that we create, not facts. For example, in the West white is the color of bridal gowns. In China brides wear red and white is the color of funerals. So whatever color seems to represent your goal in your own mind's eye is the right color, and nobody else's opinion matters. (For more information about color, seek out the wealth of books in your library or New Age sec-tion of your bookstore.)

Act in Accordance

The focus now shifts to everyday, ordinary, secular life. We have many names for the world outside of Circle: the world of form, the plane of manifestation, the Clockworld. Whatever you call it, this is where you hope to see results, and it is also where you need to direct your efforts now. Action in the material world requires that you expend time, energy, and possibly money, which will not then be available for other purposes. By committing your resources you show the Gods and your own deep mind that you are serious about your goal. Secular follow-through also provides your magic with a channel for manifestation. (This, by the way, is why the best time to work a healing spell is when the patient is actually undergoing a course of medical treatment.)

For example, you might want a new job. Start by making a realistic and sequential plan—big projects are done in small steps. What can you do this week—update your résumé, get a haircut, check your interview wardrobe? What can you do when that's done—contact headhunters, look at the want ads, send out résumés, schedule interviews? Some goals take longer than others. If you want not just a new job but a whole career change, you might have to retrain. The first step might be taking some aptitude tests or researching available training.

Whatever your goal is, there is some small, immediate practical step that you can take between now and the next coven meeting. If you're having trouble figuring out what this step is, ask your covenmates to help you. Make a formal commitment in Circle, as you prepare to raise power for your goal, to take this immediate step. Be prepared to report back to your coven on how it went.

Evaluate Your Progress

There's a tale told many times, about many different peoples. I've heard it ascribed to indigenous peoples from upper New York State to far Australia. They say there's a spot in the village where the old grannies gather. Their hands are busy grinding the grain or spinning the yarn or whatever it is grannies do in that place. As they work they talk over all that is happening around them, and share their long, long memories. If you have a problem you can come and sit with them. They may ask you many questions, bringing out aspects of your problem for you to consider. They may make suggestions from their hard-won wisdom and rich experience. They will send you away with some sense of what to try.

If you try it and return they will talk with you some more. They will help you figure out what worked or did not work, and perhaps even to understand why. They will give you further suggestions, as many times as you need. If you do not try it and still return, once, they will repeat their first advice, making sure you understood it.

But if you still take no action and return a second time, the grannies will pick up their work and move.

Just so with a good coven or a good secular growth and support group. It's one of the major convergences between the two. Respect is one of the "necessary and sufficient conditions" for an effective counseling relationship, and one of the five points of the counselor's pentacle. To be respectful is to hold the attitude that the other person has the internal capacity to make and implement good decisions in her life, to expect that she will do so, to hold her responsible. This was the core teaching of Carl Rogers, one of the great psychologists of this century. Precisely the same teaching is found, of course, in the Charge of the Goddess: "If that which you seek you find not within you, you will never find it elsewhere." (See Appendix B.)

So you return to your coven and tell them what you tried, how it worked, what you discovered, how you feel about it. They will hear you out, perhaps ask a few more probing questions. They may have some insights to share, some related experiences, even some bits of advice. Together you may or may not decide to raise power again. You will either celebrate success or decide what your next small step will be.

But what about the one who comes back without having done what he said he would do? What about the one whose actions seem to contradict his words? In love and respect, we owe him honesty. We tell him, caringly and as gently as possible, but firmly and clearly, about the inconsistency that we perceive.

Here are some sensible guidelines for confronting inconsistent behavior. Loving confrontation increases your involvement. Don't offer it unless you are willing to stand by him while he works through the contradiction you've shown him. Pick a calm and grounded moment for both of you. Speak gently. Only address one or two key areas at a time. More than this is more than a person can process at once. Only discuss things the person realistically could change. Be as specific as you can about how the behavior is interfering with his stated beliefs or goals. Check that communication was clear. Have him restate what you said if possible. Allow time for discussion of what you have presented. Be prepared to handle a defensive or angry initial reaction. Be as firm and as patient as stone.

Confrontation is a black mirror that we hold up to him in love. When he can look into it openly, in trust, he receives the gift of increased choice. Perhaps this was a goal he thought he should want, and never really did. He needs to find a new goal, and a good one might involve self-exploration. Perhaps some catastrophe took place elsewhere in his life. Things do happen. But what if he continues to avow this goal while failing to act in accordance? How much time and attention does he get? When does the Circle move on?

This judgment call is the coven leader's responsibility, and a very hard one to meet. We like to think of ourselves as loving and generous. We typically have a deep need to be needed. Drawing the line goes against our nature, but it saves the group's energy from wasteful dissipation and can be salutary for the person who is confronted.

Here's one of my stories: A member of my coven repeatedly sought job magic. The tasks of his job were far below his capacity. He was bored and spent a lot of time daydreaming and speaking on the phone with friends. This was getting him into trouble. We raised power again and again to no effect. Then I realized that this man was six credits—two incompletes—short of a college degree. I told him we would do no more job magic for him until he completed his degree. He did, and shortly after received a promotion to a more appropriate position where a degree was required.

> *Those people who weren't able to take charge of their lives and handle situations, and who did crumple up under them or have life start to overwhelm them, these were the people whom I would ask to leave. They weren't what we needed. It's not that they weren't good people. But their needs were so great that I felt it would vampirize the group.*
>
> *Using magic is not to give up and turn it all over to the Gods or to anybody else to do for you. It's working toward something, and the magic is enhancing what you're striving and working for.*
>
> —THEOS

Willed change requires active participation. Your coven, your family, your friends, all can help, but none of them can do it for you. Sometimes tough love is saying to someone, "Come back when you're ready."

Far more often, the magic works. Small successes empower further efforts, and positive change is self-reinforcing. Yes, there are setbacks. No path is perfectly smooth. The coven is there, a source of power, a collective best friend, to console us on the bad days and to cheer us on when the going is good. We can achieve most of our worthy goals, with the help of the Ancient Gods and in Their service.

Predictable Change: Life Passages

Through most of our lives we experience long periods of slow and steady growth. We call these life stages, although we are not static even then. Sometimes we choose and manage our own changes in accordance with will. At other times we encounter stuck points or spontaneous growth spurts. Certain moments of particularly intense change feel like gateways—clear and irreversible transitions into another life stage or period.

Some of our changes are natural and inevitable, predictable bodily changes like puberty and menopause. Others are happily chosen commitments, like marriage and initiation into the priesthood. Still other changes come without choice or warning: illness, violence, and natural disasters that, if navigated successfully, may render us wiser and deeper.

Life passages are primarily psychological in nature, but they are also among the traditional concerns of religion. One of the things all religions have done for their people is to guide and support them through life's gateways with rituals of passage. In these rites an individual, witnessed and supported by her community, acknowledges, integrates, and honors some experience that has forever changed her. Rites of passage also establish a new personal, social, or religious status consistent with the candidate's internal changes.

Passage rituals generally work through a sequence of three steps:

1. *Separation*—also called the pre-liminal stage (*limen* is Latin for "threshold")—requires a removal from or yielding of former roles or social statuses.

2. *Transition*—also called the liminal stage—the time between two ways of being, at the threshold, where challenges are met, lore is imparted, oaths are given, and change is made.

3. *Reincorporation*—also called the post-liminal stage—the passage completed, the person is welcomed back to a new role and status in the community and in life.

Be aware that this is not an absolute. The three steps are not always fully present or clearly defined. Shortcuts happen. Still, it's good to bear these steps in mind when planning a passage ritual, since they do describe the full process.

You may have inherited some rituals of passage from your tradition: a handfasting, a baby-blessing, a memorial. Still, there will be other, perhaps unanticipated, passages for which you have no preexisting script. In any case it's far better to adapt even an inherited rite to make it more personally relevant to the candidate.

If you are creating or adapting a passage rite, start with a good look at the way the change actually manifests—whether that change is expected, in progress, or already here. What is tangibly different about this person's life? Is his daily routine different? Will he be moving house? Will he look or dress differently? What old responsibilities will he be laying down? What new ones will he be taking up? Will she be perceived differently by family, friends, covenmates, or neighbors? How will her community status or role be changing? Will she have different expectations of herself? Which of these differences will matter most to the person or people most directly affected?

The answers to these questions will guide you in choosing what will happen in the liminal space at the heart of the ritual. What will most clearly and strongly show the person's deepest self what's changing or changed in his life? Which stories will give him a model of how to proceed for the next while? What commitments should he be making at this time? What energies should she be calling into her life right now? What energies should she be releasing? Would she do well to ask the guidance and protection of any particular Deities or Guardians?

Having structured the liminal part of the ritual, you can then plan an effective separation. What is the person leaving behind? Is he really ready to yield it, or is there still some ambiguity? Give him a space to appreciate and grieve what he will miss, to make peace with what he will gladly be rid of. Give him a moment to experience the freedom and the terror of a nakedness far more profound than merely going without clothing.

And then, finally, you can plan how best to reincorporate her into her family, coven, and community, not returned as the same person to the same position, but as a changed person to a new place in life. The youth has become an adult. The single person is now a spouse. The worker has become an elder. She looks forward to a new life, different challenges, and dif-

ferent pleasures. Others follow behind her to take the places
she has left, and so the community continues. Those who live
with and around her recognize and honor the change. The passage is accomplished.

Initiations and Elevations: A Witch's Passages

In many of the lineage-based Wiccan Traditions new
Priest/esses work through a degree system, which includes a
series of sequential passage rituals called initiation and elevation. The specific number of advanced degrees varies. There are
some complicated issues around these particular rituals, in part
because they serve two purposes.

They are the graduation exercises of our priesthood training
system. Our degrees are comparable in some ways to the ranks
of Apprentice, Journeyman, and Master in the old craft guilds
and in others to the modern academic sequence of bachelor,
master, and doctor. As such they are celebrations of learning
accomplished, skills demonstrated. They convey a status that is
already earned and objectively measurable. This is the meaning
of the paradoxical statement, "All initiations are either redun-
dant or invalid."

That's the truth about graduation exercises. I didn't actually
learn anything at my college commencement ceremony. But it's
not the whole truth, because our initiations are not just graduation exercises. Partial truth can be profoundly misleading. In
our covens we train, but we don't train dentists or tailors. We
train clergy: Priest/esses of the Ancient Gods.

Clergy conduct the rites and mentor the spiritual development of others. None of us can do this properly without first
doing some real work on our own spirituality. So our training
is not just the transfer of information or skill, it is itself a spiritual growth path. Our initiations do celebrate the completion
of a stage of training, but they are also . . . initiations, profoundly transformative rituals of passage that bring people
through critical thresholds of their spiritual growth. They are
not, however, the only possible kind of initiation.

You can become a Witch by saying "I am a Witch" three times, and thinking about what this means. All who declare themselves to be Witches have offered their lives to the service of the Old Gods, exactly the same as those of us who stepped into some Tradition's initiatory Circle. The Gods are fully capable of providing powerful and effective initiatory experiences directly, without any human mediation. For the most part, however, it's easier and safer to seek initiation within a Tradition, where elders can look after you as you work through the process.

Easier and safer, and more verifiable. Here's the problem: Just as a traditional initiation might not take, the Gods might reject the offer made by a self-initiate. And how would the rest of us know? Whether a certain rite was done is an objective question, easy to answer. Whether it worked is a much more subtle and subjective determination, which may not be clear for years. If we can't even be certain that a rite was done, how dare we evaluate the person's initiatory status?

It's tempting for those of us who were initiated within a traditional lineage to confuse form with substance, to convince ourselves that we have some exclusive claim to the power of the Gods, and to disrespect the self-initiated on this basis. Here's how Vivianne Crowley, an experienced, and thoroughly traditional, elder explained the problem:

> An important part of Wicca is that of the ancient Pagan mysteries—a way to inner transformation. There has always been exoteric religion, the religion of the state and of public temples. However, behind this were rites, ceremonies, mysteries, that were available to those who sought mystical union with the Divine and to transform their innermost being. This is the way of initiation.
>
> There are many types of initiation. One is the initiatory process that is part of all our lives; the painful path of growth and change which life and the Divine force within us demand. This is ongoing until the day we die. There is also another form of initiation—initiation into a magical or spiritual tradition whereby we are grafted onto its group mind. . . .

There are benefits in an initiatory tradition. We have
the opportunity to be trained and advised by others, but
initiation also has dangers, not least that of ego inflation.
Possessing secrets or undergoing ceremonies that are the
prerogative of a privileged few can be a way for us to prop
up our inadequate egos. . . .

If you are attracted to initiatory systems because you
like achieving things and collecting badges, then initiatory
Wicca will do you more harm than good. . . . Collective
identities can become personas which inhibit our spiritual
and magical progress rather than helping them. Titles such
as priest and priestess are heady enough; how much more
so are those of High Priest or Witch Queen?

Self-initiates, and members of self-generated covens, take a
more difficult and riskier path to the same goal. Perhaps fewer
of them make it. But those who do are creative, resilient, dedicated Witches, a pleasure to know and a joy to work with. I
am a traditional Witch, nurtured within a lineage. If I limit myself to others who took that same route, I deprive myself of
good company and many opportunities for learning and
growth. I risk spiritual and intellectual stagnation. Perhaps I
also put myself at risk of ego inflation. Perhaps my behavior is
evidence that I have already succumbed to ego inflation.

It is certainly evidence of total lack of empathy. Snobbery
hurts the snob, but it doesn't hurt only the snob. Try feeling
into this angry description:

RHEA   Because ours was a start-up coven without a lineage,
we found that covens with lineages often denigrated our
work and belittled us as ignorant children.

Far from being supported, we were undermined by lineages, traditions, and organizations. I had the experience of
being told more than once that I had not been initiated because there was no one in the room at the time who had
been initiated at an earlier time (we all initiated ourselves
and each other) and because we weren't initiated into some
tradition the speaker recognized as preexisting. I had the ex-

perience of being called ignorant because I did not have a Third Degree in someone's hierarchy. I have often been un-invited to discussions for the same reason.

This is not the way the Goddess wants Her children—or Her clergy—treating each other.

Instead, I propose that we start thinking together about spiritual substance, rather than ritual form. There are some fas-cinating studies about how different faith traditions have dif-ferent understandings of what it means to be a religiously mature individual. Their different descriptions of religious ma-turity are closely consistent with their different models of the Sacred and different theologies. What's ours?

If we know what Pagan maturity looks like, we have a basis for recognizing those who are mature. If we know how an au-thentic Pagan mystic might act, or how it feels to be around one, we can begin to discern who to trust.

If we know the destination, we can start mapping out the path. We have sixty years of collective experience to reflect on now. That's enough to start with. What are the experiences, rit-ual and other, that shape a mature Pagan? How can we safely and reliably replicate those experiences? Can we identify deep common structure that supports stylistic variants in teaching or ritual design? What are the landmarks of the Path, the indica-tors of progress? What are the pitfalls, the ways people typi-cally go astray? How can we help those who have strayed to find their way back?

The term *initiation* denotes a Path of self-development for Pagan Priest/esses and mystics—one that should follow upon the general human developmental issues of love, work, and self-actualization, and reach for effective conscious contact with the Ancient Gods of Nature. It also can denote a series of passage rituals that bring a person through significant gateways along this Path. These rituals are helpful, but not essential. What matters is that the doors of perception are opened, that contact is made, and that, from this moment, the power and guidance of the Old Ones informs all our being and doings.

Long-Distance Magic: Directing the Power to Others

Can we send magical help to someone who is not present in our Circle? Of course we can, and very often do. When you have a need or desire, it helps to know that your friends are pulling for you, whether they are close enough to touch or across the continent. For distance work it's particularly helpful to bless and charge a talisman and send it to the person, so he has a tangible reminder that the work was done. This can be as simple as passing a piece of stationery around the Circle and asking all present to write down a few words of encouragement. Tuck in a few petals from the altar flowers. Think how good it would feel to open a letter like this.

If we can work magic without a person's presence, can we also work it without her knowledge, even without her permission? Yes, we can. Should we? This depends on whether you believe that magic is effective. For me the answer to this question hinges on whether you believe in telepathic communication—and the evidence in favor of it is mounting up.

It's possible that our magic simply works through the placebo effect. Knowing that someone cares enough to root for you encourages you to mobilize your own forces. In this case distance magic still works if we inform the recipient that we're doing it, send him a token to reinforce it, and so on. But magic done without the person knowing of it at all has no effect on that person. All it does is ventilate the feelings of those who work the magic. If this is the case, even a curse is harmless.

If telepathy is a reality, however, then all well-worked magic reaches the recipient's unconscious mind and has an effect there. To intervene in someone else's mind and life without her permission is an act of the profoundest disrespect.

Here's why: It's like breaking into a friend's house when she's not home and redecorating her living room. You may do an excellent job, going to a lot of trouble and expense, but it's still an invasion of her space and her privacy—and how do you know she agrees with your choice of wallpaper, or that she wanted the room redecorated in the first place?

The bottom line is, you cannot run other people's lives for them. And there is no way to know what anyone wants without asking. This goes for healing and protection spells as well. Maybe your elderly grandmother is very sick and tired, at the end of a long struggle with cancer. A "healing" spell might just prolong her pain. It's frustrating to have the power and feel that you shouldn't use it, but magical manipulation is bad karma, and sometimes nonaction can be more helpful than meddling.*

Consider this: If the person were there, standing at your altar in the middle of your Circle, you would never dream of raising power for him without his full agreement and participation. What changes when he leaves the room, or even leaves town? The courtesies of the situation do not change, and neither do the ethics. *Always ask first!*

Conclusion

A coven is a safe space within which each member's psycho-spiritual growth is gestated. So is any secular growth and support group, and many of the characteristics and processes are the same for both coven and counseling group. The difference lies in the coven's particular spiritual orientation. The changes that are nurtured in coven must be in accord with specifically Pagan spiritual values. If they are they will be activated by the power of the Ancient Gods. The reason we undertake personal change rooted in our spiritual values is to become not just better people, but also better Witches, clearer representatives of the power and beauty of the Old Ways, in service to the Gods, the People, and the Earth.

---

*Hunter, Jennifer, *21st Century Wicca: A Young Witch's Guide to Living the Magical Life* (Secaucus, N.J.: Citadel, 1997): 49–50.

To Learn More

Blacksun. *The Spell of Making*. Chicago: Eschaton, 1995.

Bonewits, P. E. I. *Real Magic*. Berkeley, Calif.: Creative Arts, 1979.

Carroll, Marguerite, Marilyn Bates, and Clarence Johnson. *Group Leadership: Strategies for Group Counseling Leaders*, 3d ed. Denver: Love, 1997.

Corey, Gerald. *Theory and Practice of Group Counseling*, 4th ed. Pacific Grove, Calif.: Brooks/Cole, 1995.

Crowley, Vivianne. *Wicca: The Old Religion in the New Millenium*. London: Thorsons, 1996.

Garfield, Charles, Cindy Spring, and Sedonia Cahill. *Wisdom Circles: A Guide to Self-Discovery and Community Building in Small Groups*. New York: Hyperion, 1998.

Houston, Jean. *Life-Force*. New York: Delacorte, 1980.

———. *The Possible Human*. Los Angeles: Tarcher, 1987. (Jean Houston has written several books that contain sequential exercises for willed self-development. All are worthwhile.)

Kennedy, Eugene, and Sara C. Charles. *On Becoming a Counselor*. New York: Continuum, 1990. (This is the definitive book on ancillary counseling for members of other professions.)

Macy, Joanna Rogers. *Despair and Personal Power in the Nuclear Age*. Philadelphia: New Society, 1983.

Starhawk. *Dreaming the Dark: Magic, Sex and Politics*. Boston: Beacon, 1982. (This book and the one above by Macy are primarily about collective magic, such as peace work and Earth healing, a very important topic that was outside the scope of this book.)

———. *Truth or Dare: Encounters With Power, Authority, and Mystery*. San Francisco: Harper & Row, 1987. (This book and the one above are primarily about collective magic, such as peacework and Earth healing, a very important topic that is outside the scope of this book.)

———. M. Macha Nightmare, and the Reclaiming Collective. *The Pagan Book of Living and Dying*. New York: HarperCollins, 1997.

Yalom, Irvin. *The Theory and Practice of Group Psychotherapy*, 4th ed. New York: Basic, 1995.

7

To Learn In Order to Serve

COVEN AS TRAINING GROUP

The whole teaching is about grasping our humanity, honing it, and putting it into the Gods' service and thus our own.

—David

The Craft must ever survive. Only by thorough and competent training can we ensure this. Our covens serve us as classrooms, mini-seminaries in which we both train the Priest/esses of the future and offer ongoing education to the Witches of today.

I believe there are only two types of Priest/ess: Priest/ess-in-training and Priest/ess retired. There's no such thing, anywhere, as a completed education. As new discoveries are made, there is always more to learn. Furthermore, learning doesn't just add to our knowledge, it actually helps keep our minds young, active, and alert. Many secular professions now require their members to engage in continuing professional education, and to prove that they have done so, in order to retain their licenses to practice.

What is important and beneficial for doctors and lawyers is absolutely critical for Witches. European Pagan Nature spirituality was long suppressed. Whether you believe our ways survived underground or went completely dormant, it's certain that a great deal of ancient lore was lost. The current neo-Pagan renaissance is just about sixty years old. We are still very much in the initial phases of reviving, reconstructing, learning as we go.

It's not only that no single one of us can know it all. It's that all of us together are still very far from recovering the knowledge and skills that eroded during the silent centuries.

So it behooves every one of us to put serious effort into:

- Contributing to our collective knowledge base through both archival and experiential research.

- Staying aware of the contributions that others make to our body of information and skills.

- Sharing this heritage with new Witches in such a manner that they are empowered to continue the process of learning, discovering, and contributing.

Covens are places where Witches can learn together. They are also the nexus points of a larger learning community, collaborating to reconstruct and create a way of Earth spirituality that will both honor our ancestors and serve our own current needs.

One powerful way to learn is to teach others. Figuring out how to present something requires us to delve more deeply into it than we otherwise might. Then we are challenged to go still further by the fresh insights and unpredictable questions of new students, people full of enthusiasm and relatively free from preconceptions.

Continuing education for all of us develops our collective knowledge base and helps the Craft to thrive. Perhaps that's a luxury. Nothing thrives unless it first survives. The simple survival of the Craft utterly depends on the training of the next generations of Priest/esses, and that is the focus of this chapter.

Three Dimensions of Training: Students, Competencies, Roles

Students

No two people are exactly alike, not even at the outset, as newborns. By the time a person is ready to seek training in

Witchcraft, she is uniquely formed not just by her genetic endowment and her upbringing, but also by myriad other experiences—educational, cultural, occupational, and so forth. Some of these experiences were intentional, others apparently pure coincidence. Some may be early hints that the Gods will eventually call this person to priesthood.

People differ in many different ways: gender, race, class, appearance, and more. Which of these differences matter depends on the circumstances, on what you are trying to do. For vocational purposes, including Wiccan training, two important things to understand about all seekers are their talents and their temperaments.

Talent means a natural endowment, a mental or physical aptitude, an inclination. Some examples of talents are verbal ability, manual dexterity, and spatial perception. *Temperament* refers to a person's characteristic manner of thinking, behaving, or reacting. Temperaments would include patience, spontaneity, or assertiveness.

Many different kinds of contributions are needed for the reconstruction of our lifeways. For this reason we cannot say that any one neatly defined cluster of talents and temperaments predicts success as a Priest/ess. Still, these aspects of all our students can guide us both in training them most effectively and in helping them discover their own unique path of service. They are also useful in matching students with teachers. Which talents do you feel qualified to train? Which temperaments mesh well with your own?

Competencies

These include the subject matter, the content of the training. Remember, we are training adults. We are hopefully training well-rounded, healthy adults who have lives, jobs, and families. We are training them in something that, although it is one of the central commitments of their lives, will, by religious principle, be entirely a part-time and voluntary activity. Out of respect for the people we train, our training should be efficient, effective, as free from superfluity as we can make it.

This means our curriculum design should focus on the future, on the way we hope these students will function in service, rather than on whatever was customary in the past. There's no time for make-work anymore, if there ever was.

The Association for Specialists in Group Work, in their Professional Standards for the Training of Group Workers, divides competencies into two basic types: knowledge competencies and skills competencies.* To simplify: Sentences describing knowledge competencies would begin with, "Be able to explain . . ." while sentences describing skills competencies would begin with, "Be able to do. . . ." It's the old pairing of theory and practice, stripped down to what we actually expect of our students.

ASGW has lists of required knowledge and skills competencies for each of the subspecialties of groupwork. They can give the reasons why they included each item on these lists. So should we. We also should be able to identify core competencies that we require of every student, competencies needed for major subspecialties, and competencies required to enable each student to actualize his or her personal vision of priesthood.

To knowledge and skills competencies I would add a third: perceptual competencies. Strictly speaking, trained perception is a type of skill. However, I think the ability to observe, notice, or perceive certain things is so critically important that it warrants an independent category.

This is not only true of Witchcraft. Consider: Anyone with normal hearing can put his ear against a person's chest and tell whether that heart is beating. Medical students work with recordings of the subtly varying sounds of heartbeats, and learn to hear differences that will aid them in diagnosing a variety of heart conditions. Consider also how the specialized vocabularies of tea tasters, sound engineers, and perfumers enable them to observe and work with fine distinctions that are generally unintelligible to the rest of us.

Having a set of structured categories helps us notice subtleties we would probably otherwise miss. The specialized tech-

*Conyne, Robert K., F. Robert Wilson, and Donald E. Ward, *Comprehensive Group Work: What It Means and How to Teach It* (Alexandria, Va.: American Counseling Association, 1997): 245–254.

nical vocabulary that identifies these categories allows specialists to share their observations with each other, and to teach trainees and beginners to do the same. You'll have heard the old cliché about Inuit having twenty different words for "snow," describing various snow conditions. You'll hear something similar on the ski reports. We notice those differences that matter to us.

Spirituality and magic are concerns of the deep mind and the heart. We work on the inner planes and in the Otherworld, realms that can only be apprehended through imagination and symbolism. We work with spiritual and psychic energies that our culture chooses to ignore. Most of us were not taught as children to notice these energies, make fine distinctions among them, or direct their quality, intensity, or movement. I also suspect that, as with learning languages, these skills are far easier to learn in childhood. Without support, guidance, or nurturance, childhood psychic and spiritual propensities wither. Be assured, the rootstock is still alive, however deeply buried.

Roles

In the English-speaking world most clergy members have one of three titles: rabbi, minister, or priest. We tend to define all three similarly as "a member of the clergy of the ____ faith." By doing so we obscure an important distinction among their working orientations:

- A *rabbi* is primarily concerned with lore, with studying a large body of traditional writings, perhaps making original contributions that apply old wisdom to new circumstances, consulting and answering questions regarding this material, teaching interested community members of all ages about it.

- A *minister* is primarily concerned with people, with counseling, mentoring, guiding, advising, offering spiritual direction.

- A *priest* is primarily concerned with ritual, with mystery and sacrament, with the unconscious mind and the spiritual realm as the particular church conceives it, with mediating the connection between worshipers and Deity.

It's interesting, and slightly embarrassing, to me that I cannot so define the role of an *imam* or a *sensei*, and I don't even know the proper term for a member of the Hindu clergy.

These roles are certainly not opposed to each other. Neither do they often occur as pure types in real life. No doubt different working clergy members combine them in different proportions in their practice. If they were three corners of a triangle, a person could find a place anywhere within its area.* All of us locate ourselves in accordance with a complex combination of our own talents and temperaments, how our community understands and prepares its clergy, and the needs of those we serve.

My contention is that a fully functional religious community, one that seeks both conscious contact with Deity and the manifestation of this contact in daily life, needs to be well served in all three of these capacities. Since no single person is likely to do well by all three roles, this argues for a decentralized clergy network, each of us recognizing and honoring the specialties of the others. This kind of network also works best to share the work and responsibility, protecting our volunteer clergy from burnout.

Application

The next section of this chapter gives various perspectives on constructing a Wiccan training curriculum. As you read through it ask yourself questions like these:

- Is this something all Witches need to know? Is it part of the specialized knowledge base of my coven, lineage, or Tradition? Even if it is not a core competency, would it be helpful to have some of us become very good at this?

- Do I know this well enough to teach it? If not, do I think it's important enough to put energy into learning it? If not, is there somebody else in the coven qualified to teach it or

---

*Lady Brigantia first proposed the tripartite division of clergy roles. Margarian Bridger contributed the very helpful spatial metaphor for them. Deep thanks to both.

someone we could invite to come as a "guest instructor"? If not, do I know where to refer a student who wants to learn this?

- What talents and temperaments would incline a student to learn this well and be good at doing or teaching it?

- For those working in degree systems: What level of competency in this would I expect at each degree? Would I require this of everybody, or make it part of an interested student's "learning contract"?

- Is this topic important to the role of rabbi, minister, or priest? Is this student aiming for the role of rabbi, minister, or priest? Beyond the core curriculum, which topics should I emphasize in the training of which students?

What We Teach: Thinking About Curriculum Content

Coven leaders and elders think incessantly about what to include in a basic "Wicca 101" training curriculum. We discuss, debate, compare and contrast, exchange paperwork. I have a notebook section, over an inch thick, consisting entirely of curricula, reading lists, and assignment sheets from friendly covens. It's encouraging to note the large amount of overlap among these. We really are beginning to develop a communal sense of what a Priest/ess needs to know or to be able to do.

Still, there is no required central curriculum and no central authority or agency to enforce such a curriculum, thanks and praise to all the Gods! Diversity is theologically appropriate for a polytheistic religion. It is also pro-survival, since we are not dependent on an easily destroyed headquarters for ideas or direction. Most important of all, coven autonomy gives us multiple venues for research and experimentation, multiple breeding places for new ideas.

We have the ideal combination: well-networked autonomy. As each coven develops its own curriculum, we have access to a rich variety of sources of ideas. Here are some of them:

Your Memory of Your Own Student Years

If you trained in a lineage-based system and you were wise, you still have your old notes and journals, plus whatever training handouts your teachers gave you. (Advise your present students to keep journals. There is no better resource.) Review this material to see what your teachers considered important. As you refresh your memory, ask yourself the following questions:

- Of the material in your training curriculum, what has been the most useful to you in your own practice and teaching?

- Is anything you found useless still part of "Pagan cultural literacy" in your local community?

- What was missing? What do you wish you had known before you started your own group?

- What did you have to learn the hard way? Is this necessary (it is, for some things), or might there be a way to give people some prior preparation?

Observation of Respected Coven Leaders

This is the classic method of occupational research and job analysis. The commonsense premise is that we design a training program best by working backward from success. First, observe what is actually being done by people already successfully employed in an occupation. Then figure out what knowledge and skill they need to be able to do these things. Finally, determine what preparatory experiences would impart this knowledge and build these skills.

Professional occupational research involves observing large samples of people. This is not feasible for us. But the process still works if we scale it way, way down. Better yet, if we then compare notes we can eventually build up a more complete picture, based on many observations of coven leaders in different Traditions and different local areas.

Here is a good exercise for people preparing to hive: Find a few coven leaders whose work you really respect. Since no one Tradition of Witchcraft has a monopoly on truth, competence, or good ideas, it's best if your sample includes members of more than one Tradition. Ask these people if they are willing to have you observe and interview them, and perhaps even interview their students. Spend a fair amount of time with each one, looking for the following:

- What do they actually do? How do they perceive and explain what they do? What seem to be their priorities?

- What seem to be their strongest talents and temperaments? How would you place them in the "rabbi, minister, priest" triangle?

- What knowledge competencies do they seem to most often use? Can they recommend any books or articles that would help a new student acquire this knowledge? Can you?

- What perceptual or skills competencies do they seem to most often use? How did they learn these skills? Can they recommend any ways for a new student to acquire or practice these skills? Can you?

- What do they perceive as their weaknesses or lacks? How do they seem to work around these?

- Any other perceptions, associations or thoughts? Note them in your journal—these unstructured insights can be the richest sources of ideas as your practice deepens.

Comparing Notes With Colleagues

As I said before, coven leaders share ideas about training all the time. For this book I wanted to consult with some coven leaders in a more systematic way. I asked a group of experienced and generous coven leaders what they considered the three to five most important topics to include in a beginners' training curriculum.

Nobody likes a forced choice, so some of them growled at me for limiting them to three to five topics. One even went ahead and gave me her whole list anyhow! But the point of the small number was to get a sense of our collective priorities. After I'd tallied up the topics, I fed back the information to the group for their comments. Here's the tally and some of what they had to say about it the most important training topics.

Ritual design was chosen by eleven people.

GAWAINE   Elements of ritual. We spend an evening walking students through all the various parts of a ritual, explaining why they're done the way they are and the meaning behind them. I think this is crucial. If people are going to be effective Priest/esses they need to know why they are doing what they are doing. Especially if they are going to write their own rituals.

HOLLY   We take a lot of time demonstrating and explaining each and every step in the circle ritual that we do. We stress the magical purpose of each step, explaining the many ways in which different Traditions or groups accomplish the same magical goal. If they don't know the purpose, they can't possibly put the proper magical energy into it.

GREY CAT   Number one, of course, in my view is ritual training. Our classes on ritual come extremely early in training and the students are required to memorize the frame of the ritual (Quarter calls, invocations, empowerment, cakes and cup, and closing). Students begin calling Quarters pretty early and each one leads a ritual before receiving First Degree. After First, they should be able to take charge of their own relationship with the Deities, and that seems to me to include doing their own ritual.

JEHANA   Primarily as a participatory experiential thing. Ritual is a way of drawing members of a coven closer together in a sacred sense, and a way of honoring the Gods. One element of a coven working together is energy sharing—learning how to connect with others on that level in trust and love, without overpowering each other.

Techniques, purposefulness in ritual, and such are all important here. Effective design is important.

KATHY We have a run of classes on ritual design that we call Ritual as Theater (we borrowed the title from a workshop). We look at what theatrical techniques can be applied to ritual work. Discussions include symbolic meaning of various events, staging concerns, costuming, and props. I also like to throw out the question of whether or not theatrical stuff has a place in ritual. Usually a lively time as people work out the difference between symbolic acts and "playacting."

MARGARIAN Especially important in eclectic Craft, where you can't just fall back on the standard rituals in the book, because there isn't a *The Book.*

RHOMYLLY Ritual composition—especially stressing different ritual needs or settings: indoor/outdoor, small group/large group, single sex, holiday/rite of passage/healing/Moon, et cetera. You can never have too many ritual ideas up your sleeves.

The subject of ethics was chosen by ten people.

HOLLY I think this is such a critical issue! In spite of the ways that various Wiccan "flavors" differ, we all seem to be united in our acceptance of the Rede. We spend a lot of time in class examining what this means exactly: How do you define *harm*, who is included in *none* (most don't think to include themselves!), what specifically is it that you *will?* I think it's important to start early with this discussion, if only so that *I* can assess whether their ethics are such that I would feel comfortable teaching them more advanced techniques.

The subjects of theology, cosmology, and worldview were chosen by eight people.

GAWAINE If they don't know what the religion is all about, how can they practice it? I'll grant you, in Wicca our theology is somewhat different for different people. The variations in beliefs are part of what students need to be taught. I want my students to be informed believers who have thought about what they believe in, not mindless followers who blindly follow whatever they are told.

HOLLY   The Wheel of the Year, cosmology, all the usual stuff. How can they know if they belong with us if they don't know who we are? I think it's important to stress the differences among us as well as the similarities. Students don't know these as a rule, and I want to provide enough information to them so that they can choose an appropriate path/teacher/group. We also try to impart a sense of what it is like to live your life as a Witch: the effect and impact of initiation.

JEHANA   Students will come to their own concept of what this means to them, from the literal-minded to the essentially agnostic. Some of what this is about is book-knowledge, but much more is experiential, and learning your own ways of reverencing the Sacred as a part of magical and daily life. Meditative work is important here, as well as in other regards.

The subject of magic and energy work was chosen by eight people.

GAWAINE   While related to ritual in some ways, I think this is a separate topic. It's probably more important than ritual in some ways. I think this is important for the same reason that you don't let people drive heavy equipment, handle firearms, or work with electricity if they don't know what they're doing. Someone might get hurt.

The subject of mythic and symbolic vocabulary (elements, tools, Wheel of the Year, and so on) were chosen by seven people.

GAWAINE   Symbolic vocabulary is an excellent choice, and probably one of the more neglected areas. I'd say it's really a prerequisite for doing good ritual or magic.

CAITRIN   [Re the Wheel of the Year]   This is something all Wiccan Traditions I'm familiar with hold in common. It provides a beginning set of symbols, a proto-language that is in some ways easily understood, and yet holds deep layers upon layers of meanings to be explored. [Re tools] If they know the history and they know the language, they next need something to do with that knowledge.

The subject of inner work and self-development was chosen by seven people.

GREY CAT   We think that it is important for the students to begin their internal work at once. For one thing, the best students end up with us because they started looking inward and found that their birth religion didn't satisfy their needs, so we capitalize on what has been begun. We start with a personal cleansing ritual. We go on with meditation training. We also have a personal inventory and balancing based on the four Elements, which I have found to be very enlightening and useful.

HOLLY   I view this type of training as having two major benefits. First, this is the kind of mental discipline and training that can really help with effective magic. Second, it gives the students a resource in terms of knowing themselves on the deepest of levels. One of my very early teachers continually stressed to me the importance of being familiar with the "flavor of your own self." Students may have trouble with this at first, or may need to experiment to find the most effective meditative techniques for them. That's okay . . . as long as they aren't afraid to confront the Shadow side. Personally, I believe that most of my own magical power comes from my Shadow side operating in accordance with my directed (and controlled) will. I have found that the students who can't (or won't) tap into that often can't handle much in the way of magical energy.

JIM   Relaxation is essential to allow optimal energy flow. Whether this is creative energy, chi, or other magical energy, tension will cause restriction. With relaxation and meditation,

we open access to deeper self, that part of us that is om-
niscient, omnipresent. There can be no greater source of
information or education.

MAGENTA   I think grounding and centering is the most important. Next would come shielding and warding. Part of this
would be casting a Circle. I think people should learn several different ways to cast a Circle. Also, I think people
should be trained to do at least a few basic things without
props, and without words if possible. I can cast a Circle in a
minute or so by visualization alone. This has come in handy
a few times. Too many Witches and magicians are bogged
down in forms and props, and cannot function without
them. At least, Witches should learn to improvise, to grab a
cup of water, some salt, and a candle, and cast a Circle with
what they have available.

*The subject of group dynamics was chosen by five people. History was
chosen by four people.*

CAITRIN   History is important because a lot of seekers come to
the Craft with all kinds of strange ideas about its origins and
sources and founders and history that at best clutter up
their minds, and at worst can cause them to behave like
some kind of elite because they've found this path. You just
have to disabuse them of the notion, which wastes their
time and yours.

GAWAINE   It's hard to know where you're going if you don't
know where you've been. I think a knowledge of the Craft,
its place in human history, and its more recent history in
modern times is important. I think it's important for us as
Wiccans to understand ourselves and our beliefs in context
with what has happened in our culture. I may be a bit preju-
diced here, since I have degrees in both history and cultural
anthropology, but I've heard and read an awful lot of clap-
trap (I'm being polite) passed off as history explaining why
we do certain things.

MARGARIAN   It's very important for beginners to get the quick summary: "It wasn't nine million, the Inquisition wasn't about us, and we started about half a century ago." It's not especially important to give them a lot of historical detail at the beginner stage.

The subject of counseling was chosen by three people.

The leaders also brought up two other interesting points about appropriateness.

Two of the coven leaders who responded listed basic life skills such as balancing a checkbook, cooking, swimming, or driving. More felt strongly that teaching basic secular life-management skills is not our job. For them a seeker whose life is not in order should be sent away and told to come back when it is.

This makes sense to me. In addition, in Proteus we specifically require that every student have a secular career plan and be either working or in school, pursuing a secular career. A good job is the best way to avoid any temptation to sell the Craft.

On the borderline are the skills associated with learning: research, analysis, synthesis, and communication. The schools should teach these essential skills, but often don't. Some coven leaders are willing to fill this gap, others are not.

At the other end of the spectrum, many of my respondents felt that two of the topics listed—group dynamics and counseling—properly belong to a more advanced level of training. In a degree system these would be essential skills for a coven leader, but irrelevant to initiates. They feel it's best to let beginners focus on the basics: ritual, ethics, thealogy, and so forth.

THE CASE FOR GEOCENTRIC EDUCATION   None of the other coven leaders mentioned nature study, which we strongly emphasize in Proteus. Since our religion is centered on Mother Earth, we expect our clergy in training to learn about Her. We use an environmental awareness questionnaire as a preliminary screen before we accept a candidate for dedication. This asks questions about where your water comes from and where your garbage goes. For most people completing it requires library research. This tells us who is serious about the Earth and who is willing to work.

The Seven Trees exercise, which comes later in the process, is my personal favorite. In this we ask each student to identify the seven trees within walking distance of her home that seem to represent the spirit of that place. The next step is to celebrate each of these trees in her chosen art form. We've received drawings, photographs, poems, even preserved fruit. The Seven Trees exercise serves two important purposes. It helps people get in touch with the land spirits around their homes and develop a sense of place, and it connects their creative self-expression with their homeplace and its spirits.

Checking Out the Neighbors

Our neighbors have seminaries, university-level professional schools where people who aspire to join the clergy study full-time for several years. The tradition of unpaid clergy is important to us. Much of what attracted us to this religious community would be destroyed if we ever compromised or abandoned it. But it has its costs, and this is the major one: Our students, who must prepare to earn their livings otherwise, have not the leisure for this amount of preparation. This is another important reason why lifelong continuing education is so important for us.

We are working from very different theological bases, so I became curious to see a comparison between the subject areas we each include in our training. A friendly minister helped me select a representative sample of seven mainstream Protestant seminaries. I wrote away for their catalogs and looked at what they require of students completing a master of divinity degree, or whatever degree they consider to be preparation for congregational ministry rather than academic religious studies.* Here's what I found:

*The catalogs I consulted were from Andover Newton, University of Chicago, Drew, Fuller, Harvard, Union Theological, and Yale.

Seminar Training and Wiccan Equivalents

SUBJECT	REQUIRED AT	PAGAN COMPARISON
Bible	7 (all)	Mythic and symbolic vocabulary, chosen by 7 coven leaders
History	7 (all)	History, chosen by 4 coven leaders
Theology	7 (all)	Theology, chosen by 8 coven leaders
Ethics	5	Ethics, chosen by 10 coven leaders
Counseling	5	Counseling, chosen by 3 coven leaders, considered an advanced topic by others
Teaching	3	Not mentioned by coven leaders—but probably should be
Worship—liturgy	3	Ritual design, chosen by 11 coven leaders

The central core of our training programs are pretty comparable. There's a difference of emphasis that is consistent with our differences of theology and organization. The seminaries require some subjects that are not especially relevant for us: preaching, church administration, biblical languages. We put a lot more emphasis on the experiential: ritual design, magic and energy work, inner work. But there's a lot more similarity than I think either group would have expected.

One important difference, however, is that nearly half the seminaries require courses in teaching. Teaching was not mentioned by any of the coven leaders. Thinking about it, I don't know of any coven that teaches how to teach. Yet teaching is a lot of what we do. I know I feel quite unprepared in this area. I strongly recommend that we add methods of adult education to our curricula. Of course this is an elder-level skill, not needed by beginners. But we need it *for* beginners, to do as good a job as possible of sharing our ways with them.

Student-Directed Learning

In student-directed education students pursue their own interests, while elders act as resource persons. We answer questions, recommend books, suggest exercises upon request, but we do not tell them what to study. All initiative comes from the students.

The problem with this is that beginners may not know enough to identify what they need to learn. Elders have a responsibility to ensure that new students are exposed to the core Wiccan curriculum, as defined by the coven, lineage, or Tradition. Of course, nothing prevents any student from also studying whatever else catches his interest.

As the student progresses, the locus of control gradually shifts to him. There is far more to our Craft than any one person can master, particularly on a part-time and voluntary basis. So people should be encouraged to specialize, to pursue their own particular interests, develop their own talents, find their own role within our clergy. In Proteus, to make this clear, we ask each person approaching Second Degree to "choose a major"—to state what they think their primary path of service will be, and pursue studies specifically related to that goal.

In time people take Third Degree and hive off to form new covens of their own. They are still and always Priest/esses-in-training. But the transition is complete. Their continuing professional education is and must be completely student-directed.

Before we leave the topic of curriculum, one important reminder:

DEBBI   All the topics stem from one: Why? Why are we here? Why are we doing this? Why do we worship the Old Gods? For me, all serious training is based on this. The "what" seems almost an afterthought to the why. Especially for newbies, searching the heart, learning the self, and exploring the Divine all come from why. Prayer, magic, spiritual work flow from the search for why.

How We Teach: Method

Remember the distinction between knowledge and skills competencies? Education, cognitive learning, imparts knowledge. Training, behavioral learning, builds skill. Cognitive learning changes what we understand. Behavioral learning changes what we do. Both are willed change; both are magic.

Both are important, but for different purposes. Each nurtures the other. Understanding the biological processes of yeast is not the same as being able to perceive when the kneaded dough in your hands is ready to form loaves. You need the sensory, experiential knowledge to bake good bread. You need both kinds of knowledge to create new recipes. A Witch needs knowledge, skill, and trained perception in order to be effective on the inner planes, and in order to serve the Gods well.

Cognitive Learning: Developing the Knowledge Competencies

I have a mental model of the world, an understanding that I've built from all the many experiences of my life. So do you. Every human does. Psychologists define *cognitive learning* as changes to that model, changes of understanding. Of course, changing that inner model is precisely the same thing as changing consciousness in accordance with will.

This simple division between understanding and skill is complicated by the realization that there are skills involved in acquiring and assimilating new information, in developing our understanding. To learn we need to be able to use a library (and, these days, the Internet), to weigh evidence and balance it against contradictory information, to arrive at reasonable conclusions, to communicate what we have learned, and more. Although coven leaders are divided about whether we should be the ones to teach these skills of learning, there is no question that they are necessary for any effective learning, and critical for effective self-directed continuing education.

The learner's skills complement those of the teacher. Unless the learner engages actively in the process, she will not be able to assimilate the new information, integrate it with what she already knows, and make it a usable part of her mental model of the world. A passive learner may get something by rote, but she never really makes it her own.

Here is a widely accepted model of the stages of cognitive learning:

1. *Memory:* Recalling or recognizing information. Rote learning.

2. *Translation:* Ability to understand information, restate it in own words.

3. *Interpretation:* Able to perceive relationships among facts, generalizations, definitions, values, and skills.

4. *Application:* Correct use of the information to answer questions or solve problems.

5. *Analysis:* Ability to identify component parts of the information and the relationships among them.

6. *Synthesis:* Ability to relate this information to information already held and to see overall patterns; ability to do original, creative thinking.

7. *Evaluation:* Ability to make judgments about the accuracy and value of information, ideas, solutions, events based on own values.*

Without a doubt, a person can do this alone. Many have. It may actually be better to learn alone than in a competitive classroom where the game is to flatter the teacher, get one-up on the classmates, and cram for the test. Best yet, however, is to learn within a warm, supportive group atmosphere. It's

*Rabow et al., *Learning Through Discussion* (Thousand Oaks, Calif.: Sage, 1994): 23.

more pleasant, which makes it easier to keep going. In addition, since several alert minds are bringing different backgrounds and perspectives to the same material, the process of assimilating the material is made much more efficient.

Here's how it works. Your group has had an educational experience. Perhaps you all read the same article or book, watched a relevant film together, or took a group tour of the local botanical gardens. In a group of beginners, probably the coven leader assigned this experience as part of a structured curriculum. More advanced students may have decided as a group that this was something they wanted to do together. You've picked up some information. Now you gather to figure out what this information means to you. Here is a series of steps you can follow together (and that a teacher can facilitate):

1. Look up any words or phrases that you are not absolutely sure of. List these words and their definitions. Share all such definitions in group.

2. What is the overall theme of the material? What are the major subthemes or topics included? Restate or summarize in your own words. (Note: Suspend your reactions or opinions. It is important simply to understand what the author was saying first.)

3. How does this relate to material you covered previously (other readings, viewings, and the like)? Does it reinforce, contradict, expand, deepen, what?

4. How does it relate to your own experience, in or out of this group, in or out of ritual context?

5. Do you agree or disagree with the author's perceptions, reasoning, or opinions? Give your reasons.

6. Does this material evoke any emotional reactions?

7. Does this material evoke any insights or intuitions for you?

8. Are there any significant similarities or differences in the reactions of various group members?

9. How does this material apply to your practice or your life? As a result of engaging with this material, do you want to make any changes in the way you practice Witchcraft? In the way you live your life in general? How do you antici- pate working toward these changes? Can the group help you with this in any way?*

Note: A solitary learner can use very similar steps. It's a good idea for either a group member or a solitary to record the re- sults in a journal.

Behavioral Learning: Building the Skills Competencies

There's a classic sequence to learning a new skill. It applies equally well to baking, welding, and invoking the Guardians in a Wiccan ritual.

EXPLANATION   The first two steps could just as easily be con- sidered cognitive education. Learning to do something starts with understanding how the process works, why we do it in a certain way, and how to do it safely. The instructor explains all this.

DEMONSTRATION   The instructor performs the task, slowly, explaining each step. The student observes and asks questions. Repeat until the student feels ready to try it.

SUPERVISED PRACTICE   The student performs the task. The in- structor observes, directs, corrects, and encourages. Repeat until both instructor and student feel that the student is ready to do it alone.

SOLO PRACTICE   The student becomes the worker. The worker does the work over a long-enough period of time to encounter and adapt to varying situations, and develop his own style. This is recognized when he makes a creative contri- bution to the field (a "masterpiece").

TEACHING   The worker becomes the instructor. Having be- come adept at the task, the worker teaches it to beginners. The

*These questions are based on Rabow et al., *Learning Through Discussion*, 8. I adapted them for coven use.

effort to form a coherent explanation and respond to unanticipated questions completes the learning cycle.

Of course, it's much more complicated than this. Learning a trade or profession is learning a series of skills, and these are usually understood to have a logical order. Each new one draws on what was previously learned. Before you could read this book, you had to learn how to read. Learning to read can be understood as a series of even smaller steps: letter recognition, vocabulary development, and so forth. There are cycles within cycles, depending on how close you look. We use the level of analysis that's relevant to the task at hand.

Degree Systems: Steps to Competency

The fact that training people in skills seems to fall into an inherent, graded sequence of steps suggests that the degree system used in many Wiccan Traditions is not just an arbitrary exercise in ranking. The historical root of the typical three degrees of Wicca, many of us suspect, goes back to the three divisions—Apprentice, Journeyman, and Master—used in the medieval craft guilds. This is how I think they correspond:

WICCAN DEGREES	LEARNING STEP	RELATIONSHIP WITH MENTOR	CRAFT GUILD LEVELS
Dedicant	Explanation and demonstration	Dependency	Apprentice
First Degree	Supervised practice		
Second Degree	Solo practice	Differentiation	Journeyman
Third Degree	Teaching	Autonomy	Master

So the degree system can function as another guide to planning your curriculum. Having identified the topics you want to include, ask yourself what level of understanding, skill, or functioning you would hope to see before granting each degree.

Another virtue of the degree system is that it gives us a way to acknowledge and celebrate the intermediate steps. Recognition feels good, and so functions as a reward. Rewards, reinforcement, help people keep working toward goals that may seem far off.

Behavioral Psychology: The Power of Praise

Behavioral psychology is the specific study of how to change what people do. Behaviorists talk in terms of "conditioning." Two generations of behaviorists developed two different models, called "classical conditioning" and "operant conditioning." Operant conditioning, which includes the important concept of reinforcement, is something about which every teacher should know.

Psychology students tell this joke: B. F. Skinner, one of the first researchers in the area of operant conditioning, liked to pace the platform while lecturing. One semester the students in the first couple of rows conspired. Whenever Skinner came close to the edge, they would look very interested and write in their notebooks. Within a week, they say, Skinner fell off the platform.

The story about Skinner pacing is either a fable or an example of baneful use. Either way it illustrates the two most important things Witches can learn from operant conditioning: successive approximation and positive reinforcement.

Skinner did a lot of his own research with pigeons, and the pigeon lab is still the popular image of his work. It's also the source of a good illustration of how we can teach new skills by reinforcing successive approximations. Suppose you want to train a pigeon to peck at the center of a target on its cage wall. At first you give the pigeon a pellet if it even faces toward this particular wall. When it's doing so regularly, you wait till it takes a step toward the wall before feeding it. Then you increase the number of steps required to earn a pellet. Eventually, the reward comes when the bird actually touches any part of the wall. Next you wait till it touches the outer ring of the target, then the next ring, and so on. Finally, bull's eye!

Positive reinforcement for a pigeon may be a food pellet, but notice that the front-row students did not offer Skinner a cookie as he paced a little closer to the platform's edge each day. Most of the people we're likely to be training, like Skinner, already get enough to eat, but still hunger for attention and approval. For lecturers this might well take the form of students taking note of what they say.

One of the major applications of operant conditioning is biofeedback. The only reinforcement these machines provide is information. Just by giving people a way to see how they are doing, biofeedback allows people to assume control of bodily functions such as blood pressure that, until recently, were thought of as entirely involuntary.

Initiations and elevations are certainly a form of attention and approval, major positive reinforcement. They are, however, very big rewards, spaced far apart and requiring a great deal of work and major personal learning and change. If those are the only reinforcements available, it's something like withholding the pellet till the pigeon actually pecks at the bull's eye. Without the intermediate recognition conveyed by degree elevations, it's even more difficult. The odds of success improve greatly if we provide smaller and far more achievable rewards in between.

Put this way reinforcement sounds like common sense, but it goes against the habits of mainstream Euro-American culture. We tend to take note of problem behavior—"the squeaky wheel gets the grease"—or of extraordinary achievement. Quiet success, everyday competence, gets ignored. When somebody is "just" doing her job it is not considered even noteworthy, let alone praiseworthy. But from the perspective of operant conditioning, behavioral extinction results from the repeated performance of any behavior in the absence of reinforcers. In plain English, ignore it and it *will* go away.

From Skinner and his pigeons we learn that behavior can most effectively be changed—that new skills can best be taught—if we divide the grand goal into many small incremental steps, and warmly acknowledge each small achievement, even the ones we fully expected.

Quandaries

Wiccan training raises two special problems.

TIME DEMANDS   In the religious sense Witchcraft is a vocation, a calling from within to serve the Old Gods. In the secular sense Witchcraft is, and will always be, an avocation. Our students are adults who have all the other normal obligations and delights in their lives. We are not celibates without family ties. We are not full-time religious functionaries. We live fully engaged secular lives, congruent with our theology of immanence.

There's an old joke about "three-day wonders." In the first generation Wiccan training actually took about a month. Our predecessors bravely asserted that they were practicing a religion, but all they expected of their clergy was the ability to perform a pre-scripted ritual by rote, hopefully with some fluency and appropriate expression. This may seem pathetic now, but what we have grew from these simple beginnings.

Clearly people who knew no more than this could not provide anything barely resembling the level of clergy services we have every right to expect. So over time material got added to the curriculum, and the training period got extended. Today three years is considered normal. Is it adequate?

Three years is comparable to the length of time a student spends in seminary. But seminary students attend full time. Our students need to give primary attention to their secular careers. It seems to me we have three options here, and that only two of them are good:

- *Pack it in:* Meet more often. In my observation, a terrible idea. I knew a local coven that met three times a week or more for rituals and classes. Their membership was largely composed of marginally employed people without social skills or family lives. Such an intense schedule will screen out people who live in balance and wholeness, the very ones we want.

- *Strip it down:* Get rid of nonessentials. Make sure every single task we assign to our students adds to either their knowledge or their skills in a significant way. Some of what our predecessors required was a plain waste of time.
- *Stretch it out:* Extend the time still more. Yes, I know that the number three reflects the Triple Goddess. There's still nothing sacred about a three-year training period. The number five, for example, represents the Elements and the points of a pentagram.

Consider this. I went to graduate school in the evening, after work. My classmates were all employed adults, and the majority were also parents. The rules of our program did not allow us to schedule classes for more than one evening a week. We were working toward our master's degrees in counseling. Our program head felt that he could not prepare humane counselors by an inhumane process. And yes, a night-school counseling master's usually takes two years. Ours took four. I think the same principle that applied to humane counselors applies to humane and Spirit-led Witches.

ROLE CONFLICTS Because covens serve several different functions, so do coven leaders. Two of these roles, mentor and evaluator, can come into severe conflict at times.

If coven is a growth and support group, which it is (see chapter 6), then the leader serves as facilitator, mentor, and counselor. Our primary duty is to the current members. We need to give them safe, nonjudgmental space for self-exploration, and to offer them warm empathy.

However, if coven is a training group for the next generation of Priest/esses, which it is, then the leader serves as teacher, evaluator, and gatekeeper. Our primary duty is to the next generation, whose teachers we are now training, or to the community as a whole. Our work demands above all clear-eyed objectivity, and it certainly is our job to judge.

With each yes or no decision to initiate or elevate, we serve as our community's quality control. Each time we elevate a student to elder status or empower him to hive off within our Traditions, we are vouching to the community—and most significantly to future seekers—that this person is ethical, competent, and dedicated.

Beyond this, judgment is also our obligation to our trainees. They are entitled to our help in discovering any blockages or habits that will impede them from eventual full and joyous functioning. Here's a hard question: If I refuse to elevate, if I prevent a candidate—who is (presently) unsuited to function as a coven leader—from hiving off, am I violating the trust she showed me when she revealed her vulnerability? Or am I saving her the far worse experience of failure, offering her tough love?

These are inevitable and basic conditions of coven life. They aren't going away. So we need to think through what we can do about them. Because we are the elders, the coven leaders, it is our responsibility to create and maintain those conditions that will best help our students learn and grow. Here are two safeguards:

1. Informed consent and ongoing discussion. We should explain to our coveners the multiple functions of a coven and the multiple roles of a leader, and how these complicate the learning and growth process. Whatever issues come up in the leader-to-member relationship should be clearly and openly addressed. (This may not be comfortable for leaders who have their own unresolved problems with authority.) Coveners should certainly also be clearly informed about what is expected of them in order to qualify for initiation or elevation.

2. Get a more objective opinion by asking an elder or coven leader of some coven related to your own to make a final assessment of your students before initiating or elevating them. If we can do this for each other—and trust each other as elders well enough to accept the help—we can ease a lot of the tension that comes from the contradiction of mentoring and judging the same people.

Mini-Ritual to Begin a Course of Study

1. One of the best talismans for a learning process is a decorated and consecrated notebook. Have each student create one. If your group prefers hand-copied Books of Shadows, they can start with bound blank books. Those who prefer to compile a scrapbook of many different kinds of materials (which can still include some of your own handwriting) should use loose-leaf binders. Ask people to decorate their books according to their own tastes and talents, but using colors, materials, pictures, and symbols that are related to their learning goals.

2. Then, in Circle, have all the students explain what their books' decorations mean to them. The group can consecrate and empower the books by chanting, drumming, and dancing. These notebooks can also be blessed as part of the ritual of Dedication (see chapter 8).

(from Brigantia)

Here are some points to bear in mind:

- All power, all raw talent, comes from the Goddess. She bestows it wherever She wills, regardless of the recipient's affiliation, if any.

- All knowledge and skill come from the person's own hard work. Structured training, cooperative covenmates, wise and kind teachers, all make learning easier. None of them is absolutely necessary for learning or growth. None of them accomplish anything unless the student really wants to learn.

- Credentials are bestowed by the human community, to give community members peace of mind. If a person is credentialed it's a reasonable assumption, but not a definite fact, that he is qualified. However, a Priest/ess may well be talented, skilled, and ethical and still not have any credentials at all.

Conclusion

Last year our coven started a new study group, the fabulous Proteus class of 1997. I decided it was finally time to collect what we had in teaching papers and write the ones that were still missing, to compile the Protean Book of Shadows. We set up a schedule of classes. You've heard of teachers staying one chapter ahead of the class? Well, that's what I was doing, but mostly not reading the chapters, *writing* them.

In any profession, to train the young is to take the future into our hands. This responsibility is even greater in a new field like ours. We are indeed writing our books, inventing our curricula, as we go. But this grants us the first-generation freedom to work from our own vision, rather than follow somebody else's.

Teaching is a source of joy and sorrow, pride and anxiety. That enthusiastic and contentious group of new students walking in the door may just be the Gods' way of helping us keep our own minds young.

To Learn More

Brown, Nina W. *Psycho-Educational Groups*. Philadelphia: Accelerated Development, 1998.

Christensen, C. Roland, David A. Garvin, and Ann Sweet, eds. *Education for Judgment: The Artistry of Discussion Leadership*. Boston: Harvard Business School Press, 1991.

Conyne, Robert W. *Comprehensive Group Work: What It Means and How to Teach It*. Alexandria, Va.: American Counseling Association, 1997.

Coover, Virginia, et al. *Resource Manual for a Living Revolution*. Philadelphia: New Society, 1985. (See part 6: "Training and Education," pp. 180–200. This has information about how to design a weekend workshop.)

Holt, John. *Instead of Education*. New York: Delta, 1976.

Luhrmann, T. M. *Persuasions of the Witch's Craft*. Cambridge: Harvard University Press, 1989. (Parts of this book will offend you. All of it is written in boring academese. Hold your nose and read it anyhow. Her two middle sections—pp. 115–263—give the best explanation that I have ever seen on how to develop perceptual skills.)

Rabow, Jerome, et al. *Learning Through Discussion*. Thousand Oaks, Calif.: Sage, 1994. (Only seventy pages long, and an excellent resource on cognitive learning in groups.)

Rogers, Carl. *Freedom to Learn*. Columbus, Ohio: Merrill, 1979. (The classic on student-directed learning.)

Wlodowski, Raymond J. *Enhancing Adult Motivation to Learn*. San Francisco: Jossey-Bass, 1985.

8

SPIRIT IN THE WORLD OF FORM

COVEN AS TASK GROUP

The tale of the heroic quest is as old as recorded history. In Sumer, where writing was invented, people inscribed clay tablets with narrative poetry about the Goddess Inanna's journey. We've had many retellings since—the *Odyssey*, the Grail stories, Tolkien's ring cycle—all expressions of the same central insight. The seeker leaves home to encounter many experiences, most of them frightful and arduous, all delivering a lesson or developing a capacity. Eventually the seeker reaches a perilous and climactic confrontation. Finally, tempered and transformed, the wanderer returns home bearing a gift. This is also the model for all rites of passage, including initiation. Without reincorporation, the process is incomplete. The initiate must come home.

Inspiration must be expressed. Power must move, to complete its circuit. Skills must be used, or deteriorate. Perhaps these are three ways of saying the same thing. If our rites and spiritual practices are unconnected with the rest of our lives, if we do not bring them home, they cannot be more than an elaborate hobby. More probably, blockage will cause stagnation, frustration, corruption. Consistently ignoring sacred inspiration or personal creativity is the surest way to extinguish the spark. We must reconnect.

In doing so we accept the limits that give form to our dreams and ideas. The Otherworld is the timeless realm of all possibilities, the dreaming place. Choices in the world of form are usually "forced" choices, requiring us to let go of some other good thing we want. We can't spend the same dollar, or the same hour, twice. We can't right all wrongs, nor can we realize all our dreams. We cannot actualize all of our own potentials. Some of the choices are hard.

- At times we have to choose the lesser of two evils. An indigenous group's ancestral shamanic rites, for example, may require the use of feathers from an endangered species of bird.
- At times we have to balance conflicting rights. At a gathering, you want to drum and dance in ecstasy till sunrise. I want quiet to dream in.
- We all have many competing obligations. Do I spend a day with a coven member who just lost her father or meet a writing deadline?

Confused by situational ambiguities, constrained by practical limits, we do the best we can to live authentically from our values, hoping to let our faith shine through all our deeds. All sincere Pagans, all religious people, do this. Witches, like other committed religious practitioners, do something more. We are Priest/esses of the Old Ways, ones who venture within and beyond and who return to the community with gifts.

> *I think I have told you, but if I have not, you must have understood, that a man who had a vision is not able to use the power of it until after he has performed the vision on earth for the people to see.*
>
> —Black Elk

Priest/esses bridge the worlds of spirit and form, each of us according to our unique abilities. We paint pictures and write poems. We create and conduct rituals. We do research, both archival and experimental, and then write articles and present workshops. We facilitate groups, and we counsel and mentor individuals. We do all the things that dedicated religious workers everywhere do. For the most part our covens are our sounding boards, our cheering sections, and our main sources for helping hands. They are the supportive context within which each of us finds our own way to express our personal priesthood.

But in the world of form, there are worthy projects that require a broader range of talents and skills than any one person is likely to have. There are also projects that are simply too big for any one person to do. So we pull together to make good things happen, sometimes in ad hoc groups gathered for specific purposes, but most often as covens.

Special thanks to the three people I interviewed for this chapter. Debbi's coven has been putting on a weekend-long annual conference for seven years. Deborah's coven, along with others of their Tradition, offers open Sabbat rituals for their local area. Jehana's coven published two Craft-related anthologies.

Can a work of sacred art be done by a committee? Every symphony concert, every play, every wonderful piece of architecture, is a collaborative work of art. Working together, overcoming obstacles, and sharing the pride of accomplishment, can bolster a group's sense of identity and cohesion, while providing valuable services to the community. Projects are good for covens.

DEBBI   Projects like this bring out the most incredible things in us. They give us an opportunity to be the best we can be and the worst we can be and all of our extremes. You get an opportunity to see the people whom you love rise to heights that they never dreamed they could rise to.

In Praise of Conflict

Projects are stressful for covens. The hard choices presented by the world of form become harder when multiple perceptions, opinions, desires, and aversions must be taken into account.

The radio program has just so many minutes of airtime and no more. The newsletter has a page limit. The ritual can enact just one myth, although many are relevant to this season. There's enough in our coven treasury to buy reference books or a new drum, but not both. I know your ideas are good. I know you believe mine are good. But we can't implement both of our ideas, so how do we choose?

When we move our faith from theory to practice, we inevitably face conflict over limited resources. Performance anxieties and deadline pressures add to our tension. We want to do a good job and to be recognized for the good job we do. Our egos get involved. We are free-thinking, free-spirited people, passionately engaged with the work at hand. We will not agree about every question. Because we care on so many levels, the arguments can get intense.

These conflicts test the web of relationships that is the coven.

DEBBI   Doing a project together places your members in a position of great power. But it also places them in a position of great humility. Sometimes no matter how hard you try, things are going to go wrong, and horribly wrong. And no matter how much you screw up, things are going to go tremendously right. So you learn as a group to be both prideful and humble.

In the secular world groups encounter conflict in three areas: personalities, principles and values, and practical issues. In theory covens are shielded from two of these three. If the work of formation, and of incorporating new members, was done well, personality conflicts were long since worked through. In a group bonded in love and trust, every member matters. Because we value each other, we insist on inclusive decision making. Even more important, covens are religious groups, gathered on the basis of shared values. If we differ in major ways on basic principles, the sooner we discover this, and dissolve, the better. Of course weaknesses can be short of fatal, precious warnings that allow us to correct internal contradictions before they take the group down—if we want to.

What's left is conflict about such pragmatic matters as logistics, priorities, the best way to get things done. Such conflict is very manageable and can actually be an important protection against unhealthy enmeshment, or "groupthink." All groups need a certain amount of cohesion in order to work together effectively (see chapter 2 for the process by which this necessary cohesion is formed). Taken to extreme, however, cohesion can bloat into a mind-killing conformity.

In a classic 1952 study by psychologist Solomon Asch, experimental subjects were placed in what they thought was a group of people like them. Actually, every other group member was an experimental collaborator. The "group" was asked to make some comparisons of the lengths of lines. After doing some rounds correctly, the collaborators made deliberate errors. Three-quarters of the actual subjects agreed with the majority's wrong answers.

Asch's subjects were ordinary people, randomly selected.* We aren't.

An important part of a Witch's training is learning to perceive subtle energy flows, connections, and changes. We learn this from our teachers and from our covenmates, and so we form the habit of allowing our perceptions to be guided by theirs. Furthermore, our relationship with these people is, and should be, one of deep trust. For both of these reasons we are far more open to their influence over our perceptions than people were to be influenced by the random strangers they met in Asch's lab.

Our covenmates and elders will not lie to us, but they might be mistaken, or even delusional. So being part of a warm and close-knit coven, which is good for us in so many other ways, actually increases our risk of falling into group delusion.

I've seen it. At one point in the history of Proteus, we fell victim to a collective delusion of psychic attack. Some members believed they saw an entity in the form of a purple blob in the park opposite my living room window, placed there by a hostile

*Rathus, Spencer A., *Essentials of Psychology*, 3d ed. (Fort Worth, Tex.: Holt, Rinehart & Winston, 1991): 544–545.

magician. They claimed this entity fomented dissension in our coven, and for several meetings we actually did experience terrible dissension and chaos. Members who did not see the blob were accused of being "headblind." I was urged to cover my living room windows with aluminum foil, to block the blob's disruptive influence. At least nobody tried to locate our "attacker" or urged that we strike back. What finally burst the bubble was a trusted elder, not a member of our group, telling us the tale of a similar group delusion that had taken place in a local ashram.

"Groupthink" is a group delusion compounded by hostile defenses. Typically, a group afflicted by groupthink uses a fantasy of external threat to bolster internal conformity. Such groups tend to stereotype outsiders and discredit any information that contradicts their delusional view. Members who question the group's false beliefs are accused of being allied with or influenced by the evil outsiders.* This may sound familiar. It was the underlying dynamic of the witch hunts in both Renaissance Europe and Cold War Washington.

A group afflicted by groupthink is very cohesive. They can work efficiently together toward a stupid, dangerous, or even evil purpose. When we're all excited about the same thing, those who say, "Wait a second, what about. . . ?" can be inconvenient, or even annoying. We're tempted to discount what they say, perhaps even to freeze them out.

Two classic teaching stories come to mind. One is of the Trojan seeress Cassandra, whose prescient warnings went unheeded. The other is the children's tale of the emperor's new clothing. When an entire city shared the delusion, only a child too small to have been affected could speak the truth that shattered it. Our own Cassandras, annoying though they can be, help keep us safe, sane, and congruent with our own core values. Cherish them.

Warning: Honest dissenters can make honest mistakes. Even more serious warning: The world also contains people who enjoy conflict; they are often adrenaline addicts and sad souls

*Rathus, 550.

who know no more constructive way to feel important or gain attention. Most serious warning of all: Sometimes the adrenaline addicts are also correct. The boy who falsely cried "Wolf!" from boredom and loneliness yesterday may be facing a wolf in truth today. It's better to check out a false alarm than to ignore a real one.

In summary, conflict, when handled fairly and openly, can benefit a group in the following ways:

- Prevents collective delusion and groupthink.
- Brings hidden problems to awareness.
- Generates new ideas and approaches.
- Arguing for their views forces people to state those views clearly, gather evidence, and test those views against reasoned opposition.
- Promotes healthy group cohesion by allowing any reservations to be explored and resolved.

The Facilitator's Contribution

Some definitions: *Content* refers to whatever the group is working on, the project, the task at hand. *Process* is the group's way of working, their ground rules or operating procedures. *To facilitate* means "to free from difficulties or obstacles; make easier; aid; assist."* Task group facilitators help groups establish and maintain good process ground rules, which make their work both easier and better. The facilitator's focus is much more on process than on content.

To facilitate a group engaged in a project requires some specific skills. The Association for Specialists in Group Work recognizes task group facilitation as one of the major subspecialties of groupwork. This is their definition:

> Task/work groups: Much work in contemporary Western society is accomplished through group endeavor. The task/work specialist is able to assist groups such as task forces, committees, planning groups, community organizations . . . and other similar groups to correct or develop

American Heritage Dictionary, 1st ed., 1969.

their functioning. The focus is on the application of group dynamics principles and processes to improve practice and the accomplishment of identified work goals.*

Professor Roger Schwarz, who studies such work groups, makes a useful distinction between what he calls "basic facilitation" and "developmental facilitation." In basic facilitation, a facilitator manages a group's process for them in order to help them work through a substantive problem. Developmental facilitation, while helping to solve a substantive problem, also uses the work at hand as an occasion for helping the group learn how to improve and ultimately manage their own process.† Thus the group takes time, when process issues come up, to reflect on them and learn better ways to interact.

The developmental approach is far more demanding and time-consuming. For most work groups the task is the primary function and focus. Their reason for engaging in developmental facilitation is to improve their performance on future projects. A group not anticipating future projects would be wasting their time.

For groups, like covens, that expect to keep working together after the current project is long completed, the extra work is worthwhile. In fact covens use projects as occasions to improve their skills at communication, problem solving, conflict resolution, and collaborative work, while also serving the community and the Gods.

Debbi When you get a chance to allow others to see your weaknesses as well as your strengths, to see that everybody in the group has weaknesses and strengths, it does create an extra-special bond.

Using developmental facilitation, and even formally teaching how to do it, becomes even more important when you consider

*Association for Specialists in Group Work, "Professional Standards for the Training of Group Workers," in Conyne, Robert K., F. Robert Wilson, and Donald E. Ward, *Comprehensive Group Work: What It Means and How to Teach It* (Alexandria, Va.: American Counseling Association, 1997): 246.

†Schwarz, Roger, *The Skilled Facilitator* (San Francisco: Jossey-Bass, 1994): 6–7.

that many coven members eventually hive off to lead new covens. Developmental facilitation is an investment not just in the well-being of this coven, but of all its daughters.

When a coven engages in a project, leadership involves three important roles: project coordinator, process facilitator, and spiritual mentor. These three aspects of leadership correspond with the three major criteria of a successful coven project:

- Accomplish the project (content).
- Maintain and develop the group (process).
- Meet the needs of members (spirituality).

Please note that the order of importance of these three goals and roles is, for a spiritual group engaging in a project, exactly inverse the order for a secular task group. It's also important to remember that any facilitator is first a role model. Authority depends on credibility. Credibility absolutely requires that we visibly practice the skills and live the attitudes we are attempting to convey.

DEBBI   They have seen me break down and cry because we did not break even. They have seen me angry, and power crazy, and set me gently on my ear. I feel I can be so much more honest in ritual with these people, and they can be the same with me, because we've seen so many sides of one another.

It would be very difficult for any one person to encompass all three roles. Often, working partners assume complementary responsibilities (see chapter 10), but they're still two people handling three roles that sometimes carry contradictory imperatives. One suggestion: The spiritual mentorship role must remain with a coven leader, but the role of process facilitator can be delegated to a mature covener who is contemplating hiving. Hands-on practice in the presence of your mentor is always excellent training. The role of project coordinator can be delegated to any covener who has both the relevant technical skills and those of good communication.

If delegation is not feasible, please remember that any person handling multiple roles needs to be very careful and very conscious. Talk things over with your own peers and elders.

Seek divine guidance through divination, meditation, and dreamwork. A coven leader should be doing those things anyway.

Here are some of the components of the three major roles:

PROJECT COORDINATOR   (focus on task or content)

- Good communication skills, diplomacy.
- Ability to motivate people, help the group maintain enthusiasm.
- Relevant technical expertise—being able to advise people on how to do specific tasks, offer suggestions and corrections.
- Understanding of schedules and deadlines and what needs to happen in what order. Ability to prompt people diplomatically.
- Flexibility; ability to respond to unexpected circumstances.

PROCESS FACILITATOR   (focus on communications, relationships)

- Direct and maintain focus during group discussions.
- Balance members' participation.
- Active listening and observing, empathic response.
- Summarize and clarify statements.
- Link ideas and concerns of members.
- Reflect on interactions and process.
- Conflict management and resolution.
- Block and confront inappropriate interactions.
- Ensure that decisions are fairly made.
- Attend to both relationships and task.

COVEN LEADER   (focus on values, spirituality)

- Coven's designated expert resource for matters of spirituality, religion, and magic. Repository of coven and lineage memories and wisdom.
- Maintain priority of spiritual and magical development over any particular project.
- Set and maintain limits regarding ethics and safety. This responsibility can never be delegated or abdicated. In a good coven its exercise is almost never required.

DEBBI   Yule is just a few weeks before our conference. We all get together and tell stories far into the night. That is almost the entire ritual, just sitting down and doing some story-telling. We're sharing with one another, which helps us to re-focus that the conference isn't everything. The conference is not our whole lives. Yes, the conference is almost here, but we're still going to be here as a coven family, even when the conference is over. I think that we've been lucky enough to use that holiday to really soften and connect with each other and bond with each other before the last push. That holiday is so very important to us all. It's turned into one of our fa-vorite times of year, even despite or because of the pressure.

Conflict Management Techniques

For our purposes let's define *conflict* as "a strong *and emotion-laden* disagreement." Such conflict is inevitable, and can even be salutary, in groups composed of strong, free-spirited people who care about what they are doing together. Conflict man-agement is an important part of the process facilitator's role. Here are a few suggestions for process facilitators to use when conflict comes:

• Ask the parties to be very clear about the nature of their conflict. Does it stem from principles or pragmatics? How in-tense is it? Might any of the emotional intensity attached to this conflict be transferred from similar situations elsewhere in the parties' lives? You may even want to ask the people in conflict to take time out for self-examination and meet privately with you before the next group meeting.

• If necessary, use a talking stick (an object that passes back and forth, giving the holder the right to speak) to prevent interruption. If you do this ask both parties to limit them-selves to one major point per statement. If it seems neces-sary to cool things down even more, ask for ten seconds of silence before each response.

• If either party seems to feel unheard, require each one to paraphrase the previous statement *to the satisfaction of the other* before responding to it.

- Remind all concerned to focus on their actual interests rather than their positions. Here's a good technique for helping them understand the difference: When they say what they want, ask, "And what will that do for you?" Keep repeating the question till you reach their actual desire. (There's a wonderful teaching story so prevalent among groupworkers that I don't know the original source. Two sisters are arguing over an orange. Finally, in fairness, they decide to cut it in half. Then one sister squeezes out the juice and throws the shell away. The other grates the peel off her half to flavor a cake and discards the pulp. The moral is that if she had only said what she wanted the orange for, each could have had 100 percent of what she wanted. Tell them this story.)

- If necessary, use the "single text" technique. Start by crafting a solution that seems fair to you. To make it inclusive, bring it first to one party, then the other, asking them to make corrections and suggestions. Keep going back and forth until neither side suggests anything else.

- A fair solution can be imposed; an inclusive one cannot. Inclusive solutions require full and wholehearted participation. If both sides do not cooperate willingly, a facilitator can't force them. And if each side does not actively want the other side's concerns to be honored, why are they covening together?

The Project Sequence

Work groups gather to address concerns and problems, to explore new ideas and opportunities, to plan and carry out projects. Along the way they will make a series of decisions. Strong, emotional disagreement around some of these decisions will take the group into the realm of conflict resolution.

There's a typical sequence to a project. It's very similar to the cycle of personal change described in chapter 6. Again, this pattern will vary depending on specific circumstances. And again, it's easy and feels natural to integrate our magical techniques with those of secular groupwork.

The major difference is that our focus before was on individual development as nurtured in the coven. Our focus now is on the group itself, so we need to attend to the perceptions, opinions, desires, and aversions of all participants.

Here's the sequence:

Identify and Explore a Problem or Opportunity

Somebody notices a problem, or has a great idea, and brings it to the coven. For example:

DEBBI   A former conference went defunct. We were asked if we would run a similar conference by the people who got left in the lurch by that. A lot of the teachers and a lot of the vendors didn't have a place to go. They said, "If you do it, we will come."

DEBORAH   For a while our coven took over the September ritual. People had lost interest and weren't doing it. We revived it. So for several years, we just took responsibility for that one every year. Nobody else wanted to do it 'cause it's complicated to do, so we didn't have any competition.

JEHANA   We realized that there didn't seem to be many books out there on the God aspects of Witchcraft and Paganism. There are the classic mythologies, but there didn't seem to be that much contemporary discussion of the God form. This was mainly noticed by the male members of the coven. I don't remember how the idea of doing an anthology suddenly came up.

Start by exploring how other coveners perceive the same situation. Do they also feel strongly about the need or opportunity? What would they hope to change or create? What do they fear would happen if no action is taken?

For this kind of preliminary exploration consider using a talking stick. This allows the holder to speak without interruption, and with everyone's undivided attention.

There are two main ways to work with a talking stick. At first it simply goes around the circle. Each person in turn either says what is on his heart or passes. The stick makes as many rounds as it takes until there is a complete round of silence. This technique draws out the quieter members, making sure that everyone is heard.

Later, as people begin to get excited over possibilities, place the stick on your altar. People can pick it up as they feel moved to speak, in any order, and replace it on the altar when they are done. This allows members to build on one another's thoughts, but it also can let the more assertive members dominate the discussion. To balance inputs, switch back to the previous "round" method to conclude the session.

By now you've either decided this idea isn't for you or you've formed a general goal. A goal is not a specific action plan; nor are you yet ready for detailed plans. Before anybody plans a trip, they need to choose a destination. The criteria for a good personal goal given in chapter 6—positive, possible, ethical, ecological, and observable—apply just as well to collective goals. Try checking your goal against these criteria.

Gather Information

There's one more thing to figure out in this exploratory session. What additional information will you need and how will you gather it? Does someone need to check out site availability, or printing costs, or relevant law, or what happened to the old mailing list? Be clear about who is undertaking to research what. Set another meeting time and draw closure.

If you can, circulate whatever information is gathered before your next meeting, so people have a chance to digest it. If not, open your second work session with these reports.

Generate Alternatives

At your next session, list as many ways as possible to reach your goal. You can do this through facilitated discussion, or by using the talking stick again. It's important that someone take notes.

Brainstorming is the optimal method. Have people call out ideas as they occur, without any internal censorship at all. Weird and far-fetched ideas are welcome at this point. If we limit ourselves to the things we already know will work, all innovation is precluded. Some of the ideas may build upon other ideas or even be reactions to them. That's fine. Just for now, suspend analysis. Simply jot the ideas down as they come, preferably on a large sheet of paper that everyone can see.

When the brainstorming slows down and stops, the facilitator might want to group similar ideas. If time allows, do no more analysis at this meeting. Schedule another session. Circulate a list of the brainstorm results, or of the possibilities raised in other ways, as soon as possible, so people can both ponder and sleep on them for a while before you meet again. Save the list, too. When the project is completed and you're doing your critiquing and feedback, you may want to revisit some of the roads not taken.

Extrapolate

Start with facilitated discussion. Work through the list of alternatives. Consider the resources that are available to you, within and beyond your own coven: time, energy, money, and talent.

Remember, in the world of form there are many good projects you are simply not able to do. Eliminate ideas that are obviously not feasible. Divide those that remain into probables and possibles.

Now, having assessed feasibility as best as you can, explore the probables. Imagine together where each of these would take you. You might want to use some combination of guided fantasy and divination to explore these probable outcomes. Pay careful attention to any intuitive or emotional response that comes up for any member. Make sure to check whether anyone in the group feels strongly about including any of the possibles in this process.

If possible, try to let some time pass before you make your decision. Schedule another meeting. In between, pay attention to your dreams.

Decide

The task before you right now, your present *content*, is to choose which of the feasible alternatives, if any, your group wants to pursue. The *process* of decision making is the same for this and all the other decisions your coven will make. There are some very helpful books on how to structure your decision making in this chapter's bibliography. Rather than summarize or replicate what they say, I'd like to go a bit deeper into the matter of fair and inclusive decision making.

- *Fair* means impartial, just, equitable, and consistent. *Inclusive* means comprehensive, taking everything (or in this case *everyone*) into account.* These are neither linked nor opposed; we can have either, neither, or both.†

- Which particular formal decision-making method we use matters far less than most of us think. People have created various sets of procedural rules to ensure fairness, but any human-designed system can be subverted or corrupted by other humans. Nothing guarantees inclusiveness and fairness except our determination to have them.

- What really matters is the quality of the discussion that precedes the actual decision. When people genuinely want to know what others are thinking and feeling, they listen to each other. Open, active listening gives us courage to speak our truths.

- Inclusive solutions take whatever time they take. The group must listen until everyone feels heard and all concerns are satisfied. Time limits—and especially stopwatches—give an unfair advantage to the glib. Worse, they advantage those who come to the meeting with their minds already made up and their sound bites already prepared.

  Some issues really are time-critical. These are better handled by a fair vote, even though the outcome is unlikely to be

*Both definitions are excerpted from the *American Heritage Dictionary*, 1st ed., 1969.

†For a lot more about the distinction between the ethic of rights and fairness and the ethic of caring and affiliation, see Gilligan, Carol, *In a Different Voice* (Cambridge, Mass.: Harvard University Press, 1982).

fully inclusive. If you can't have the reality, you are better without the appearance.

- Love and trust are the keys to true inclusiveness. The word *love* doesn't only indicate romantic or sexual feelings. Sibling love is what supports our covens. However, the general definition of *love*, "a condition in which the beloved's happiness is integral to that of the lover," applies to family at least as well as it does to romance. If someone's happiness is integral to mine, we can't be adversaries. How could I feel good about getting my own way over hers? Instead, we will both *want* an inclusive "win-win" solution, and work together to create one.

- Trust is our reliance on one another to tell the truth and to keep our given word. In working through a decision we must be completely open with each other about our perceptions, opinions, desires, and aversions. Without full self-disclosure, inclusive solutions are impossible.

  Undiscussable issues poison trust. Sweeping conflict or other difficulties under the rug eventually causes bumps in the rug. In time someone will trip over one of these bumps and get hurt.

  Beware of hidden agendas, in yourself or your coven-mates. A hidden agenda usually stems from an ulterior motive. If you have some purpose or desire that is extrinsic to the shared goal of this project but that you think might be achieved through this project, this purpose or desire will color your opinions and make your positions less flexible. Those who work from hidden agendas are lying by omission. Lying kills trust.

  Lying is also a symptom of distrust. The distrust may be valid. Openness is vulnerability. Telling people exactly what all our deep needs and sore spots are is an act of deep trust. Your impulse to hold back may reflect an accurate intuition that these people don't merit your trust. If so, what are you doing covening with them?

- You can only tell the truth that you know. Attend carefully to your own personal perceptions, opinions, needs, and aversions. Notice their relative intensity and especially notice their bases. Some come from core values; some come from pragmatic considerations. Questions about what *should* be done and what *can* be done are both important, but they are very different in nature.

- Interpersonal power—disproportionate influence in decision making—is an inevitable reality. (For all the ways people accrue power, see chapter 2.) However, power itself is ethically neutral. What matters is the method and purpose of its use.

  Where there is love and trust, those who hold power will not use it to dominate, hurt, or exploit. External constraints on their power are unnecessary. Where love and trust are lacking, external constraints are easily circumvented. Worse, observing the outer forms of fairness can conceal and protect dominant, hurtful, and exploitive behaviors.

- Unless all members are free to speak their minds, neither fairness nor inclusiveness is possible. If those in power seek to protect themselves from criticism or otherwise limit members' expression, beware!

- Pragmatic concerns can usually be worked out. If your concern is pragmatic, you probably derived it from evidence and reasoning. It's respectful, and may be persuasive, to share these. If you think the group is wasting time on a dumb idea, you can simply stand aside without blocking the rest. They'll learn better—or you will.

  Concerns related to conscience and values are qualitatively different. Do you actually want to be part of a group that is doing something you believe to be not just dumb, but evil?

- In a group joined in love and trust, core values are shared or, at the very least, honored. When one member expresses an intense and values-based need or objection, all members will want this concern to be satisfied. Any group that would do less is not operating in love and trust.

- When the group has fully and fairly deliberated, in love and trust, honoring each member's viewpoints and values, members are ethically obligated to abide by the decision reached.

Any concerns should have been shared and worked through during the process.

- Groups significantly larger than covens may not have either the need or the ability to weave such closeness. Without love and trust, groups may not always be able to find fully inclusive solutions. It may not be appropriate to spend the necessary time and care on trivial decisions. It may not even be possible when the group is working against time constraints. Fairness, however, is always possible.

- Coven leaders bear an inalienable and ultimate responsibility for the safety and ethics of their group. Leaders are generally more experienced than other coven members. In lineage-based groups, leaders also carry the oral tradition and collective memory of the line. On rare occasions they may have to draw limits. Anyone who finds this intolerable can leave the group.

Make a Plan

You've decided that the need or opportunity is real. You've decided that the goal is both worthwhile and within your realistic abilities. Now it's time to make a specific action plan. The questions before you are those of the world of form. For example:

- Who is the overall project coordinator?
- Who is responsible for which part of the work? Is the project large enough that we should designate committee heads? If so, how much autonomy do they have?

DEBBI Decision making was left up to the person who was doing the job. We always said that the buck would stop with the coven leaders. If you didn't feel comfortable making a decision in your area, you could always come back to Tom and me. We would either make the decision if you didn't feel comfortable making it, or back you to the hilt if you were getting flak for your decision.

JEHANA   When we had differences of opinion, we discussed why certain things were better to do. As far as the actual articles went, we pretty much agreed on the articles we would include in the anthologies. That wasn't really a problem. Most of the disagreements were on technical issues about putting it together. I'd look at it and realize that I didn't really have that expertise. I'd let somebody else decide that. I trusted the people who had that background.

- If we need any special talents that don't exist in our own group, who can we ask for help?

DEBBI   We had an artist in our group. She felt very comfortable doing all our graphic design for the first conference, and getting the program booklets together. Another person in our group had volunteered to do some security. Other people whom we knew from other covens volunteered to work with us because they had certain specialties, such as medical staff. Basically people picked up the roles they were most comfortable with.

- What is our budget? Do we need seed money? If so, how much? Where will it come from? Who is keeping our financial records?
- What needs to be done in what order?
- Does this work have a deadline? If so, what are the deadlines for the component parts?
- What is our definition of *success*?

The answer to this question is not as obvious as it seems. Take this example: A group announces that they will be offering a series of workshops on the third Saturday afternoon of the next six months. They may be doing this to share important skills or to raise money for legal defense. Skill sharing is best done in small groups. You only need to raise enough money to cover expenses. If you feel strongly about sharing the information, you may even be willing to offer it as a gift. But if your goal is fund-raising, you want to attract as many people as possible and generate a large surplus.

~~~~~~

Mini Ritual
Invocation for Guidance

Lady and Lord, to You we call
For guidance and power in the work we do
Let it bless many, let it harm none
Let it give glory unto You!

~~~~~~

Ritually Consecrate Your Project and Raise Power for Its Success

You've undertaken this project in service to the Ancient Gods. It's appropriate to formally offer your work to Them, and to seek Their guidance and empowerment. Some possibilities during this rite:

- Share visions of what you hope to accomplish by this work.
- Seek divine guidance through divination or other means.
- Use an affirmation something like this: "May the work we do together bring good to many and harm to none!"
- Formally install a project coordinator and committee heads.
- Consecrate some object that symbolizes this project. It might be a special talking stick for use at your working meetings. Raise power for your project's success and load it into this object.

As time goes on you will find other occasions for magical empowerment. Take them all! For example, if you're going to be sending out a mailing, consider invoking magical power into it so that it might find its way to the people who would best enjoy and benefit from your work.

Remember, you are doing this work in service to the Gods and in Their name. Take all opportunities to invite and welcome Their participation.

Do It! Begin Working on the Project

Remember that this is a coven project. Find ways to keep all coven members involved and participating.

JEHANA We drew on all our different skills. There were a couple of people in the group who said, "Well, I really don't have any skills," but none of us wanted to have anybody feel excluded, which I think is important too. Even a job like physically collating or putting things together, or reading over articles to decide which is a good one, that's all skill, too.

It's very important to include everybody. Some people got more involved than other people, but the point was that everybody was involved.

Keep each other apprised of progress and problems. If your coven is doing this project alone, short check-ins before your regular Circle will usually be sufficient. If you find these are in any way distorting your Circles, have the meetings at other times. If other people or other covens are helping, you'll probably need to schedule periodic meetings. Also consider round-robin letters, E-mail lists, conference calls, et cetera. If things are not quite going according to plan, or if new and wonderful opportunities are appearing, gather again and adapt or fine-tune your plan.

Remember, there will be moments of stress and tension, particularly as deadlines loom.

DEBBI We realize that tempers are short. Everybody takes a pact not to take it too seriously if somebody snaps at someone else. It's just group tension happening. A month after the conference is over, if peoples' tempers are still in an uproar, then we know we have something serious to handle.

Some of these crises may even seem funny in retrospect.

DEBBI Once our graphic designer decided that a pentagram on a cover needed to be upside down rather than right-side up. We overruled that! She felt that artistically it looked better upside down. I said, "I'm sorry. It doesn't work when this is on the cover. This is kind of showing who we are. As much as it looks better that way, I can't justify it."

Remember to take care of each other. Remember to take care of yourself. If you find yourself getting behind schedule or feeling overwhelmed, let someone know as soon as possible, before the problems compound. Remember to take time to rest, laugh, and worship.

Celebrate Your Success With Mirth and Reverence!

If the show went well, take your curtain calls, then have a truly memorable cast party. People who have worked hard together, and negotiated all the interpersonal stress with their coven bonds intact, deserve to relax and blow off some steam together.

Obviously, you'll have a meeting for feedback and critique to figure out what ideas you want to keep or even expand, and how you can do things better next time. Of course you'll give formal thanks to the Gods at your next ritual. Just as a party could not replace either of these, they cannot replace a party.

Keeping pleasure in the picture is, for us, nothing less than a matter of theological principle. "Ye shall dance, sing, feast, make music and love, all in My presence."

Another important theological point: Pride is one of the seven deadly sins . . . *in somebody else's religion*. If you've done well, go ahead, preen yourself, brag—you deserve it! Only remember to share the glory, because you did together what you could not have done alone.

DEBORAH   If we spent all of our time just meeting by ourselves, and having rituals and so on, after a while it gets to be a little bit routine. I think you need to have some kind of input from the outside world to stay fresh. Also, we have ideas about how things ought to be done. Doing an open Sabbat gives us a feeling of pride, because we know we've created something that's valuable to the community and we've shown other people what we can do.

~~~~~~

Mini-Ritual for Completing a Project

Our work is done, let the gift go forth
Like the dancing wind, like the blessing sun
Like the healing rain, like the fruitful earth
With the blessing power of the Ancient Gods
Bringing good to many and harm to none.

~~~~~~

JEHANA   I think it helped the coven know that they could do something together as a team. We felt that we could have an idea and be able to work on it together and bring it to fruition. That's a valuable thing. Being able to say, "Here's our project. We can do this." And then doing it, and saying, "Look at what we did!"

Conclusion

There is an entirely normal human need to believe that what we do matters, and that it makes some kind of helpful difference in our world. For Erik Erikson, the psychologist who described human developmental stages from infancy through old age, the focal decision of adulthood is between self-absorption and generativity—contributing to the human future, usually through teaching or mentoring (for more on generativity, see chapter 9). Abraham Maslow, generally considered one of the fathers of humanistic psychology, placed self-esteem and self-actualization at the top of his well-known hierarchy of human needs (for more on Maslow's hierarchy, see chapter 6).

All kinds of research and theory point toward the same conclusion, which I can reduce to three simple and obvious statements:

- We need to know that what we do in this world makes a difference.

- Knowing that we make a difference helps us feel good about ourselves. We need to feel good about ourselves.
- There is nothing wrong with either doing or feeling good.

Priest/esses manifest Spirit in the world of form, each of us according to our unique abilities. This is an outward and visible expression of our inner interactions with the Sacred. The rewards for this are inherent in the work itself. Who needs to be "compensated" for deep satisfaction or pure joy?

Our sacred traditions forbid accepting payment for the practice of our priesthood. There are many reasons why this seems to us to be the better way. What we do for love, we do not subject to market forces. Instead we are guided by our own inner sense of what is good and beautiful. Most of us pay for this purity by meeting the time and energy demands of the "day jobs" by which we support ourselves. But have you noticed how payment turns joy to obligation? Did this ever happen: You thanked someone who had done well by you, and he responded that he was only doing what he gets paid for?

Some things are priceless—just too precious to sell. Spirit is one of them.

Priest/ess, nobody is paying you for this. There is no extrinsic reason to do it, no reason at all for compromising your standards. You do it for love. Your reward is the gratitude of your kindred and your own self-esteem—the very things your maturing soul most strongly needs.

To Learn More

Task Groups

Heerman, Barry. *Building Team Spirit: Activities for Inspiring and Energizing Teams*. New York: McGraw-Hill, 1997.
Schwarz, Roger M. *The Skilled Facilitator: Practical Wisdom for Developing Effective Groups*. San Francisco: Jossey-Bass, 1994.

Conflict Resolution and Group Decision Making

Coover, Virginia, Ellen Deacon, Charles Esser, and Christopher Moore. *Resource Manual for a Living Revolution: A Handbook of Skills and Tools for Social Change Activists*. Philadelphia: New Society, 1985. (See part 2: "Working in Groups," pp. 43–99.)

Fisher, Roger, and William Ury. *Getting to Yes: Negotiating Agreement Without Giving In*. New York: Penguin, 1981.

Gastil, John. *Democracy in Small Groups: Participation, Decision Making and Communication*. Philadelphia: New Society, 1993.

Haugk, Kenneth C. *Antagonists in the Church: How to Identify and Deal With Destructive Conflict*. Minneapolis: Augsburg Fortress, 1988. (This is a Christian book, full of Bible references, and so on. Nevertheless, it is an excellent description of how conflict addicts operate within a religious community, and so is useful for religious people of all faiths.)

Janis, Irving L. *Groupthink*, 2d ed. Boston: Houghton Mifflin, 1982. (Although the case studies are drawn from government and politics, the pathological pressures to conform that are described in this book can take place in any kind of group. Janis's perspective is an important counterbalance to Haugk's.)

Kaner, Sam, et al. *Facilitator's Guide to Participatory Decision-Making*. Philadelphia: New Society, 1996.

9

WE CHOOSE EACH OTHER

COVEN AS SECOND-CHANCE FAMILY

Some come looking for the coven to be a surrogate family, the family they would have chosen given the choice. That sort of coven is the kind that helps the widowed member into her flannel nightgown after the wake and sings her to sleep, the kind that turns the big deep bathtub into a candle-lit wishing well where the pregnant member who is due to give birth that week floats amidst fragrant blossoms while the coveners drop good luck coins in for her and the baby.

—CAROL

I remember two women. We'll call them Tigress and Mermaid. They were in Proteus at the same time. It seemed to me like all I ever heard from either of them was complaints about the other. For Tigress ritual was an art form. She spent hours writing poetic scripts and creating beautiful decorations. Mermaid, in contrast, wanted deep inner work, emotional catharsis, and personal change. Tigress said Mermaid was sloppy; Mermaid said Tigress was shallow. Once, in a coven forum, one of them threw a wastebasket across the room in frustration. I don't even remember which one.

No question that these women's opinions about ritual were serious. No question that their complaints about each other were equally sincere. But it's also true that each grew up in a home with an older brother. Both had the habit of competing for Mom's attention, by good work and by deriding a dominant sibling.

Then Mermaid, who was unsatisfied with her career, went back to school to retrain in Tigress's field. When she needed help with her homework, where do you think she went for tutoring? Tigress, of course! That's the way it works in families. Siblings fight, compete for attention, complain about one another incessantly—and pull together whenever there is real need.

Intentional family, family by choice. Marriage is this, of course. But can we choose other relationships as well—surrogate parents, adoptive siblings? Of course we can! They say blood is thicker than water, but love is strongest of all.

My "chosen" brother is an only child. So am I. Long, long before I found the Craft, when we were both fifteen, we sat in the park across from our high school and talked about our feelings for each other. Neither of us had any inkling back then of making a formal, ritual commitment to each other. Neither of us had heard of intentional family. We simply decided together that we wanted to be brother and sister. That was 1960. He is my brother still.

People move around a lot these days, often separating themselves from extended family and neighborhood networks. We replicate these networks in our new locations. An existing structure, like a coven, eases the process:

THEOS   Part of the reason I think there was a resurgence of interest in Witchcraft was that after World War II, people spread out into the suburbs. When I started practicing, people were still coming here. Almost everybody out here was a transplanted city person. Their families were still in the city. There was no longer the grandmother, the aunts, the uncles, the sisters, and brothers right nearby. There wasn't the mixture of the older people. Everybody was the same age. Everybody had the same house. Everybody had the same-aged children.

Covens, in many ways, helped with the loss of that extended family. Baby-sitting, or puppy-sitting, or cat-sitting. The car broke down, whom did you call? You called the other guy in your Circle to come help you get your car started. And "I've got a new baby, and what do you feed it?" There was this group of people, like family, that you could turn to.

Circle, in some ways—not in all ways, because the people don't live close together, but in some ways—is a little bit of a taste of the village we lost, along with the magic, and the Mysteries, and the rituals, and a thousand and one other reasons why they come. I don't think that on the surface they even realize it, but it's something deep within, the need to seek out others.

I've seen it in action over and over again.

Or we create intentional families hoping that they will do for us all that our original families did not or could not:

PATRICK   Many of us in our group feel that the coven experience is one in which we get to create the trusting family environment that we've never been able to achieve in the secular world. And like any family, we fight, scream, tell each other to go hang ourselves. . . . But we also know that these people are the people we can go to with our concerns, hang-ups, hopes, dreams, fears, and know that they/we will support each other in our search.

That's the lovely ideal. We come together by conscious choice, not by accident of birth. We come together as mature and spiritual people. We come together with others who share our deepest values. Of course we will be able to create together the ideal family life we wish we had had, the perfectly nurturing environment we were sadly denied as children. Of course.

The paradox is that each of us is formed by all of our prior life experiences. We bring to our covens the habits of interpretation and interaction that we learned in our families of origin. Very, very few of these families were perfect. Sometimes they were dysfunctional. Good or bad, they remain our largest single formative influence. As adults, in and out of coven, we act the way we know how to act.

What follows is taken from a basic textbook on group psychotherapy. As you read it, try substituting the word *coven* for *therapy group*, and *coven leader* for *therapist*:

> The therapy group resembles a family in many aspects: there are authority/parental figures, peer siblings, deep personal revelations, strong emotions, and deep intimacy as well as hostile, competitive feelings. In fact, therapy groups are often lead by a male and female therapy team in a deliberate effort to simulate the parental configuration as closely as possible. . . . Sooner or later, the members will interact with the leaders and other members in modes reminiscent of the way they once interacted with parents and siblings.
>
> There is an enormous variety of patterns: some members become helplessly dependent upon the leaders, whom they imbue with unrealistic knowledge and power; others blindly defy the leaders, who are perceived as infantilizing and controlling; others are wary of the leaders, whom they believe attempt to strip members of their individuality; some members try to split the co-therapists in an attempt to incite parental disagreements and rivalry; some compete bitterly with other members, hoping to accumulate units of attention and caring from the therapists; others expend energy in a search for allies among the other patients, in order to topple the therapists; still others neglect their own interests in a seemingly endless effort to appease the leaders and the other members.*

*Yalom, Irvin D., *The Theory and Practice of Group Psychotherapy*, 4th ed. (New York: Basic, 1995): 13–14.

Does this sound embarrassingly familiar? Here's how a veteran coven leader describes the same phenomena:

THEOS   The whole coven is set up as a family, with the mother
    and the grandmother and the siblings. The dynamics that
    take place within it and the interaction among people are
    very much that way. When you get new people coming in,
    they're like very young children. They're enthusiastic, bubbling, I don't care what their age is. They want to go out and
    tell the whole world. It's all you can do to sit on them until
    they calm down a little bit. Then eventually they settle in.

    There's also the rivalry with the sisters and brothers who
    were there first, about you bringing in somebody new.
    There's a lot of nit-picking and bitterness that takes place,
    and jealousy and feelings that they're going to be cast aside
    because you're favoring somebody else now. It's very much
    like a family.

    And then, when you've had somebody in your group approximately three years, you reach the rebellious teenage
    stage. They know more than you do. They want to lead their
    own group. They start to give you a lot of headaches and a lot
    of problems, and it's time to let them go. Just like a teenager.

The technical term for all of this is *transference*. Some therapists
in the early twentieth century believed that transference explained everything that ever goes wrong in the human mind, and
resolving transference was the universal cure. This is patently
ridiculous, and only succeeded in making a joke of the concept.

Still, it makes obvious sense that we are shaped by all our
prior experiences and we carry over habits of perception, interpretation, emotional response, and interaction from earlier times.
Transference explains a lot of behavior that otherwise seems to
be excessive, inappropriate, or even completely irrational.

Bookstores have shelfloads of self-help books explaining how
families assign their children a variety of cutely named roles.
We then endlessly replicate roles like these in adult life, often
to our detriment. This is true, but highly oversimplified. No two

people are alike. We do not all fit into any neat set of four or
six or eight categories. If you understand that these are crude
first approximations, the books are a decent starting place.

Also, although the largest single influence on each of us is
certainly our childhood environment, some of what we carry
over comes later: from school, work, previous marriages. If the
person was in the military, and especially if in combat, you can
be sure some interactive habits come from this.

The source of the transference doesn't matter. Therapists
used to believe that the only way to resolve transference was
to identify its origin, but nobody has ever proved this.* Still, to
create ideal families of choice we must understand and resolve
our transference issues. Current understanding doesn't mean
we have to wallow in early-childhood trauma. Instead we need
to notice when some of our habitual responses seem irrelevant
or inappropriate in the here and now, and learn better ways to
deal with one another.

HOLLY   The coven as a family is a very good working model
. . . but all families, even those selected by choice, are bound
to run into some difficulties eventually. Fallible beings that
we are, it's inevitable. Dysfunction happens. I think the key
is to recognize and deal with the problems. Yes, it's ugly. Yes,
it's messy. Yes, it's painful. But unless we do that, the family
dies. I've seen a case where serious problems were ignored.
The coven suffered *terribly*. Virtually everyone knew the
problems were there, but since they weren't being acknowledged openly, they not only couldn't be resolved, but no one
could develop any viable strategy to even cope. Honesty is
essential. And I think that "perfect trust" also means that
you extend to your covenmates *your* belief that *they* also will
be honest and willing to help resolve sticky issues.

Our bright hopes are also true. We *can* work this out together. In a good coven we really do come together as mature

*Yalom, 46.

and spiritual people. We truly are joining with others who share our deepest values. In a lineage-based coven we even have one or two people around who have had a couple of years' head start in working this out for themselves, which should give them a clearer view, and possibly some facilitative skills with which to help the others.

Transference and the Coven Leader

Coven leaders are convenient targets for transference reactions. You have taken the position of the Big Person: the parent, teacher, or boss, the authority figure toward whom coveners can react. This is some of what can happen:

- They may ascribe superhuman powers to you, expecting you to be all-wise and able to solve all their problems, and then react angrily when you can't.
- They may expect you to read their minds, and then react angrily when you can't.
- They may attach tremendous significance to your most casual or trivial statements.
- Some of them may become childishly dependent and compete for your attention.
- Some of them may become compulsively rebellious, finding occasions to fight with you.

It's disturbing to be treated as a position, a symbol instead of a person. When the members of your chosen family treat you so, it really can hurt. This is hard advice to follow, but try to stay grounded and centered. Remember that their anger, although directed toward you, is not about you. The coven may be the first safe space they've ever had to release some of this long-contained pressure.

It's hard on them, too. Besides all their old hurts and scars, they are also wrestling with current feelings of inadequacy. It's the same for secular professionals. These difficult feelings were reported from a group of student therapists:

> There were two opposing sets of concerns about the "big people," and both were equally troubling: that the "big people"

were real, that they possessed superior wisdom and knowledge and would dispense an honest but terrible justice to the young, presumptuous frauds who tried to join their ranks; or that the "big people" themselves were frauds, that the members were all Dorothys facing the Oz wizard. The second possibility had more frightening implications than the first.... As frightening as their judgment may be, it is far less terrible than the other alternative—that *there are no "big people,"* and that one is finally and utterly alone.*

A Witch's concerns are startlingly similar:

BRIGANTIA   Sometimes I feel like a placeholder, a temporary replacement worker, keeping the Craft alive until the Real Witches come to town. I used to hope that the Real Witches would come whirling into town real soon now, and that they would see that at least I had tried, and take me and my initiates into their wise and caring arms and make things all better.

This was a scary concept, because there was always the possibility that the Real Witches would look at me and mine and snort, "You aren't worthy. You never wrote a book about the Craft, or got asked to be a consultant for a movie company, and we don't know who you are. Why should we care about your initiates? They couldn't possibly be worthy either." I got to thinking that if the Real Witches came to town, I'd probably go hide in a cave somewhere and hope they didn't find me.

And then one night the dreadful realization hit me. Maybe there are no Real Witches elsewhere. Maybe nobody will ever come from afar to take over from me. Not tomorrow. Not next month. Not ever.

The Real Witches are right here in our own covens. I still feel like a placeholder sometimes, but now I realize that my initiates, and their initiates, and their initiates' initiates, are

---

*Yalom, 200. It's instructive to compare that statement to this one: "If you do not find what you seek within you, you will never find it without."

the Real Witches who will take over from me. And that feels all right by me.

You are the standard against which your coveners judge themselves. They would be intimidated and resentful if you were perfect. They are terrified and resentful that you are not. Growth, for both coveners and coven leader, depends on dismantling this pedestal.

Your second-chance family will be real to the extent that all of you deal with one another as you are, warts and all, in the here and now, rather than with images transposed from other times and places. A coven leader who stays grounded acts as a lightning rod for excessive transference reactions, eventually draining their energy. Here are some more strategies that will probably help:

- Encourage coveners to check in with each other. If one member's perceptions or reactions are very different from the others', this is probably due to transference. Comparing notes will often help this member realize that she holds a distorted view. This is risky for an authoritarian leader. What would it mean if most of the members actually did have the same problem?

- Be as real as you can. Don't retreat behind a role. Stay in the here and now yourself. Therapists of the past believed that maintaining a blank, impassive mask would help identify transferential reactions. In reality, authenticity disables them far more effectively.

- Encourage meditation. In insight meditation we detach from our own thoughts and simply watch them as they pass by. This gives space to notice which of these thoughts are not presently relevant. Over time regular meditation also fosters serenity, a quiet center from which we can make wiser choices.

- Remember, the difficulties you are experiencing are growing pains, and the goal is very worthwhile.

SUSAN   Yeah, we sometimes act out old roles in our coven. One of us tends to see the others as a threat, especially when that person perceives that they are being challenged. One tends to play a clown role out of the belief that no one would be interested in seeing the person beneath that mask. And I have a tendency to lose myself in the role of Priestess, not giving myself permission to be fully open to my coven because it's my job to support them. I play the invisible child a lot. But it's only by expressing our habits that we can change them and grow into new ones. If we did not get angry at one another and behave badly toward each other, if we never took risks in our relationships but instead sat safely within the bonds of conventional etiquette, we would never change or heal or grow or even truly *be* with one another.

Counter-Transference

A group leader's transference is called counter-transference. Group leaders usually are more experienced and presumed to have already begun to work their way to clarity. It's only fair to expect this of anyone who proposes to teach or mentor others, after all.

Still, we are the imperfect products of a training program that's still in its research-and-design phase in a newly reawakening community. In addition it seems that psychological clarity, like physical fitness, requires concerted, lifelong maintenance. So it behooves us to periodically look long and hard into the black mirror of truth. Partners and elders can help, as can peer support networks, but the ultimate responsibility is our own.

VESTO   A coven leader should become aware of the sorts of people s/he is typically drawn to, for what reasons, and how s/he tends to interact with them over time. This can often shed some light on why s/he feels inclined to admit one person over another (or everyone who comes along!).

Many spiritual traditions speak of frightening and difficult moments along the Path: the dark night of the soul, that lonesome valley that you've got to walk all by yourself. Here's one

of ours: We need to face and to moderate our burning need
to be needed.

Consider medicine: The correct dose heals, but overdose poi-
sons. Many good things become bad things with excess. Here
are some good things: our human needs for affiliation, self-
esteem, and self-actualization; our desire to make a difference
in this world. One word sums up all of these, and it has been
identified as the focal issue of mature adulthood: *generativity*.

> Generativity is primarily the interest in establishing and
> guiding the next generation, although there are people
> who, from misfortune or because of special and genuine
> gifts in other directions, do not apply this drive to offspring
> but to other sorts of altruistic concern and of creativity,
> which may absorb their kind of parental responsibility.*

Mature adults need to feel that they are somehow shaping
the future. Once people did this through parenthood. Times
have changed. For love of our overburdened Mother Earth,
many of us chose not to have children. Without offspring, we
have found other ways: mentoring younger colleagues, writing
books like this one. Our need to be needed drives us to develop
our talents, make meaningful contributions, feel good about
ourselves. Our work is fruitful.

Good fruit can become overripe. Many people in the helping professions, including clergy of all faiths, are drawn to this
work because of transference issues. They may have grown up
in chaotic, dysfunctional families. Perhaps they coped by taking on responsibilities their parents abdicated, trying desper-
ately to fix what was wrong or at least to smooth it over. As
adults they become "a *codependent*, one who is fixated on solving others' problems in a way that ignores their own and
allows the others to continue in self-destructive behavior,"† because they fear that they are only acceptable if they can make
themselves useful.

---

*Erikson, Eric H., *Identity and the Life Cycle* (New York: Norton, 1980): 103.
†Anodea, Judith, "Out of the Frying Pan—Into the Fire: Dysfunctional
Families and Group Energy," in *Green Egg*, Vol. XXII, No. 87: 7.

This risk multiplies for women who are High Priestesses. Mainstream culture still expects women to be compliant caretakers, making nice and not being too assertive. The pressure escalates further in some corners of traditional Witchcraft, where the role of all-giving mother is projected onto us. Some tired bits of verse urge a truly sick self-abnegation on the Priestess, acclaiming her unlimited ability to absorb exploitation, disrespect, neglect, and abuse without complaint or reproach. Frankly, it's a 1950s male fantasy, detrimental to all concerned. It denies our right to protect ourselves and our option, and occasional heart-wrenching obligation, to set clear behavioral limits (see chapter 2 on power, chapter 8 on conflict).

Overripe fruit eventually becomes rotten. The excessive need to be needed becomes, in corrupt form, the need to control. We can guarantee that we will be needed by deliberately retarding our students' growth, infantilizing them, keeping them dependent. That this happens is demonstrated by the sad and bitter jokes about "the rest of the Book," (for example Your Coven's Book of Shadows). There are people—thankfully few—who have been elevated to higher degrees, even some who are already leading their own covens, who have still not been given all the information or materials to which they are entitled.

I would remind these people that the Old Gods are not anybody's private property. Human-created boundaries are irrelevant to Spirit. Although you have been unfairly denied some of the lore that is appropriate to your degree, you don't need it. You can reach to all the same Sources from which that Book was written in the first place.

And here's where the fruit analogy breaks down. Rotten fruit will never be sound again, but people heal. Codependency and even corruption can be confronted. People can come to understand how certain behaviors betray their calling, and can learn better ways of being and relating. The sick control addict can transform into the wounded healer, the one best able to help others see through their own transference issues and come into vibrant relationship with a second-chance family of choice.

Mostly, We Make It Work

GAWAINE   I like to think that our coven is a pretty good intentional family. We all take a great deal of joy in getting together, both for Circle and on just social occasions. In fact,
it's not unusual to have someone lamenting that we don't
get together more often. I think the keys to our success are
love for each other, a shared vision, a willingness on the part
of all members to do their share, a lack of competition for
place in the pecking order (we all peck on each other
equally), and giving everyone the space they need.

RONALD   Part of the two long-running covens' success is that
they do function very well as substitute families, not least to
myself. All remember the birthdays and other moments of
passage of each member, all lend moral and practical aid to
comrades in moments of difficulty, and all provide a safe
space within which any feelings can be shared or thoughts
discussed. It is fairly clear that the success and stability of
these covens are due to the fact that participants generally
feel more tension with the outside world than with those inside the enchanted space.

SUSAN   I have absolutely definitely been building an intentional family. I have created a fairly supportive bunch of
folks who can tease me, take care of me, tell me when I'm
being stupid, make me laugh, and generally love me. Although I have biological family living and involved with my
life, it is the coven, along with certain other friends, that I
turn to when I am in need of anything. I have also made
my working partner my health proxy, legal proxy, and ex-
ecutor, along with some Craft-sympathetic friends.

   Working with people, the way I do the coven, creates a
strong bond. Especially in my coven, which is not a "three
degrees in three years and then you're out" type of group,
we have people who have been together for a long time. For
me, as someone who trusts with difficulty and reservations,
if ever, the Craft has handed me a set of people I can allow

past my defenses. I get upset or disappointed with them sometimes—we're all imperfect after all—but I get past it amazingly easily.

Anyway, the impact spills over and changes the other areas of my life. I am a different person, and a happier one, because of this. On a less personal note, I know that of the other four members, three have stated that they feel more attached to the coven than to their families (as a whole, some of us have strong relationships with specific members), and that they find in the coven relationships things they never had as kids.

Branch Sculpture Mini-Ritual

Find a fallen tree branch about the right size to make a nice wall decoration in the room where you have your rituals. Ask each member to bring a small token of himself, about the size of a Yule tree ornament. Also provide or encourage others to bring an assortment of ribbon, yarn, and so on, for decoration. Place some hooks in your wall so the branch can be hung when ready, and attach some picture wire to the branch.

In Circle each person explains her personal token, then attaches it to the branch. Then all of you can further adorn the branch with the decorative materials, as you feel inspired. Empower the branch by chanting, drumming, and dancing. As the power peaks, hang the branch on the wall hooks.

To Learn More

Carlson, Kathie. *In Her Image: The Unhealed Daughter's Search for Her Mother*. Boston: Shambhala, 1989.

Downing, Christine. *Psyche's Sisters*. San Francisco: Harper & Row, 1988.

Erikson, Erik H., ed. *Adulthood*. New York: Norton, 1978.

———. *Identity and the Life Cycle*. New York: Norton, 1980.

10

Soul Friends

WICCAN WORKING PARTNERSHIP

orking partners are playmates, workmates, and soulmates; best friends, confidants, and mutual spiritual
directors. Their bond is deep and intimate. They are
the lovers of each others' spirits and souls. In classical Wiccan
practice, and often still today, they are also romantic and sexual lovers, lifemates, spouses who share a home and children,
as well as a coven, in common. Around this warm and living
center a happy and creative coven gathers.

Like raising children, coven leadership can be done and
done well by a single person, but at a cost. There will be far
more moments when the stress overbalances the joy, far more
risk of burnout and dysfunction.

Here's a secular view of group leadership:

Facilitating groups is mentally challenging work. It requires
simultaneously paying attention to content and process,
verbal and nonverbal behavior, those who are speaking and
those who are not, and comparing what is apparently happening in a group to what has happened in the past and
what will likely happen in the future. While considering all
this, the facilitator must also be thinking about whether to

intervene, what interventions to make, how deep to make them, to whom to address them, and the effects of the interventions on the group once they are made. Then the facilitator must intervene. The facilitator often must do all this in less time than it takes to read this paragraph."*

This is what's involved in facilitating a simple task group, a committee, people gathered to work together on a problem or new opportunity in their organization. No deep inner exploration, no attempt to create or nurture a connection with the Sacred, no craving for self-transformation. A work group is very much simpler than a coven, yet even this group is difficult for one person to facilitate alone. In addition, most organizational facilitators in academia or business are professionally trained, while the majority of coven leaders have only experience and intuition to guide them.

No wonder solo coven leadership can get so overwhelming. In the eighteen-year existence of Proteus Coven, people have come and gone. This includes my partners. I've had four, and some long solo stretches in between. These were not our golden periods. But partnership also has its problems.

The Bad News: Disagreement and Conflict

Coven leaders are strong-willed people who care passionately about Witchcraft and about the people in their group. No two such people will be able to agree on every question. The inevitable disagreement and conflict are hard on us, particularly so because of the closeness of the relationship. Sometimes we can work through and heal our conflicts, but not always. The undeniable risk of painful separation exists in every relationship, but so does the hope of closeness, support, and joy. If we pay attention to each other, the risk can be minimized.

From groupwork theorist Roger Schwarz we can learn the very useful notion of a "zone of deference."† This is the extent

*Schwarz, Roger M., *The Skilled Facilitator* (San Francisco: Jossey-Bass, 1994): 210.
†Schwarz, 222–223.

to which I can tolerate seeing my partner do things I would not do myself. We can work much more comfortably together if we understand the extent—and the limits—of our mutual zone of deference. Generally one partner will have to intervene in another partner's action if:

- It seems that a group member will be endangered or harmed.
- The partner's action violates core values. (Note: This implies that you must share core values.)
- The partner's action would prevent or hinder the group from achieving their goals. (Note: This implies that you must share goals.)
- The partner's action would change your roles or your relationship with each other or with the rest of the group.

In short, neither partner has the right to violate safety or ethics or to *unilaterally* change the group's operating principles. Both partners have the right and responsibility to intervene immediately and assertively if they believe these things are happening. Think of this as a specific application of the Wiccan Rede: "An it harm none, do what you will." Understand, though, that such immediate intervention will damage your relationship with your partner, perhaps beyond healing. Also, visible conflict between leaders can result in group members feeling uncomfortable and insecure. Unless your partner's action seems likely to cause irreparable harm right now, discuss it as soon as possible *in private*.

In private, at leisure, is the time to talk about the things that really matter to you. In a healthy partnership, nothing is off the table. Beware of the poison phrase *agree to disagree*. When people agree to disagree, they are saying that some topic is out of bounds, too stressful to work on any further. The problem is that any topic you place in this category becomes a dead zone in your relationship, a stuck place. As these accumulate, your communication, your relationship itself, becomes more and more stuck and inflexible. If this goes on your partnership will be reduced to cold and careful civility, and your hearts will starve. Agreeing to disagree is the beginning of the end of your partnership.

Working your conflicts through is tough, but it is your best chance of keeping any relationship alive and growing (for much more about conflict-resolution methods, see chapter 8). If necessary, find someone you both trust to facilitate for you. Talk about your hopes and dreams, and also about your comfort zone, your limits. Listen carefully and openly to what the other has to say. If you find you don't trust or believe your partner's statements, think carefully about what this implies. Ask the Ancient Ones for help. Seek Their wisdom through meditation, divination, and your dreams. Tentatively define a mutual zone of tolerance. Then try it. Be ready to negotiate adjustments till you reach stable comfort. Stay aware. Check in with each other often.

If you are in wholehearted agreement about safety, core values, goals, and basic operating principles, don't just tolerate variations of emphasis and style. Celebrate them! Conflict can weaken a partnership and a coven. Avoidance of conflict can kill it dead. But complementarity enlivens the partnership and offers the students a far wider range of ideas, knowledge, and skills.

If you have different views of history, theology, or the like, please let them show. Respectful debate is very different from an ugly quarrel. Instead of lecturing, dialogue. You will give your students a message far more important than any planned lesson: that our religion is safe space for free thinkers and free spirits.

Disagreement can strain a partnership, or it can be a source of power. The difference depends on whether the partners are working from the same basics on safety, values, goals, and operating principles. Open communication and honest negotiation when needed are the essentials for any healthy, functional relationship, including Wiccan working partnerships.

Sharing the Work: From Each According to Ability

Partnership halves the workload, a blessing in itself, but that's the very least of the blessing. Leadership is not simple work, like dish-washing, that we might just split in half. Covens are multifunctional groups. Leading them calls for a broad range of talent, knowledge, and skill. Complementarity of skills is just as important as complementarity of viewpoint.

Fortunately, people are not interchangeable parts. We each have different natural gifts, a unique set of talents and temperaments. We each have been formed—nurtured and challenged— by different life experiences. Consequently, each of us brings to the coven a different perspective, different abilities, creating a whole that is so much more than the simple sum of its parts.

There are many ways to divide the work. Some of them seem to be related to particular aspects of coven functioning. Here are some examples:

Gender Roles

Most, but certainly not all, working partnerships consist of one woman and one man. Often, during rituals, the High Priestess represents the Goddess while the High Priest represents the God. The Deities are easier to see that way. But it's a simplistic view, a caricature of human function. The energies that we represent as Goddess and God actually move within all people. The true Sacred Marriage is their balancing and integration in each individual as we move toward wholeness. Ritual gender roles, while convenient, may reinforce conventional gender role stereotyping over the long term, to the detriment of personal growth.

A more immediate problem comes when stereotypical gender roles dictate the division of labor *outside* of the rites. When this happens the High Priestess is expected to act as the all-nurturing Mama, while the High Priest, as Papa, is cast as both stalwart guardian and exacting standard setter for the group.

The debate about whether perceived differences in function between men and women comes from nature or culture is still unresolved. Either way, we come to the Craft as adults, already formed by this culture, already inculcated with different interactional styles and perhaps even different ethical sensibilities. However we got this way, and whether or not we like it, we are different.

Those who believe that the difference is primarily natural also tend to feel that members of a Nature religion should accept the way Nature made us. Those who believe most of the difference is culturally imposed, as I do, typically also feel that it's worth the disorienting and sometimes painful struggle of working through these artificial barriers to wholeness.

Perhaps having one coven leader of each gender allows Wiccan students to observe the full range of human functioning in the clergy role. The custom of having women teach men and men teach women may give each of us those pieces of the human pattern that were denied us in early childhood, so we can grow to be Priest/esses in the fullness of our sacred humanity.

Inside/Outside

One partner sets the tone for the group. This partner's self-image may be as one tending the hearth or holding the mystical charge for the coven. Typically, this person also carries the group's memories and stories, and shares them at appropriate moments with new members. The other partner has a more administrative function: scheduling, keeping records, setting expectations and limits, maintaining boundaries, and handling relations with other groups and with the community as a whole.

Seer/Moderator

In worship we seek conscious contact with the Ancient Gods (see chapter 5). Toward this end one partner may reach for insight and guidance through a variety of meditative and divinatory techniques. The second partner watches over such altered states of awareness and eventually guides the seer to a safe and complete return. The second also models appropriate response for the group, and guides the group in discussion of the meaning and application of whatever insights the seer has received.

No person is more favored of the Gods than any other, although some are more practiced in meditative techniques. If the same person acts as seer each time, the group may become dependent on him, or even begin to think of him as holier than the others. This is a particularly disempowering delusion. If the same person always acts as moderator, he may be typecast as second best, as just an enabler for the "real mystic" of the group. Even worse, the person acting as sole channel is in severe danger of ego inflation. This is one of the main causes of "High Priestess's disease."

In contrast, one of the major goals of our practice is to help each person find her *own* direct connection with the Gods, rather than limiting her to dependent and indirect contact through some sort of channeler. As a quiet demonstration that contact with the Sacred is every person's option, partners should alternate acting as seer or moderator.

Teacher/Scribe

We all have our specialties, areas of knowledge that we have explored more deeply than others. My partner is expert in herbalism, and in nature study in general. I know more about psychology, counseling, and group dynamics.

When the coven is functioning as a training group (see chapter 7), partners take turns teaching the subjects they know best. While one lectures or facilitates a discussion, the other records the main points. The mental image of a blackboard or flip chart in Circle may seem incongruous or even slightly silly. Still, these are useful aids for workshops and classes, which some of us prefer to teach within Circle. Or the scribe might simply keep notes for a group journal or a handout summarizing the discussion.

Task/Relationship

Covens sometimes take on collective projects in service to the community (see chapter 8). When they do, one partner may coordinate or manage the work. This partner will assign, direct, correct, even enforce deadlines when necessary. Serving the community in truth, in the world of standards, limited resources, and deadlines, is an excellent reality check and balance for the inner work that we do—and very good training for Priest/esses-to-be. But these pressures can strain interactions and fray the web of love and trust that is essential to a coven's shared spirituality. So the second partner should attend to "process"—to communications, relationships, and the general mood of the group, making sure that productivity never becomes more important than kindness or laughter or spirit.

Focus/Monitor

In our covens we find safe space and support for personal healing, growth, and self-transformation (see chapter 6). As we feel ready, each of us brings our issues, needs, and goals to the Circle. When this happens, one partner may work intensely with the person who has requested the group's help, while the other observes the reactions of other members and of the group as a whole.

Again, these are just some of the possibilities. Every set of working partners should apportion the work based on their joint sense of their own abilities and their coven's needs. Here are some working coven leaders' descriptions of how partnership contributes to their work as a coven leader:

ALEXEI The burden isn't all on the shoulders of one person. One of us is better at communicating with coven members and creating personal links with them; the other is better at teaching and improvising ritual. One of us is more affected emotionally by coven issues and more likely to get discouraged; the other can compensate by taking a more detached and practical view.

GAWAINE Our different perceptions and viewpoints serve as reality checks for each other. We have different strengths and insights that create a synergy that is much, much greater than the sum of its parts. Quite frankly, losing that partnership would be more crippling than losing an arm.

HOLLY I think for both of us, the partnership is essential. I really can't imagine it any other way. It would be so hard! A partnership is great because it really prevents one person from getting dictatorial tendencies. (Gawaine and I both have strong personalities and neither of us would like if the other were always dominant!) It also provides two perspectives, instead of one.

MARGARIAN   The biggest thing is that we can bounce ideas off each other. We think very differently. Hergest notices things I don't; he's usually more diplomatic than I am, and is sometimes able to pull my foot out of my mouth.

The other big thing is that we can split the workload. We're not too good at sharing a task; we tend to end up fighting. But we can divide things up between us. If he teaches a class, I can sit back and kibbitz, or even stay home and put my feet up for an evening.

Most of the time, I end up leading. That's partly because of the difference in our personalities; I'm more comfortable with leading than he is, and have a better developed "extrovert mask" (we're both introverts, but sometimes I can play extrovert for a few hours). It's partly because he has an exhausting full-time job, and I work only part-time.

SUSAN   I rely on him to catch things I miss with our students, to jump in where I can't be neutral, cue me if I forget that it's time for me to do something in ritual, write rituals with me and make mine better with his insights and inspirations. We bounce off each other and depend on each other.

We have a good way of handling conflicts. In general the person who cares more gets their way, and if we both care then we discuss the matter until we agree. We listen to each other pretty well, too.

I get upset sometimes because he gets his way more often than I do, because he cares about more things, and more intensely, than I do. At times I end up feeling like I give more then he does. Then I remember all my romantic relationships—and I recall having the same worry. Then I realize that this is about my baggage, and not really about my partner at all. And that's one of the very best things about having a partner (one of the hundred or so very best things): It forces me to see things more easily avoided.

IONTAS   We are the check and balance for each other. We are best friends. We brainstorm together. We bounce ideas off each other. I couldn't imagine doing it without him.

I really think that the best way to run a coven is with a two-person leadership . . . but not all of us have that luxury. It can be done alone, as many people do, but there are so *many* benefits of having a partner to work with that, as I said, I couldn't imagine doing it alone anymore.

Please do notice, though, that I gave contradictory advice about work sharing. Should working partners each do what they feel they do best, or should they switch tasks periodically? There are arguments for both.

Specializing is most efficient. Developing new skills is an important part of our own personal growth, and sets a great example for our students. Both are good, desirable, even necessary, but they are commonly understood as being opposites or reciprocals. In Wiccan terms, this is another polarity. Instead of settling into any one rigid division of labor, you and your partner can experiment with role sharing till you find your own optimal balance between convenience and growth.

One caution, though. People move, die, lose interest, discover deep-seated incompatibilities. There is no more guarantee of permanence in our partnerships than there is in any other human relationship. Partners who opt for inflexible specialization, however they may divide the work, will be in trouble if the partnership ends. Think of the stories of widows who had no idea how to change a fuse and widowers who could not prepare a simple meal for themselves. Just as every adult should be competent in basic life skills, every coven leader should be competent in the basic skills of coven leadership.

Becoming Partners

We don't so much choose our partners as recognize them. The working relationship is usually added on to a more conventional friendship, romance, or marriage. This is how it happened for some of my friends:

PATRICK   Barbara and I became friends first, working partners second. Nurturing the relationship came first at a human level. We share a mutual love for each other. Being working partners is simply an extension of that love into a much more internal space.

GAWAINE   We both wanted to find a working partner. We had been working in the same group together for some time. We grew close. It was a lot like falling in love. Matter of fact, both happened together.

HOLLY   Hmm . . . well, we both wanted a partner, and it was clear that we liked working together since we had been working in the same coven for quite a while. Our energy seemed to fit together and balance well, and we have very similar perspectives on how we like the magical energy to "feel." Like our relationship, "it just growed." [Holly and Gawaine are partners.]

IONTAS   Well, falling madly in love with each other helped. There really was no question for the two of us; the Gods saw fit to put us together so we may be more together than we are separately.

ALEXEI   We were already romantically involved when my partner was High Priest of our coven in a conventional working relationship with a High Priestess. When the High Priestess left, we became working partners as well—with some trepidation, because we are a same-gender couple. But this doesn't seem to have affected the functioning of the coven: There's sufficient polarity between our personalities to provide the necessary complementarity.

Working partners who are also lovers or spouses are in two different relationships with the same person. Dual-role relationships, as they are called, are often contradictory and complicated, so much so that the secular counseling profession considers them to be simply unethical. And yet the work we do together doesn't merely require this level of intimacy,

it seems to actually *create* it. Some of the older Craft documents simply assume that those who work together will fall in
love. Why?

Soul Friends

The term *working partner* is widespread and traditional among
Witches, but it falls so far short of communicating the real
depth and intensity of the relationship that it can be misleading. The kind of pleasant cooperation that we might reasonably
expect from an officemate doesn't even come close! We typically spend many more hours with our officemates, but bond
far more deeply with our spiritual partners.

The contexts and goals of these relationships are so very different. Covens exist to nurture the spiritual and magical
growth of their members, in service to Pagan community and
culture, and to the Ancient Gods. Coven leaders are elders. An
elder is not necessarily holier or wiser than anyone else, but he
is more experienced. One of my favorite definitions of an elder
is "someone who started sooner." But a new coven leader may
be only three or four years more experienced than her own beginning students—that's all I was at the start.

So there we are, putative elders, committed to coven leadership and expected to teach, guide, and nurture our students
as they grow to be Witches in truth. We are doing all this in
accordance with a thealogical tradition that has long been
dormant and is, after half a century, still in the quite early
stages of reawakening and reconstruction. We are writing the
operating manuals as we go. To be honest, much of the time
I've considered myself lucky to be one lesson ahead of the class.
The responsibility is daunting.

Whatever we can offer in the way of teaching, guidance,
and nurturance is hollow if we do not also model it. Showing
is far more powerful than telling. It follows that whoever is
acting as elder to others must also be actively working on his
own spiritual and magical growth in a way that is visible to
the students.

If we are to be effective as leaders, we must have the resources to support our own growth. The covens we lead are the wrong place to seek these resources.

Our students do have insights to offer us. They are adults, with their own richness of prior learning and life experiences. But it is unwise and unfair to rely on them for primary spiritual direction, guidance, or nurturance. There is a secular parallel: Single parents who use their children as confidants and companions force them to grow up far too soon. Similarly, when coven leaders use the coven to meet our own needs, the resulting role confusion deprives coven members of an important perception of security. They need to believe that we know more than they do in order to trust our guidance. Covens exist to meet the needs of the members, not those of the leaders.

Also, valuable as beginners' fresh perspectives are, they cannot substitute for perceptions informed by long experience. Those of us who work within a lineage will usually have our own elders to rely on, just a phone call away. But not always. Elders lose interest, retire, move away, die. And not all of us are rooted in a lineage. Most of us network in various ways with other coven leaders. Peer support is a valuable resource. But the best source of nurturance is the closest.

The heart of the working-partner relationship is mutual spiritual direction, a specialized kind of love. From our partners we receive the support and challenge, the nurturance and guidance that we need and deserve. Secular group leaders, who may be tempted to work on their own "stuff" in the groups they lead, are advised instead to join a "maintenance group." (The name is somewhat misleading. These groups do not assist their members in staying as they are. What they maintain is their members' ongoing growth.) Similarly, spiritual partners help each other avoid misusing the coven for their own needs by helping one another with these needs.

The concept of spiritual partnership is both ancient and widespread. In Malaysia, where Gerald Gardner, the founder of modern Witchcraft, worked for many years, the native traditions of spirit shamanism rely on the dual leadership of a seer (called *bomoh*) and a moderator (called *minduk*).* Buddhist tradition also recognizes the "noble friend," the *kalyana-mitra*:

> Your *Kalyana-mitra*, your noble friend, will not accept pretension but will gently and very firmly confront you with your own blindness. No one can see his life totally. As there is a blind spot in the retina of the human eye, there is also in the soul a blind spot where you are not able to see. Therefore you must depend on the one you love to see for you what you cannot see for yourself. Your *Kalyana-mitra* complements your vision in a kind and critical way. Such a friendship is creative and critical; it is willing to negotiate awkward and uneven territories of contradiction and woundedness."†

Because the tribal, shamanic, and Earth-based traditions of Europe were destroyed and repressed, contemporary Witches avidly learn and borrow from analogous traditions of any place or time. But the people we most identify with, whose religion we hope to retrieve, are the ancient Celts. So we can note with great pleasure that the concept of a soul friend is as native to green Ireland as it is to the exotic East.

> In the Celtic tradition, there is a beautiful understanding of love and friendship. One of the fascinating ideas here is the idea of soul-love; the old Gaelic term for this is *anam cara*. *Anam* is the Gaelic word for soul and *cara* is the word for friend. So *anam cara* in the Celtic world was the "soul friend." . . . It originally referred to someone to whom you confessed, revealing the hidden intimacies of your life. With the *anam cara* you could share your innermost self, your mind, and your heart. This friendship was an act of recognition and belonging. When you had an *anam cara*, your friendship cut across all convention,

---

*Laderman, Carol, *Taming the Wind of Desire: Psychology, Medicine and Aesthetics in Malay Shamanistic Performance* (Berkeley: University of California Press, 1991).

†O'Donohue, John, *Anam Cara: A Book of Celtic Wisdom* (New York: HarperCollins, 1997): 25.

morality, and category. You were joined in an ancient and eternal way with the "friend of your soul." ...

In everyone's life, there is great need for an *anam cara*, a soul friend. In this love, you are understood as you are, without mask or pretension. The superficial and functional lies and half-truths of social acquaintance fall away, you can be as you really are. Love allows understanding to dawn, and understanding is precious. Where you are understood, you are at home. Understanding nourishes belonging. When you really feel understood, you feel free to release yourself into the trust and shelter of the other person's soul."*

The soul friend is the one with whom we can fully share ourselves, including all the parts that are tentative, fragile, and vulnerable. She will hear us out, and will never use what she has learned to hurt or control us. But she can and will use it to help. A soul friend can hold up a mirror that allows us to see parts of ourselves that we might otherwise have ignored or denied. Our fears and shames, yes, but also those hidden potentials and strong points for which we might have evaded responsibility. So we ultimately come to know ourselves, and to grow ourselves, through the process of deep, intimate, and mutual sharing with a soul friend.

Our immanence-based theology (see chapter 5) holds that all living things, perhaps all things, have a sacred aspect. As a step toward developing this perception, we are taught to seek the God or Goddess in the eyes of a friend. In an *anam cara* relationship we move beyond simple perception toward the blessed possibility of close interaction with the sacred dimension within a soul friend's soul. Even better, when a loving and trusted partner perceives and honors the Indwelling Divine, he draws It out. This Inner Light becomes stronger, clearer, more able to shine for other coven members and for all those we meet and touch. Thus the tragic separation between the worlds of form and spirit is, little by little, healed.

*O'Donohue, 13–14.

This is not a relationship that can be arbitrarily chosen, and certainly not assigned from outside. Neither should we take a partner by default, working with whoever is sufficiently experienced and conveniently present. Although it need not become sexual, spiritual partnership must always and only be a love relationship. Understanding this, it becomes clear why our soul friends are so often also our spouses or lovers.

Married Working Partners: Layered Relationships

Dual-role relationships are always complicated and difficult to manage. So I asked my friends, the coven leaders, whether their Craft relationship has had any effect—for good or ill—on the other aspects of their relationships. Their answers revealed some of the complexity that faces married working partners.

BEAR   I was not aware of the Craft before I met my wife [Otter]. Although I knew the God, I never knew or heard of the Goddess. When she first said, "Bear, did you know I'm a Witch?" my response was "You mean like Samantha on TV? I'm set for life, for life!" Otter later explained what being a Witch is really all about.

 The effect on our life has been to enhance it for the most part. The Craft gives us one more thing to share together. It does, however, also create some conflicts.

 Since I wasn't originally involved in the Craft, my ideas about Circle and ritual were different from those of Otter and most of my covenmates. This added some "spice" to our religious discussions, especially when I was asked to take a more active role in ritual and ceremony. Nothing big, I just thought that there should be a balance of feminine and masculine both in symbol and participation. Otter's original idea was to swing the pendulum toward the matriarchy to counter all the generations of patriarchal dominance. We decided that the latter would only serve to create a new generation asking for payback, so we now work under a balanced idea system.

DEBBI   Tom and I are married working partners. I feel that the
Craft relationship does play a huge role, both good and ill,
in our marriage. It is a bond between partners that in many
ways parallels raising children together. Differences of opinion over styles or philosophies go deep, because the subject
involves emotion, thought, dreams, ideals, and prejudices.
Name me a couple with kids whose parenting disputes don't
affect the rest of their lives together, then kill them because
they are space aliens. But the Craft, like children, is such
an intimately shared part of life that it brings unequaled
joy sometimes.

DEVYN   This question is a tough one for me, emotionally
speaking. I'm not working with a Craft partner now, but did
for almost ten years. Our relationship ended two years ago.

My partner began as an absolute novice in the Craft. First
I taught her what I had been trained in. Then both of us
began training with another couple. We entered that context
as equals, which made sense since I had only been active for
perhaps two or three years before I met her.

As the years went on, we worked together as Craft partners. Things were fine for some time. My partner was (and
remains) a highly intelligent woman with a strong and keen
sense of where she needs to go, even before she can articulate her feelings. We experienced interesting debates and
discussion when, at times, she sensed that what we were
learning wasn't entirely all she felt she wanted to do. This,
of course, was completely fine, and as time progressed, she
developed her own personal spiritual niche.

Our relationship had multiple other problems, but yes, I
think the fact that we began to grow in radically different
Craft directions played a large role in our breakup. This kind
of makes sense to me, since what we are doing in Craft work
can be such a large part of how we identify ourselves.

Of course, there were also wonderful, positive moments.
We shared private ritual experiences that I cannot imagine
sharing with anyone who was not my working partner,
lover, and spouse. Perhaps the consequences of breakup are

in balance with the emotional and spiritual rewards of partnership. We shaped each other, in many ways, and now we lead separate lives, in entirely separate covens. We each are doing what makes us happy and are continuing to find Craft in all that we do.

MAGENTA We decided in our coven a long time ago not to have both halves of a couple in the coven. Mates are invited to holidays, but it's clear who is a primary member and who is a regular guest. This has been very useful in keeping a stable coven. I know of covens that have broken up when a member couple broke up.

Personally, I cannot imagine being in a close relationship, like lovers, to someone who is *not* involved in the Craft or Paganism, at least to some extent. Not being working partners, I can understand. But how could I share my life with a person who doesn't share my spiritual beliefs, which are an essential part of who I am?

GAWAINE It has had a very positive effect on the relationship, expanding both its depth and intensity. Not only is there the joy of being able to enter so deeply in mutual worship, but I think we both find that acting together as Priest and Priestess is another way of sharing our love for each other. Certainly, when acting as God and Goddess, the fact that we are deeply in love with each other enhances our ability to reflect the Deities. At the same time, working as partners spiritually, as well as in other aspects of our lives, deepens the relationship on all levels.

Frankly, after my experience with Holly, I find it very hard to imagine having a magical partner who is not my lover, or a lover who is not my magical partner. Either way, you end up not being able to share one of the most important part of your life with the person.

I think the fact that we are working partners enhances our mundane relationship as well as our magical one. The fact that we are equal working partners on the magical level carries over to the mundane. We don't seem to have the kind of "power struggles" I often observe among other couples. Of course at the same time, the fact that we act as equals on the mundane helps to ensure that we act as equal partners in the magical realm as well. Hmm, . . . a positive feedback loop.

I suspect that the magical came first, since we worked together magically before we became lovers. I think that fact has colored our whole relationship very positively. Especially for beginners, it seems to be easier to be magical partners first and lovers second than the other way around.

I have seen several couples who ended up with considerable difficulties because they played the same kind of power games in Circle that they played in their mundane lives. In fact, we recommend to students whose significant others are also studying the Craft that the two of them should work in different groups, at least initially. That way they are free to develop magically without the interference, well intentioned or otherwise, of their partner.

An additional advantage of being both partners and lovers is that it provides a constant source of conversation. There are always theological issues to explore, classes to revise or write, coven issues to discuss. I always found stimulating conversation a great aperitif to making love.

HOLLY   I have found that there are a few occasions when the disagreements bleed through from one level to the other. Mostly this happens when I'm annoyed about some mundane item, and it gets in the way of my opening up fully to Gawaine's energy on the magickal level. It has never really happened to me in the other direction—it's always mundane to magickal. One of my early teachers in the Craft pointed out that it's easy to allow love into the Circle, because it's so easy to share with others. Anger and hate in Circle close people off, so almost always cause problems in Circle.

If I am closed off to Gawaine, I'm closed off to the others in Circle and can't really function as I should as a Priestess. My solution to this on the mundane level is to resolve the differences between us. My solution to this on the magickal level is to concentrate on leaving the mundane issues in the mundane world, and ground myself thoroughly before Circle. It (usually) works.

And I also agree (perversely, it may seem) that *in the beginning*, couples new to the Craft probably benefit from a venue and time to work separately from one another. I certainly had this time (many years of it, in fact) before Gawaine and I became partners, and I know I benefited. It gives people time to experiment and learn their own best working style before partnering firmly with someone. This is only a recommendation that we give. . . . I'd never try to discourage a couple if they really wanted to train in the same coven, only encourage them to also take time to work alone, in addition to together.

GAWAINE   A further thought, after reading Holly's comments, on the issue of couples new in the community working together. Like Holly, I had quite a few years working magically, in a couple of magical traditions, before we became partners. At the time we partnered, we had worked together for a while in the same coven, and were both Second Degrees. In other words, we each had had the time to develop our magical personas and styles. When we became both lovers and magical partners, we were already experienced and knew the other was as well.

On the other hand, I have worked in a coven with a married couple who were initiated about the same time and joined the coven together shortly thereafter. They had a number of issues in their marriage, relating to control, dominance, and individual freedom, that they were unable to leave outside the coven. Each kept on trying to correct the other in Circle, telling the other what he or she had done wrong. They eventually found it impossible to remain in coven together. The man left, tried again a year or so later, and left again very shortly.

In contrast, one of our coveners is married to a fellow who was initiated about six months to a year after she was. They each work in different covens, and then work together privately. This has allowed them each a "safe" venue in which to grow and experiment without the other looking over his or her shoulder. They can then take what they learned and share it with the other when they work at home. Both are growing rapidly in skill and knowledge and have as happy a marriage as they did before they joined the Craft.

HERGEST   Certainly Margarian and I have different styles of ritual leadership, differences sometimes as little as personal idiosyncrasies in tone or wording. Being marriage partners before being partners in the Craft, we know more than anyone our particular strengths and weaknesses . . . particularly our weaknesses, which can cast a negative light on our impressions of the other's leadership of a ritual.

REDMOND   Rhomylly is neither my lover nor my spouse; however, being working partners has bonded us in a way I never expected. I am a "solo practitioner" of life, and this new, non–sexually intimate relationship has caused me to grow, risk inciting ire, stand my own ground, grow, eat humble pie, and celebrate life. I think she does the same. We speak boundaries successfully and if not, we discuss. As with any relationship, you can choose to make it work or fail. It is a matter of focusing on the positive rather than the negative. It is a matter of respect.

RHOMYLLY   When my working partner was also my lover, I think it had a very positive effect on our relationship—one more level upon which to "bond," in other words.

I have been unable to maintain a relationship with someone outside the Craft since I became intimately involved in it twelve and a half years ago. There is just too much lack of commonality of language and cultural references.

The next comments are from a religiously intermarried couple:

HE SAYS   I am an agnostic. Wicca has no more appeal to me than any other religious belief system. Mysticism is not my strong suit, but I did (and do) accept that others can have transcendent experiences. I myself have never felt such an experience. I feel strongly, however, that my wife has the right to pursue it as her heart takes her. At this point, Wicca has become a very important part of her life. While it would be more satisfying to both of us if we could share this belief, I feel that we are both comfortable with our acceptance of each other's belief systems.

SHE SAYS   I hadn't yet realized I was a Witch when I met and married my husband, although I already had strong Pagan leanings. Both of us were fairly skeptical agnostics. When I found myself more and more strongly drawn toward Wicca, I hoped that my husband would share my newly discovered religious feelings; but it just wasn't for him. It would have been wonderful to have him as a working partner all these years, but I knew better than to push the issue.

He recognized that it *did* seem to have great spiritual and personal value for me, that being a Witch has done me absolutely no harm, and a great deal of good. So he supports me in it; and he has never had any problem with "giving me personal space" to pursue interests that he does not share.

When our son was born, and during the years when a child needs at least one adult around all the time, my husband would cheerfully take over the parenting duties while I went to Circle.

I've always been very glad that my husband was able to accept my practicing what I believe in. His support has been nearly as much of a blessing to me as his full participation would have been.

ANNE   I'm in the midst of struggling with the beginning of the end of a twenty-five-year marriage to someone who is not involved in the Craft, so this question hit deep.

I was a Witch from childhood; that was part of me my husband knew when we first got together. But it was not until fifteen years into the marriage that I both became involved with other Witches and joined a newly formed coven, and also became pregnant with our first child. The

strains of my suddenly starting to have an independent social life with the coven came at the same time as the strains
of our being new parents.

Then five years ago my involvement with the Pagan community began to intensify, and I began to realize I was functioning as Priestess. I'd come from an egalitarian coven that
did not have a degree system, and I picked up most of my
priestessing skills on the fly. I hadn't considered the ramifi-
cations of becoming so involved, hadn't chosen it—but it
chose me.

A Priest who mentored me pointed out the source of new
tensions in my marriage, that my husband may have known
he was marrying a Witch but not known he was marrying a
member of the clergy, and that these were two very different roles. As I took on more responsibilities I began to see
more resentment. I had to finally ask myself if I was growing more through being a Priestess or through my marriage,
and realized that I was being nourished far more by my relationships in the Pagan community.

It's been horribly lonely at home being in a relationship
where I can't discuss the spiritual growth that I am going
through. I've stopped mentioning the details to my husband,
as I get faced with blank incomprehension or silence. It's not
like having a different job and not having your spouse understand the shop talk, it's having a whole important part of
your identity not being granted validity by your spouse.

I try to be supportive when the discussions of non-Pagan
partners come up, because I know that there are some out
there who are genuinely concerned and supportive of their
partner's Path. When someone is getting into a marriage and
I perceive that she has not fully dealt with this issue, I try
not to scream at her like a wild-eyed fanatic that she mustn't
take this disastrous step and go marrying a non-Pagan. Instead I count to ten, breathe deep, and suggest she talk
about it with someone who can tell her what changes becoming clergy could entail for her should she get more involved in the Craft. I also suggest to her that raising children

in a mixed marriage may be more difficult for the Pagan parent, who feels strongly about raising the children in the Craft.

I don't think I could be with a future partner who didn't share my religious views, after what I've experienced. I want someone who would be supportive of my raising my children in the Craft, and active in celebrating with me.

VESTO Our Craft partnership has affected our marriage basically for good. In fact, sometimes I think if we hadn't had this common goal to rally around (coven co-leadership) and it had not come along when it did (about nine years into our relationship, which has now endured for nineteen), we might not be together now.

Through leading our coven we received the chance to develop not only joint leadership skills vis à vis our relationship with the rest of the coven, but also skills at how to negotiate more successfully with each other and to listen well when the other's center speaks (and sometimes very quietly) about matters that are occasionally extremely personal and difficult, and at other times decidedly Otherworldly. We learned that our coveners just don't believe either one of us, and things end up rocky, when we make a decision prematurely without having gone through *all* of the steps toward finding the center point.

Coven leadership came into our hands somewhat accidentally when the former leaders of the group decided to move away, and turned the group over to my spouse, who held elder status at that time. I took the elder degree a year later, and after a brief hesitation became HPS. By then, my HP had already developed a style of his own, so our relationship as leaders together did not gel immediately.

It was his trust that allowed me to grow and mature into a full partner in leading the coven. Now we continually have to trust each other, because we've come to understand that our personal styles, emotional rhythms, and tolerance for trouble differ somewhat, although we are rock solid on basic values. And having to learn to find common ground in coven matters gradually began to apply in the rest of our life together.

It's not perfect, but far, far better.

Problems and Pitfalls

It's a real challenge to draw conclusions from a set of experiences and opinions as diverse and even contradictory as these. But they are the voices of real life, of people who have lived with the joys and stresses of spiritual partnership and coven leadership for many years and who have made it work well. I want to highlight a few points.

Respect and friendship should precede any intimate bond, spiritual or marital. People who are already strong and autonomous, and who come together as equals, have the best chance of successful partnership. For this reason Holly and Gawaine suggest that even married couples should experience the first stages of their Wiccan training in separate covens.

When people are married to their spiritual partners, the two relationships will almost certainly influence each other. This feedback may be negative, as it was for Devyn, or positive, as it is for Gawaine, Holly, and Vesto. Our challenge is to find ways to make positive feedback more probable.

When a couple who belong to the same coven break up, the stability of the coven is placed at great risk. If they are the coven's leaders, or if the breakup is particularly bitter, the risk becomes even greater. Devyn reports that his breakup put a strain on his entire local community. To avoid this problem, Magenta's coven will not admit spouses or lovers of members.

On the other hand, many people reported that they could not imagine having a spouse or lover who was not involved with the Craft, because this is so important a part of their lives. And yet lovers and spouses should not have secrets between them. If your spouse is a Witch in a different coven or Tradition, will coven or Traditional confidentiality strain your marital bond?

If one partner in a conventional marriage is in the Craft and the other is not, how will this affect the marriage? If the Wiccan partner then enters a spiritual partnership with some other Witch—even if this bond remains nonsexual—will the intimacy of this partnership arouse jealousy in the spouse? If they become coven leaders, will the time and energy demands impact the marriage? If a marriage is strained, innocent children may be hurt.

For this reason, in classical Wiccan practice the only people accepted for training were married couples who were both interested. It seems horribly unfair to exclude someone because his spouse, whom he cannot control, is not interested, and even more unfair to singles. But our elders felt that to do otherwise was to place people's marriages at risk. Both positions are reasonable. Can they be resolved? And how does this play against Gawaine and Holly's feeling that people develop best if they take their early training separately?

On yet another hand, to the best of any of our knowledge, Donna Gardner, Gerald's wife, never had any interest in the Craft. Neither did the husband of my own High Priestess. Also, recall the comments of the anonymous intermarried couple on page 230. Some mixed marriages work well. What makes the difference?

There are no simple answers to be had. Various covens have tried everything from requiring that new students be married to each other to prohibiting spouses from working in the same coven. Every approach seems to have been adopted to avoid the very real risks and drawbacks of the other approaches. So we avoid some problems only by backing into others.

The closeness and intimacy of a spiritual partnership is likely to extend to all other aspects of the partners' lives. The risk of destructive contradiction exists in every sort of dual-role relationship. The risk of destabilization is part of all genuine inner or Otherworld exploration, as many mystical and shamanic traditions will attest. These two sorts of risks exacerbate one another.

People have tried to protect themselves in simplistic and ill-considered ways. Some religious traditions attempt to minimize the risk by requiring celibacy of their professed religious. This would be theologically incongruent for our religion, which celebrates sensual pleasure of all kinds.

There is such a thing as playing it *too* safe. The choice of a life of grayed-out moderation is always open to us. Both by avoiding all possible risk and by numbing out our emotional responses, we could protect ourselves from turbulence, stress, and grief. We would also lose the peak experiences, the moments of jubilation. Most Witches, however, are not this kind of timid. Is there some way, without losing life's zest, that we could take a bit better care of ourselves and each other? I think so.

Conscious Partnership: Getting Started

In my experience, what destroys relationships of all kinds are hidden and incompatible assumptions. If people's hidden assumptions are, by dumb luck, compatible, they can muddle through. That's how conventional marriages survive for years without any genuine intimacy of mind or spirit. If the incompatible assumptions are not hidden, partners can usually resolve their differences. It's the combination that's deadly.

Co-leading a coven requires basic accord in matters of safety, ethics, goals, and operating principles. If you and your partner are incompatible at this core level, and are not aware of it, you may find out the hard way—suddenly, in the middle of an intense moment of coven work. This can blow up your partnership and your coven, leaving all concerned seriously hurt.

Taking your spouse or lover as your spiritual partner is normal and natural, the expected thing in our community, but it should not be assumed. Especially not if your relationship is new, still in a courtship or honeymoon phase. The romantic rush can certainly hide deep-seated incompatibilities. By treating a working partnership as a separate and conscious choice, we create an opportunity to examine our assumptions about partnership and about coven leadership. The best time to discover any serious differences is *before* they become focal to our work. Then we can negotiate these differences in a calm and careful way. We can either resolve them or back off from a dangerous risk.

To begin with, here are some questions. Answer them separately, then later compare your answers. Do this even if you are a married couple who have studied the Craft together in the same training group or coven. Don't assume! Even better: Each of you create a list of your own questions for the other to answer.

1. How did you become interested in Witchcraft? What is the major benefit of having Witchcraft as part of your life? What is the most serious associated problem?

2. What beliefs, values, and philosophies guide your work? What beliefs, values, and philosophies seem to you to guide your partner's work? Are yours compatible, complementary, or contradictory with those of your partner? (It's important to verify, or adjust, your perceptions of your partner's guiding principles.)

3. How do you perceive your own and your partner's talents, temperaments, skills, and knowledge as complementing and supplementing each other?

4. Which of the experiences that you had while you were in training left you with the best memory? The worst?

5. What is your vision of an ideal coven? Describe the best- and worst-functioning covens you have so far encountered. Describe the best- and worst-functioning coven leaders. Describe the best- and worst-functioning partnerships you have known.

6. How do you propose to share the work and responsibility of coven leadership? How much time and energy are you realistically able to devote to your coven and other common projects? What kind of time and energy commitment do you expect from your partner?

7. If conflict arises between coven members, how do you think it should be handled? What about conflict between you and one of your students?

8. What kinds of disagreements between you and your partner are you willing and not willing to show in front of your students? In front of others outside your own coven? How do you propose to resolve your disagreements?

9. How do you think you can improve as a Priest/ess? How do you think your partner might help you improve?

10. How do you think your partner might improve? How do you propose to help your partner?

You can also try co-visioning. In Circle and in a light trance, start describing to each other your concept of an ideal coven. What kind of people will be there? How will it be organized? Will it have any particular theme or focus? If it's a teaching coven, what will be included in the curriculum? Be as detailed as possible, and see if your ideas mesh.

Divination is another possibility. Either each of you can do a separate reading and then compare, or you can seek a reading from a trusted and objective friend. Before you talk about what your reading showed, sleep on it. Your dreams may well offer even more insight.

Mutual gaze is a simple, powerful technique. In ordinary conversational contact, adults sustain eye contact for ten seconds or less. So-called lovers' gazes average about thirty seconds.* Instead, try for two to three minutes. Choose a piece of quiet and unobtrusive music of about the right duration. Use a "soft-eyed" gaze, as you would in scrying. Sit comfortably, facing one another. Make gentle eye contact and hold it while the music plays. Take some silent time to assimilate this experience before you discuss it.

Partners who are spouses or lovers can expand on the concept of mutual gaze to include their whole bodies. This exercise is called the mirror dance. Play some gentle music. Stand facing each other squarely, with your feet comfortably apart. Raise your hands to about shoulder height, with the palms facing front. Raise the shorter person's hands and lower the taller person's hands till they are right opposite each other. Touch hands briefly, palm to palm, and feel into this, then withdraw till your hands are an inch or two apart. Now start to move.

---

*Lind, Jane D., "Looking Into the Other: Mutual Gaze," in Association for Humanistic Psychology, *Perspective* (February/March 1998): 28.

Each one mirror the other's movement until you are no longer aware who is initiating which move.

You can use these and similar activities at any time to refresh your partnership. They are particularly important in preparing for a rite to bless and empower a new spiritual partnership. Whether you are entering an entirely new relationship or adding a dimension to an existing marriage, this is an important moment of change in your life. It certainly should be ritually marked. Here are some suggestions for a partnership-blessing ritual:

1. If you have trained within a coven, hold this ritual in the presence of your elders. Ask for their witness and blessing. If possible, invite the presence of all of your coven-mates. If you trained in two different covens, the presence of your elders may be more difficult to arrange, but it is even more important.

2. If you do not live together, each of you bring a small gift for the other. Get something small enough to be placed on your partner's altar, representing you when you are not present. Whatever it is, buy two of it, one for your partner and one for yourself.

3. Each of you should bring your own athame, cup, pentacle, and wand to this Circle. Set the altar with both of each item.

4. Make Circle in your usual way. If your "usual ways" are different, figuring out a new usual way is an excellent partnership exercise. Do this as fully and formally as possible. If your elders are present, ask them to make the Circle.

5. Take some time for mutual gaze. Invite the others to meditate while you do this.

6. For each of the four Quarters, each of you pick up the relevant tool and, while holding it, tell your partner how you feel you contribute the qualities of this element to the partnership. Alternate who goes first. Then put the two tools together and ask the Guardians of that Quarter to bless them.

7. Elders may offer advice and blessing. Then anyone else who is present can do the same.

8. Make whatever formal pledges you have decided to make to one another (for example: mutual honesty, mutual nurturance, mutual responsibility). Use your own words.

9. Cleanse, consecrate, and empower the gifts that will represent you on each others' altars. Exchange them, with a mutual blessing (for instance: "May my abilities always meet your needs, and may yours meet mine").

10. Bless cup and plate together. Share with all present. (If you use fruit juice, each of you can bring a different flavor and then blend them in the cup—but discuss this in advance to make sure the flavors are compatible!) This is a good time to toast the new partnership.

11. Close Circle.

Nurturing Conscious Partnership

Human relationships are something like gardens. They need our active care in order to stay healthy and fertile. Often this care is a pleasure in itself, but not always. Sometimes it gets sweaty, smelly, and makes our muscles ache. There's no guarantee, no matter how hard we work, of a good crop. But the crops are good enough, often enough, to more than repay the effort. Here are some general suggestions for nurturing your bond with your partner.

- *Communicate:* Communicate often, daily if possible. Communicate very honestly. Communicate about the coven's business, but don't limit your communication to this. Be best friends: Share ideas, gossip, problems, triumphs, dreams, and silly jokes.

- *Play together:* Go dancing, watch videos, go for long walks or bike rides, pursue a hobby. You need some "golden time" together out of role.

- *Circle together:* Just the two of you, in addition to your regular coven rituals. This is absolutely basic. My first working partner and I had a "just us" Full Moon Circle every lunar cycle without fail for eight years straight. This was easy when we lived within walking distance. When he moved away, and we got lax, our partnership soon disintegrated.

- *Work together:* Achievement feels good. Mutual achievement is the very best reinforcer of partnership. Plan and conduct rituals, teach, have common projects.

- *Keep your promises:* If external circumstances prevent you from keeping a commitment, let your partner know as soon as you realize this. Partners must be able to rely on one another.

- *When you disagree, work it through fairly and with real care for the other's feelings:* When one "wins" and the other "loses," the partnership is weakened, and both really lose. Listen to each other.

- *When real difficulties come up, don't smooth them over:* Work them through or they will come up again even stronger than before.

Here are two important specific suggestions.

Postritual Feedback

When your coven has met for Circle or any other activity, don't do any heavy analysis until you've had a chance to sleep on it. (This advice is particularly difficult, and especially important, for those who share a bed!) As soon as possible upon waking, check in with each other. How did the ritual or meeting compare with your plan or your expectations for it? What went well? If you were trying anything new, how did this part work out? What would you do differently next time? What did you notice about individual students' progress? Is there anything you need to take up with any of your students? Were there any personality clashes or differences of opinion that need to be either addressed or monitored? Is the group working well as a team?

What were your feelings and perceptions toward each other's presence and conduct in the ritual? Did you work well

together? Is there anything either of you wish the other had
done differently? Is there anything the other did that you particularly enjoyed or admired?

Most important: What were your internal reactions and feelings about this ritual? Is there anything you would like to get
out of your system? Did the two of you have the same strong
emotional response at any point? On reflection, and by comparison to your partner's reactions, do any of your own reactions—happy or unhappy—seem to be out of proportion?
Might the excessive energy in these come from some other period or aspect of your life?

In the light of all this, where do you think your own or the
coven's growth path leads from here?

Shared Inner Journeys

Pathworking—collective guided fantasy—is an important part of
the work of many covens. Leaders of groups that use pathworking would do well to first explore the terrain as a couple.
Even if your group doesn't do a lot of pathworking, it's a powerful technique for deepening your intimate contact as partners.

What you actually do is very simple. In Circle, both enter a
meditative state. You can use mutual gaze for this, or you can
focus on a candle or a mirror or the rising incense smoke. You
can alternate giving each other verbal suggestions to relax your
muscles, slow down and deepen your breath, and so on. Then,
when you feel ready, start describing to each other the land-
scape you intend to explore. Build on one another's perceptions until you have a detailed inner image of the place. If
anything happens there, observe or participate in it together.
Then return to your Circle. Again, sleep on this and then discuss it thoroughly before repeating the experience with the rest
of the coven.

Wiccan working partners share very much more than the hard
and rewarding work of coven leadership. We are each other's
companions for the spiritual journey, playmates and soulmates,

best friends, confidants, and mutual spiritual directors. We can work through the occasional and inevitable conflicts and disagreements that will arise. We bring out the best in one another, always in the service of our covens and the Ancient Gods.

To Learn More

Co-Facilitation and Partnership

O'Donohue, John. *Anam Cara: A Book of Celtic Wisdom*. New York: HarperCollins, 1997.

Schwarz, Roger. *The Skilled Facilitator*. San Francisco: Jossey-Bass, 1994. (See chapter 11, "Working With Another Facilitator," pp. 210–229.)

Yalom, Irvin D. *The Theory and Practice of Group Psychotherapy*, 4th ed., New York: Basic, 1995. (See the section on co-therapists, pp. 414–418.)

Gender Issues

Fausto-Sterling, Anne. *Myths of Gender: Biological Theories About Women and Men*. New York: Basic, 1985.

Forisha, Barbara Lusk. *Sex Roles and Personal Awareness*. Morristown, N.J.: General Learning Press, 1978.

Gilligan, Carol. *In a Different Voice*. Cambridge, Mass.: Harvard University Press, 1982.

Tannen, Deborah. *You Just Don't Understand: Women and Men in Conversation*. New York: Ballantine, 1990.

11

To See It Grow Tomorrow

A NEW COVEN HIVES OFF

If you pursue the parallel of coven to family, then the coven leaders are the parents. The children are grown, so it's more of an extended than a nuclear family model. As in any functional family, the parents have to foster the growth of their children. This means giving them the space to grow, helping them when they need it, but also giving them the freedom to try and to run the risk of failure. You can't protect them from everything, but you can be there to provide praise when they succeed and support when they fail. It also means you have to help them grow in the directions they need and want to grow, not in the way you want them to grow.

—GAWAINE

In 1980 my High Priestess received a wonderful scholarship for advanced professional study and left town for a year. Hiving was not an agonizing choice for me, simply a logical response to her departure. Not everybody has it so easy.

You love your coven's leaders. How could you not? They've helped you, taught you, opened up a whole new way of understanding and being in the world. No words or tokens of gratitude could ever begin to express the wonder of what you've shared.

But you know ... they have their ways, their habits ... their rut. They're comfortable, Goddess bless them, and not always willing to try something new. Sometimes their habits are just a little irritating. Sometimes you feel just a bit thwarted. You have some hunches about some better ways to train people and you just met some interesting new beginners and. ...

There's no way you'll ever pay them back, but perhaps it's getting to be time to "pay it forward." It's time to move on. Time to follow your own leadings.

Traditional Witchcraft is matriarchal and matrilineal. Covens gather around High Priestesses. When a Priestess leaves her original coven to form a new one, we call this hiving off. It's the same term that's used when a queen bee leads a swarm of bees to establish a new hive.

Ready

Whoever truly understands the depth and complexity of a coven leader's responsibilities will have serious qualms about assuming the role. When people ask you to teach them, ask yourself whether you honestly can. Have you the knowledge, the skill, the grounded wisdom? Dream and meditate on this decision. It is not trivial. It will change your life as profoundly as though you had borne a child. Don't do it for power, or prestige, or popularity. Do it for love, or not at all. Do it only when the ideal coven of your imagining demands to be given form, when your inner voices sing to you of possibilities. Do it when you have to, not before.

Here are a few more objective guides:

Have you completed the training program of your coven and Tradition? If not, why not? If there were extenuating circumstances, critical situations elsewhere in your life that you needed to attend to, have these now been resolved? If you simply didn't find the time or energy to do your coven work, what has changed for you? Either way, prove it by completing whatever work is still outstanding.

If some of the requirements are irritating, do them anyhow. Only this will ensure that those you bring in will be fully recognized. However, if any of the requirements actually go against your deep values, you should not do them for social or political advantage. What we do is, after all, religious—values-based and Spirit-led.

In some covens you will be expected to lead a training group under supervision as part of the requirements for your final elevation. It makes perfect sense to ask you to demonstrate your ability before giving you the authority to lead an autonomous coven. Think of it as an internship project. When you are feeling ready to take it on, have a long talk with your mentors.

Do you have a clear idea of what your new coven will be like, or what it will do? Describe your new coven in a sentence or two, as though you were writing a classified ad for prospective students. This is a good exercise in self-definition, whether or not you have any intention of actually advertising. (See the section on self definition or the "birthing" phase in chapter 2.)

In general, whether you are planning a project, a ritual or a coven, it's a good idea to start with the results you want and work backwards through the necessary antecedents. For example:

BRIGANTIA   When I started my first coven, I planned rituals in linear time order, start to finish. This very intuitive and commonsense approach inevitably led to time crunches, running out of materials, elegantly crafted bits of ritual that were so incompatible that they had no hope of working together.

Now, after many years of trial and error, I start by planning why we want to do a ritual and what we want the ritual to accomplish. Then I think about what the culmination of the ritual should be like, and work backward from there, step by step, figuring out what the necessary precursors are.

My rituals work better this way. Also, I get a good night's sleep before the rite, because things are ready. This method, by the way, works just as well for designing casseroles, workshops, and gardens.

Think about what you want your coven to be like. Ask yourself whether members of your core group have among them the necessary "starter set" of skills or competencies. If you don't yet have a core group, this list of desired skills can be a guide for your screening, just as though you were hiring workers for a new project. Here are a few questions to help figure out whether you have a full starter set (for some pointers on how to answer them, see chapter 7).

1. What knowledge and skills do you think every Witch should have? Which of these do you consider prerequisites and which are you able and willing to teach?
2. What knowledge and skills do you think a coven leader should have? Do you feel properly prepared to lead a coven? If not, how do you propose to fill any identified gaps?
3. What skills are necessary to have somewhere in every coven, but not necessarily in the coven leader? (For example, I can't carry a tune, so other members lead our chants.) Does someone in your potential core group have whatever of these skills you lack?
4. Are there any "extra" skills, or areas of knowledge, that are needed for your coven's intended specialty, although they are not essential for all covens? (For example, a coven specializing in ritual arts may need stagecrafters and musicians.) Again, which of these are prerequisites and which are you willing to teach?
5. Conversely, are there any "extra" skills that exist by happenstance among your potential core group that you expect will enrich your coven and influence its future direction?

Screening: What to Look For

Competency is important. Character is even more important, and far more deep-rooted in the individual. I gathered the opinions of my friends, the coven leaders, on screening new seekers. They shared some hard-won wisdom about people and problems to avoid.

ALEXEI   This is tricky, since most beginners on any path are immature or untried in certain respects, and you shouldn't turn away people for imperfections that could be corrected by growth. It's up to every coven leader, of course, to gauge just how bad the problems are in each separate case, and how much of a risk they pose. I've seen the following patterns:

People looking for a surrogate parent. This is further complicated by the fact that in Wicca all that relates to training and initiation tends to get presented in terms of parent-child symbolism. It should be made clear that this is appropriate in some respects, but not at all in others. This is a path for taking responsibility, not relinquishing it. People who want to become emotionally and morally dependent on their coven leader(s) are not only stifling their own spiritual growth, they risk becoming terribly disillusioned when the leaders fail to live up to the unrealistic ideals that have been projected onto them—and this can lead to severe disruption within the coven.

People who are expecting magic to solve all their problems. They think that their employment problems or romantic failures will be cleared up by a few spells, without taking any other measures that might make success more likely. When they fail to see any improvement after a few months, they blame the coven, or the religion itself. Such people have to be made to realize from the start that magic should be used to improve the self as well as external circumstances, and that it is itself only a part of a larger process (involving many mundane skills as well) through which we find our right place in the world.

People who are obsessed with the idea of "power." When the people are young I refer to it as "Teenage Witch Queen Syndrome"; but the problem, unfortunately, doesn't always dissipate with age. These people are often bright and talented but, perhaps because of early family situations, they have needy and insecure egos that crave compensation through control and power over others, and they see magic primarily as a means to this end. They cultivate "witchy" personas and make sure that others are impressed by their psychic or magical talents. At first they are hungry for the approval of the coven leaders, but later seek to manipulate them (and other coven members) for their own advantage. If they don't undergo some maturing experiences in time, they will easily resort to unethical and destructive uses of magic, and will generally sow dissension within a coven.

People just looking for a social circle. Often people who feel "different" and don't fit easily in more conventional milieus think they would like to hang out with Witches because we are perceived as countercultural and accepting of difference. They are not, however, prepared for the discipline and motivation needed to work with a coven, and if they don't get bored and leave of their own accord they can become serious deadweight within the group.

ALICE Avoid the obvious lunatics, of course, and the ones whose notions of Witchcraft and magic derive mostly from role-playing games and comic books.

GAWAINE Avoid the freeloader; the dogmatist who is always right; the person who needs to always be the center of attention; the person who can't keep coven business in the coven; the person with a chip on her shoulder; the fanatic; the person who is in the Craft because he sees it as an easy means to sex; the person who is exploitive or passive aggressive. I think it's also important to avoid those people who do not have their personal act together. I don't mean someone who has an occasional crisis in her life. We all have those. I mean the person who seems to always be in crisis, who can't hold down a job, et cetera. I also think it's wise to delay bringing in someone who is in the midst of a serious personal crisis, since he may not really be capable of making a true commitment at that time.

Also, on more than one occasion I've run into the kind of person who wants to be a BNP (big-name Pagan) as a kind of ego trip. As I see it, for such folks the Craft is not a sincerely sought path. They do no good to the coven or the Craft, and often bring harm. (Folks who want the title and what they see as the prestige, without doing the work, are a pet peeve of mine.)

SUSAN I personally like to avoid anyone mentally unstable. I mean *really* unstable. Anyone who disrupts the group *on an ongoing basis*, by needing to be the center of attention, or by being flaky and funny even when it's not appropriate. All those who can't take responsibility for themselves and are always looking to external sources for rescue and blame. The problem is, most people are like this at some time or other. I am referring to folks who are usually this way. It would have to be intense enough to be a problem.

WEYLAND I won't tolerate those who cannot be trusted to keep sober after they agree to do so. I can't help those who want "the secret Word of Power" or who need a guru, surrogate parent, scapegoat, or lover.

VESTO We have had real challenges training people who suffer from, and may be on medication for, emotional illness, or are childhood trauma survivors. In my group's observation, depression or anxiety medications, especially if the person is at a stage where she is "adjusting medication," tend to interfere with focus and the ability to keep track of several things going on at once, including communicating with fellow coveners. People with histories of trauma often seem to have skill at getting "out of body," but sometimes have a hard time coming back afterward. If possible, find out about existing conditions before admitting students, so you can decide whether you and they are up to the challenge.

RHEA Don't try to save the world. Just because they need help doesn't mean you have to give it. The Goddess may have sent them to you, but a good servant knows when to say, "I'm sorry, I can't perform that task adequately," and pass it on.

MARGARIAN   Avoid fanaticism. Also beware of—

A gossip. (This one's a biggie. If they gossip about others, they'll gossip about the coven to others.)

A substantially dysfunctional person. ("Don't coven with anyone crazier than you are.")

Those with substance abuse problems, or other addiction, unless they're in reasonably stable recovery.

Those who refuse to take responsibility for their own actions, and own their mistakes.

Those who think they already know everything, and therefore can't possibly learn anything from you. (I've had students like this—usually under twenty-five.)

Those who think they know nothing, and have no skills or life experience to share.

Those who still haven't worked out adolescent rebellion issues. They'll project all of that onto you as coven leader.

Anyone who's heavily into power games and politics. Especially the "jungle fighter" type; there's no room for love and trust when you're always guarding your back.

Those with no sense of humor. Conversely, those with an excessive or inappropriate sense of humor; they'll always be disrupting your work together with ill-timed jokes, and they may pull pranks that hurt or frighten others, destroying trust.

Anyone who doesn't respect personal boundaries.

Those who are excessively needy. If you're a codependent type (as many of us are), they'll seem attractive at first—but in the long run, they'll drain you.

And I would add: Beware of fundamentalists. The inability to distinguish metaphor from fact corrodes any religion. Beware of hypocrites. Those who are unwilling to live their beliefs are a waste of your precious time. Beware of anyone who is studying Witchcraft for ulterior motives, and of those who think their personal will is in fact the whole of the law.

The elders also had some definite thoughts about what to look for and who to welcome.

IONTAS   The true desire to learn and love the Gods that burns brightly like a flame.

MARGARIAN   Ethics. Maturity. Integrity. Honesty. Healthy self-respect, without arrogance.

MAGENTA   Compatibility. Someone can be a wonderful person, but not fit into your group. Be very clear about this.

DEVYN   I look for sincerity, trustworthiness, responsibility, and commitment. I am impatient with people who seek covens exclusively for personal gain. I look for a sense of honor, a sense of community spirit, and an understanding of the need and value of service as part of the spiritual process.

CAROL   A sense of discretion is mandatory. Other members must be able to trust that they will not be "outed" by a loose-talking new member if they need to keep their involvement private.

ALICE   Sincerity, first and foremost. Is this person genuinely searching for ways to grow closer to the Ancient Ones? A modicum of intelligence and common sense is desirable also. Furthermore, the leader needs to have a sense of how the new person will fit into the already-existing group mind.

HOLLY   The seeker first of all needs to be mentally stable. This may sound ridiculously basic, but we have turned away a few people who seemed so precariously balanced at the edge that we were afraid that opening any magical doors would be dangerous for them.

CAROL   Stability is important. The coven needs to know that they can count on every person there. It is vital to know that new members are willing to commit themselves to the coven, and will not have too many other conflicting interests that will keep them from regular involvement.

MARGARIAN   Enough room and time in their lives to be able to commit to the responsibilities of a coven. One of the most common coven-busting patterns I've seen is the slow, unstoppable disintegration of a coven whose members are too busy, or work crazy shifts, or can't find a reliable baby-sitter. You can't make a coven happen if you don't know whether you'll get all eight people to tonight's ritual, or only three or four. Even one member who is too often absent can ruin the synergy of a coven.

HOLLY   Seekers need to have their lives in some reasonable sort of order. I don't mean to imply that they can't have problems like the rest of us, but people in the midst of crisis don't need the added burden of trying to put energy into coven work. They need to put it back into their own lives first.

MARGARIAN   Having their lives reasonably together in the mundane world. In the current economy, I wouldn't insist that people have meaningful full-time jobs, but they should at least be coping well with financial necessities, relationships, and little practical details like being where they said they would be, when they said they would.

WEYLAND   I like people with curiosity and intellect. I like people with a good vocabulary and a good sense of humor (especially including the ability to laugh at themselves). I like readers. I like people who are interested in the meaning of things and not just their outward form.

CAROL   I personally like people who ask a lot of questions about what we do and why we do it, people who are intellectually curious and not just interested in being spoon-fed.

KATHY   I look for thoughtful answers. A reasonable lack of chaos in their life. An understanding of cause and effect. Enthusiasm. A willingness to learn. I ask a lot of questions about the seekers' expectations and I try to be clear about how they match what we are able and willing to do.

RHEA   Look for: the bright, the silly, the creative. Look for people who want to give as much as they want to take (avoid
people who can't do both things). Look for people who have
the potential to teach you something fun you really want to
learn (how about ballroom dancing?). Note: This is not the
same as looking for someone to teach you deep psychological truths about yourself (for example, do not choose someone to teach you why you hate men).

And I'll add a few thoughts of my own. For Proteus, I want
people who love the Earth and who put that love into action.
I want bright, talented, creative people who are free-thinking
and free-spirited, and yet understand that human life is sustained by community just as humankind is sustained by the interconnected web of life on Earth. I want people who will not
perpetrate—or tolerate—"dominator" behavior. I want people
who walk their talk, who actively seek lifeways congruent with
their values. For Proteus, which is my heart, I want ethical,
dedicated Witches in continuous training, and nothing less.

Screening—How to Look

These are a few suggestions about the process of screening.
Most would apply to either the gathering of a new group or
considering new members for one that's ongoing.

- Don't put your home address or phone number into any
  kind of public advertisement. There are still too many people out there who don't understand that Witchcraft is religion. Some are looking for thrills or for manipulative
  magical powers. Others are looking to harass you into con-
  version to their religion. You don't deserve either of these
  problems.

- Ask seekers to write a letter of self-introduction. Tell them
  to include a bit about their background, and much more
  about their hopes and expectations. Ask for permission to
  share this letter with other coven leaders. Then if they seem

like good people but a poor match, you may be able to refer them elsewhere. If you judge them on spelling, grammar, or handwriting, you may be depriving yourself of some excellent coveners.

- To screen for dedication, include some demanding, but universally beneficial, task. We use an environmental awareness questionnaire that requires some library research of most people. Even if they never enter the Craft, it's good for anyone to know how nature works in their region.

- If you decide to meet with them, have your first meeting in a restaurant or other public space.

- Before taking them into your group, make your requirements clear. This is basic fairness. If you're in an area where this is possible, ask them to visit and interview with two or more other groups before making a choice. Suggest that they read the advice for seekers in chapter 3 of this book.

- If you are screening new members for a group that already exists, I strongly recommend an additional interview with the full group, so the candidate can meet as many of your present members as possible. Questions in both directions are appropriate, whether the interview is with the group or just with the leaders.

A Bittersweet Transition

You feel ready, even eager, to start your own Circle. You have either gathered a group of people you want to work with, or determined what kind of people you're looking for and put out the word. You and your people are about to begin the process of braiding a collection of individuals into a true coven. (For a detailed description of this process, see chapter 2.)

While the group works through the formative stages, the coven leaders face one more personal challenge. You need to redefine your relationship with your own elders from that of a student to that of a junior colleague. This is a task faced by new graduates and young workers in every profession, and one that always requires tact, assertiveness, patience and humor.

Models become widely accepted when they encapsulate and reflect a lot of people's experience. Again, there is a widespread model here to help you understand what you are going through. These are the stages of transition:

1. *Dependency:* The elder teaches basic and intermediate topics, sets safe limits, and gives a great deal of guidance. This is roughly comparable to the old craft guild status of Apprentice.

2. *Differentiation:* The student pursues advanced topics and follows personal interests, learning from many elders. Students test their personal limits of talent and skill (and also sometimes test the limits of safety and ethics—this is adolescent rebellion). The elder facilitates differentiation by giving the student increasing responsibility and much less specific direction. However, the elder is still actively watching over the student, and still volunteers direction and correction when necessary. This is comparable to the old status of Journeyman.

3. *Autonomy:* The student is self-directed and under no one's protection. The elder gives advice only upon the former student's request. The elder's advice is not binding. The student is now a Master, and entitled to begin teaching others.

Sometimes elders, enmired by their own control and codependency issues, are unwilling to let go. In other cases advanced students who are hesitant to take on the responsibilities of leadership project their own reluctance onto their elders. This is another occasion for the same advice I've been giving all through this book: Talk openly and honestly with each other and use the Witch's toolbox (meditation, divination, and dreamwork) to seek your own inner wisdom and the leadings of the Old Gods. Remember that everything that lives changes, including this cherished relationship.

For every action there is an equal and opposite reaction. In many of the lineage-based traditions, an elder who has taken someone through the complete training process to the point where he is now leading a coven is given the rank of Queen or Magus. The vocabulary is overblown—Grandparent would be both warmer and more accurate—but the underlying psychological principle is very sound.

It's a loss as well as a thrill every time a fledgling leaves the nest. Both of you will miss the other. Although you were often irritated with each other as you struggled through the differentiation phase, your deep bonds of love and trust are all you see as you approach separation. Allow yourself to feel your sense of loss, like people crying at a wedding. It's just as real as your elation. The buckle on the garter is the elder's compensation for loss, reframing our grief into the deep satisfaction of a job well done.

Hiving off is a major life transition. I strongly recommend that it be ritually marked with a coven blessing. If this is also the first hive from this elder, a promotion ritual for the elder is equally in order. You can combine these rituals, but be careful to give full attention to both statements. Invite the extended family, especially all of those who are elder to your elder, and make it a great big feast!

Graduates: As you hive from your elders remember that you came to them in trust; now leave them in love.

Elders: As they hive remember that you brought them in in love; now let them go in trust.

Continuity

So here you are, in a candlelit room with a carefully collected bunch of newly introduced strangers. You also have the knowledge, passion, wisdom, and skill you've developed through the years of your own training. You have the hopes and dreams that rose within you and the plans that you created as the time for hiving approached. You have the curiosity and enthusiasm of the new beginners who have come to you.

You're probably apprehensive. Do you really know enough about Wicca to teach it to others? Can you do right by these trusting people?

You have available to you the same Source that was available to your own elders, and to Hypatia and to Emperor Julian the Faithkeeper, and to Gerald Gardner. You have the guidance of the Ancient Gods, the small voice that sings within you and through all the Earth. Listen to it! Use it! Bright blessings on your path!

Some Group Bonding Exercises:

1. THE GODDESS IS ALIVE

Start by clapping or using small percussion instruments to establish a strongly accented but fairly slow "one-two" rhythm. Have the group repeat, "The Goddess is alive; magic is afoot," as a spoken chant, softly at first, then louder, but not faster. As the energy builds the first person will call out her own name instead of "the Goddess"—for instance, "Judy is alive." The whole group completes the sentence, "and magic is afoot." Next they repeat and affirm the whole sentence, "Judy is alive; magic is afoot." Then the next person, clockwise, does the same. When all members have called out their own names and received affirmation from the group, change it to the group's name: "Proteus is alive; magic is afoot." Let this build to a peak and release.

2. SINGING THE NAMES

Have each group member take a turn in the center as the group sings or chants his name, free-form. End with singing your coven's name.

3. GROUP PRAISE

Have each member take a turn in the center. Take a moment for silent contemplation. Encourage people to say what they appreciate about this person and her participation in the group.

Another possibility is for people to say what they associate with this person: flowers, animals, foods, colors, whatever.

12

Ṫḣe Ṅvṙċvṙaṅċ Ṁaċṙix

THE COVEN'S EXTERNAL SUPPORT SYSTEMS

Although my elders taught me as much as they knew, I still found myself stuck for answers when I at last had my own coven. Some of the answers we found for ourselves, in coven. Many more answers came from conversations with other coven leaders. Craft books, magazines, and gatherings helped, too. I am grateful for all of these support systems, which I suspect were nonexistent even sixty years ago. The Gods have given us a truly marvelous gift.

—BRIGANTIA

A healthy body has several different circulatory systems: vascular, lymphatic, nervous, and so on. They deliver nutrients and information to the cells, and remove wastes. Without these systems the body could not have developed its marvelously complex array of organs and organ systems. Without these systems the individual cells would stagnate, choke, and starve.

Just so with us. During the centuries of repression local groups of Pagan worshipers were brutally persecuted. Most were destroyed, some may have survived. But because of the need to hide, we lost our circulatory systems. Long-distance communication and transportation were more difficult for everybody in those times, and the links were far more fragile. Surviving groups, thus isolated, became stagnant. Our ways died back to their living roots: perhaps a very few, very isolated faithkeeping families, some folk customs carried on without memory of their original meaning, and the ever-present, ever-living Mother Earth, patiently waiting for us to notice Her.

In hindsight it's no surprise that with the advent of railroads, modern postal service, typewriters, the earliest telephones, and automobiles, new shoots sprang up around the apparently dead stumps of European Paganism. As communication became easier for all people, we could begin again to share our knowledge, to build on each other's work, to recover and reconstruct our ancient sacred ways.

We still face discrimination in employment, housing, and—most heart-wrenching of all—in child-custody situations. As I write this chapter I am aware of three different blatantly discriminatory actions being contested in different areas of the United States. Very probably there are more that I have not heard about. Still, we are much safer than we were. In Britain the Witchcraft Act was repealed in 1951, ending legal persecution. In the United States we have established legal precedents recognizing us as a religion, and gained significant recognition in the interfaith movement. As our need to hide fades it's much easier for us to keep in touch with each other, and even to share perceptions and skills with open-minded neighbors.

Throughout the twentieth century, as both communications technology and a more open cultural climate have allowed it, we have been regenerating our precious circulatory system. It's a work in progress, of course. So is our religion itself. Every living thing is in continuous change, but I mean something more than this. Contemporary Witchcraft, in all its aspects, is young and growing *fast*. We probably have yet to reach our adolescent growth spurt as a religious culture and community. Let's take stock of what we've done so far and what still needs to be done.

What We Have

Lineages and Traditions

Lineage-based covens have access to a body of material created by their predecessors. This material is of varying quality, written with varying levels of scholarship or poetic ability and under varying levels of inspiration. Some of us have unfortunately carried over the fundamentalist habit of treating this material as sacred scripture, to be read literally and held invariant. It's a heritage to be treated with respect and affection, but not enshrined or reified.

More important are our elders. We still have among us people who were present when critical collective decisions were made. They are the culture bearers, the living record of our memories, but their time is passing. Those who have the honor of caring for our aging first and second generations should gather these memories on tape or in any other way possible.

Our own teachers, although their experience is not first-hand in the same way, also carry a great deal of oral tradition, plus what they have learned in their longer experience with the Craft. Hang out with them as much as you can.

If yours is a self-generated coven, think about adopting some "foster elders." It's good to have the benefit of somebody else's experience. Choose one or more long-term coven leaders whom you particularly admire and ask them if they would be willing to serve as resource people for you and your group.

Your elders, whether you found them when you started studying Witchcraft or adopted them well after your own coven began, are exactly that: resource people. Consider their advice carefully, for they have learned by making mistakes that they can help you avoid. Still, all decisions are yours, and you are the ones who will live with the outcomes of these decisions.

Informal Elder Networking and Coven Leaders' Support Groups

MARGARIAN   Those of our local people who travel a lot and do
live networking in other cities are our biggest source of fresh
ideas and skills. I seem to have become one of those travel-
ing networkers; one of my nicknames is "Our Lady of the
Highway." There are two or three others who have substan-
tial out-of-town connections. Some of us [from the Midwest]
travel to festivals and workshops on the West Coast; one of
our elders commutes regularly to the East Coast. Occasionally
someone moves here from another city, or one of our people
moves away but stays in touch.

HARAGANO   It's very important that a group's elders circulate in
the community. The more they move about, travel, read,
discuss, et cetera, the more gets back to the group. Freshness
gets enfolded into the training. The more the elders keep
their own minds alive, in short, the less likely it is that they
will fossilize. This is most important with a traditional group.
I have noticed that when an elder's circle of connection con-
tracts, dogmatism takes an upswing.

We keep this circle of connection open by all the ordinary
kinds of social contacts with friends who are coven leaders.

In addition, there are coven leaders' support groups in some
places. These groups meet regularly to discuss coven issues, all
the kinds of things covered in this book. Some groups are composed of members of a single Tradition, which allows them to
discuss oathbound ritual materials as well. Others prefer a
broader perspective. As with single- or mixed-gender covens,
this is a matter of personal preference.

We learned two things in the New York–area leaders' group:
First, pick a topic in advance. If someone comes in with an
emergent issue, you can always defer the topic. But if nobody
had a problem this month—and that happened about a quarter of the time—you'll have the planned topic as a fallback.

Second, a designated moderator or facilitator can help the group maintain focus.

Local Organizations or Councils

As places to meet, greet, celebrate together, share news and gossip, sponsor open rituals or workshops, and introduce seekers to coven leaders, these groups are indispensable. If you don't have one in your area, start one.

MARGARIAN Our local networking organization is our primary source of local connections and cross-pollination. It includes people from a number of different Traditions and backgrounds, talking to one another and doing ritual together. Also, a women's circle that's part of it, that I'm in, has Priestesses from several of the covens in town. In addition to being a good circle, it's also a good place to network and to learn from one another's rituals.

KATHY What helps most are the public festivals and rituals. It gives us all an opportunity to see other people work on an occasional basis and also allows us opportunities to work with other people on short-term projects. I have found that I learn a lot from these situations. I get to talk to people in an informal situation.

National or International Organizations

Organizations like Covenant of the Goddess or the Pagan Federation are also indispensable, but for different reasons. Their size, geographic spread, and longevity (CoG, for example, was incorporated in 1975) make them best able to defend our right to practice our religion. They also engage in extensive and effective public information and education activities. It's important that the media know where to find articulate Witches who are willing to make public statements.

Don't take them for more than they are, though, or your heart may be broken. Their effectiveness comes at the cost of intimacy. Strong individual friendships can grow out of working together in large organizations, but mainly they are groupings of cooperating strangers. Members live too far apart and see each other too rarely for all to bond deeply. The level of love and trust that is normal in a coven is simply not feasible at an annual corporate meeting. Instead, there are factions, lobbying, backroom dealing, politics as usual, if anything made more painful by the concealing mask of consensus process.

And these are the ones that are fairly run. Before you join any national organization, investigate. Some will attempt to dictate the internal practices of your coven, or tell you how to perform initiations. Others are set up so that their founders are designated officers-for-life and extract their livelihoods from the dues of members—who cannot vote them out of office. Read the fine print, and watch out for scams.

Publications

At any given time there are hundreds of Wiccan and Pagan magazines and newsletters. They come and go quickly, so I'm not going to name any of them. Ask around, get sample copies, and see what you like. The good ones provide a valuable flow of thought, insight, recipes, rituals, songs and even parodies. Some are Tradition-specific, for the exploration of oathbound material. Some are locally oriented, and feature a local events calendar. Others share information across localities, which helps build the broader culture.

Festivals

MAGENTA   With festivals, we not only have gotten ideas, specific chants, ritual tropes. We have gotten the sense that Paganism is more than just us, that there are a whole lot of us creating this, and that it is an ongoing process that is worthwhile. We have had the chance to perform rituals that we can't do at home, whether it is because it won't fit in someone's house or backyard, or because we can't get enough people, or whatever the reason. Just being at a festival with several hundred other Pagans is incredibly revitalizing.

The Internet

The Internet makes networking easier in many different ways. Most are well known—E-mail, listservs, newsgroups, and home pages. One caution: The openness of the medium is both its glory and its peril—there's a lot of nonsense floating around out there. Here, on the other hand, is a report from the green, growing edge:

CAROL   The online coven has given many solitaries who discovered the Craft through books a chance to have in-depth conversations with others of a like mind who may live thousands of miles away. It has pulled them into a community of Pagans, given them a chance for a coven experience that might not otherwise be possible for them.

I have been working in depth for the past year with one person who came online to describe an experience that she'd been having, an experience that was leading her to think she was going crazy. She knew nothing of Paganism or psychic phenomena; I had to start from the most basic of information.

We began to see her experience as a spontaneous shamanic development. She has been reading voraciously, asking superb questions, and recently traveled several hundred miles to attend her first Pagan conference. When I asked her how it went, she responded, "If you had told me I needed people a year ago, I would have laughed at you. But now I realize how much I need the sort of people who can understand me."

She has come home to the place she never knew she was longing for, and her progress has been one of the most satisfying processes I've been privileged to midwife as a Priestess. She lives on another continent from me, though it turns out we grew up within twenty miles of each other.

The chemistry has been just right between us, a fit that would be so difficult to duplicate in the rural areas where we both live.

Nothing in this woman's usual lifestyle or social circles would have led her to Pagans otherwise, but having an on-line coven where she could explore new ideas in a supportive environment gave her the opportunity to blossom.

What We Still Need

More Ways to Share Advanced Knowledge

KATHY   The one thing I sometimes wish we had more of was a way to train for basic skills in the larger community. While there are a number of things that work well teaching in coven, there are also a number of things that can be just as well learned from a specialist in that area. In the areas where I am weak (astrology, kabbalah), I prefer to send people to someone who has a much better grasp of the material than I have.

Institutional Support Throughout the Life Cycle

Religious education for our children, senior citizens' residences, burial societies and cemeteries—as Pagan demographics normalize, we need just what anyone needs. It's good to see the Pagan student groups proliferating on major campuses, but we need to see that they have appropriate adult advisors as well.

Pagan Yellow Pages

It would help to have knowledge of one another's secular trades and professions.

MAGENTA   I wish we had a lot more practical stuff in place. Where can I find a Pagan therapist, or at least a Pagan-friendly one? (I hesitate to do counseling because I am not trained, and don't know anyone who *is*.) A Pagan doctor or dentist? A Pagan electrician or plumber? The first is obvious, but how do I explain to a doctor that I will use magic to heal myself? I would really like to have Pagans, or at least people who know about it, if I need anything done in the house, so I don't have to put everything away.

Next Steps

If you want to join a coven:

- Do whatever you can to prepare yourself.
- Understand your local ecology and spend time in nature.
- Develop a means of creative self-expression.
- Meditate and keep a journal.

The first time you see a tree or other growing plant each morning, salute and greet Mother Earth. The first time you see the Moon each night, salute and greet Her. Participate in your local Pagan community. Help with the work as much as you can. Get to know people. When considering a group, ask if you want to become more like the members. When considering a teacher, ask if you want to become more like this person.

If you want to form a coven, ask yourself:

- Do we have a group of people who are committed to exploring the Old Ways and to supporting each other in this exploration?
- What are our mutual goals?
- Do we have the skills we need to begin?
- Do we have a plan for continuing to learn and grow?
- For those within a Tradition or lineage: Are we qualified by our own Tradition's standards to pass on our Tradition?
- For self-generated groups: Are there elders we respect and admire who are willing to serve as advisors to us?

Help Wanted

We don't proselytize. As long as people treat each other and the Earth kindly, it doesn't matter whether or not they practice any religion, let alone ours. Those who are religiously inclined should worship in whatever way nurtures their spirit. Even within the neo-Pagan community, Witches do not recruit. The call to become a Priest/ess must come from within you, for I guarantee that nobody from your local coven is going to ring your doorbell or accost you on a street corner.

But this much should be obvious: We can offer you an extraordinary outlet for your energy and creativity. All that we already have needs maintenance and improvement, and there are many good support systems that we don't yet have. The work of the Witches can and should make a real difference to the Gods, the People, and the Earth.

13

And Yet It Moves

WHY US? WHY NOW?

W hy, after nearly two millennia of brutal suppression and long after most people believed they were dead and gone, are the Old Gods and the Old Ways now coming so rapidly and so exuberantly back to life? Why now? Why us? This is what my heart tells me: All of us face a quiet but very dire threat right now which requires that we join together to awaken the land spirits of all the earth. We need Earth religion and Earth clergy right now. Here's why:

There is a sort of conversation going on in our culture among religions, with everyone else listening in. This ongoing religious conversation gives society an important part of its guidance, its values. All the well-known religions have a place at the table, and some of the newer ones are gradually beginning to gain places as well.

Some of the voices at the table argue for repressive and retrogressive actions. A few even call for the establishment of a theocracy in our land. Others, like the much-mourned Martin Luther King Jr., sound a more gracious note. But the conversation is still incomplete. Perhaps there are many voices, many views still left out. The omission that appalls and terrifies me is this: Who at this table speaks for Mother Earth?

Religion connects the Sacred with our everyday behavior in many different ways. Since at least the time of the great biblical prophets one way has been to offer correction, to "speak truth to power." So through centuries of history, religion has been the cry of the oppressed, the soul of a soulless situation, the heart of a heartless world. This has not changed, nor should it. What has changed is the terrifying scope of the present crisis. Not genocide, but total ecocide threatens us now.

Modern industrial society, having lost its heart and soul, now turns to devour its own body. Blind, psychotic greed, directed against the Earth Herself, throws Her into a life-threatening crisis. She needs Her guardians, advocates, companions, and healers. She needs us right now. She calls us to Her. Because all our lives depend on Hers, this need must be met. We must learn what we forgot: to see Her once again as a sacred living thing. We must share this knowledge with others, not to change the way anyone worships, but to change the way we all live.

My name is Judy Harrow. I am a Witch. I am a Witch. I am a Witch.

To Learn More

Look for Ronald Hutton's forthcoming book, *Triumph of the Moon: A History of Modern Pagan Witchcraft*. This is expected from Oxford University Press in 2000.

Meanwhile

Ashcroft-Nowicki, Dolores, ed. *The Forgotten Mage: The Magical Lectures of Colonel C. R. F. Seymour*. Wellingborough, Northamptonshire, U.K.: Aquarian, 1986.
Russell, Jeffrey B. *A History of Witchcraft: Sorcerers, Heretics, and Pagans*. New York: Thames & Hudson, 1980.
Valiente, Doreen. *The Rebirth of Witchcraft*. London: Hale, 1989.
And the writings of Gerald Gardner and Margaret Murray.

Appendix A

GLOSSARY

People who share a common interest tend to develop a specialized vocabulary to help them communicate fine points of technical knowledge. Often this includes ordinary words that have been redefined to be more useful for the purpose. Just so, these definitions are not always what you'd find in a dictionary. They do reflect the way these words are used in this book.

authority   the many ways in which power within a community may be granted, legitimated, or validated.

avocation   an activity we do for enjoyment, in addition to our regular work; a hobby.

base community   a small group of Christians who convene for worship and Bible study, comparable to a coven.

behavioral learning   learning to do particular things or to act in particular ways; skills training.

centering   concentration, inner focus; becoming aware of our own boundaries and of our deep selves.

chavurah   Hebrew for "group of companions"; now generally refers to a small group of Jews who worship together, comparable to a coven.

Circle   a Wiccan religious ritual, in the same sense that Mass is the name for a Catholic religious ritual. Also, the consecrated space in which a Wiccan religious ritual is held. Most Witches do not have permanent worship space. Instead we "cast Circle," which means consecrate the space immediately before use, then return it to normal use when we are finished. The process of casting and closing Circle is also our way of making the appropriate shifts in consciousness and focus to prepare ourselves for ritual participation.

codependency a fixation on solving other people's problems, thus both enabling their self-destructive behavior to continue and ignoring our own problems and opportunities. Usually arises from an excessive need to be needed.

cognitive learning learning to understand or explain certain things; education.

confrontation informing other people when we perceive their behavior to be inconsistent with their stated values or goals, self-defeating, or obstructive to the group's work. By letting them know how others see them, we increase their ability to choose.

congruence consistency between beliefs and behavior; integrity. Congruent people may be described as walking their talk or practicing what they preach.

cosmology study of the history, structure, and constituent dynamics of the universe. Speculation about the beginning of time or of the world.

covert leadership leadership that is not acknowledged, and therefore cannot be confronted if it becomes excessive, tyrannical, or corrupt.

counter-transference a process by which the group leader uses the group to work out issues that arose elsewhere, and usually in the past.

Craft proficiency, skill, technique. The word means exactly the same when used as the second syllable of *Witchcraft*.

daughter coven indicates a lineage relationship between covens. The leaders of the daughter coven were trained in the mother coven.

deep self the unconscious mind; tacitly held understandings, perceptions, and values that form the unacknowledged basis for current thought and behavior.

divination reaching into the personal and collective unconscious, and perhaps accessing the wisdom of the Gods, to gain insight into present trends and extrapolate where they might lead. May use a wide variety of methods such as Tarot, Runes, or I Ching.

dreamwork the process of remembering and interpreting dreams in order to gain insight.

dualism the understanding that the world is driven by two competing forces, usually understood as good and evil.

dual-role relationship a relationship in which people interact in two or more different ways that may create conflicting expectations. A secular example would be when the same person is both your employer and your lover. In covens the most common dual-role relationship is when the same person serves as both mentor and evaluator.

egregore the group mind of a coven, lineage, or Tradition, or of Wicca as a whole. Initiation is perceived as giving a new member access to the group's egregore.

elder "someone who started sooner." In traditional Witchcraft the term *elders* most commonly describes people who are qualified by the standards of their own Tradition to lead a coven, and to train and initiate new members of this Tradition.

elevation in Traditions using degree systems, the ritual by which a member is initiated into a more advanced degree.

empathy the ability to share another person's perceptual field and emotional responses. Translated from the German *einfuhlung*, as used by Sigmund Freud. The original word means "feeling in" to the lifespace of the other, an activity rather than a quality.

energy the power that Witches raise and direct toward a goal, which manifests as emotional and physiological arousal. Other cultures have specific terms, such as *mana*, *orenda*, or *prana*, which are less misleading than the electrical metaphor that we commonly use.

Esbat a coven's regular meetings for learning and working. Normally held on or close to the Full Moon and limited to coven members.

eschatology speculation about the end of time or of the world.

feedback information received from trusted friends about how well we are communicating, how well we appear to be functioning, how we are affecting them, and the like. Confrontation is one kind of feedback.

Gardner, Gerald B. (1884–1964) retired British civil servant and amateur anthropologist, commonly believed to be the founder of contemporary neo-Pagan Witchcraft.

generativity influence on the next generation, whether this means our children, our students, or our junior colleagues. Through them, there is some chance to shape the future. In the life-stages theory of psychologist Erik Erikson, this is the focal issue of our mature adulthood.

geocentric   Earth-centered. The term refers to training, thinking, and behavior congruent with Earth religion, such as neo-Paganism and Wicca.

grounding   1) Connecting with the Earth. One good way to do this is by actively imagining a taproot extending down from the base of your spine through the soil, bedrock, water table, et cetera. 2) Allowing energy and inspiration to manifest in behavior. "We ground our faith in service."

groupthink   unhealthy enmeshment; group delusion typically compounded by hostile defensiveness; a tendency to stereotype outsiders and blame them for all the group's problems; Procrustean pressure on members to conform in belief as well as behavior.

grove   a training group in which people prepare for Wiccan initiation. Sometimes called an "outer court."

growth group   a group whose members support each other as they work toward self-development and self-actualization.

hierarchy   literally "sacred order," a command and control system whereby some people have authority over the spiritual exploration and development of others. Military and corporate pyramidal structures are secular parallels to religious hierarchies. Hierarchies dictate how members shall think and act. In extreme cases authoritarian religious leaders can claim to be gatekeepers between worshipers and Deity. The familial relationship of a lineage is structurally similar, and so looks the same when drawn on paper. The difference is in the nature of the linkages—love and respect instead of command and control.

High Priestess's disease   a pathological condition in which coven leaders fall into the delusion that they are holier than the others and can mediate between them and the Gods. Although most coven leaders are women, similarly situated men are equally at risk.

hiving off   in a lineage-based Tradition this is when a qualified High Priestess leaves the coven in which she was trained to form one of her own, usually a joyous occasion.

immanence   the theological theory that sacred meaning and value are to be found within the manifest world, within ourselves and one another.

inner court a group of Wiccan initiates; a coven.

initiation a ritual by which a person is brought into the priesthood of the Old Gods and into membership in a coven and a Tradition.

inner plane the personal unconscious, the collective unconscious, and perhaps the Otherworld, which is the realm of the Gods. In the theology of immanence, the Otherworld includes, but is not limited to, the personal and collective unconscious.

lineage a system of relationships among covens based on descent (that is, where the coven leader was trained).

magic 1) The art of changing consciousness in accordance with will. 2) The art of causing change in accordance with will.

meditation a variety of methods for stilling the mind, calming surface distractions, and focusing on inner wisdom.

metaphor one thing conceived as representing another; a symbol.

model 1) Model *of*: a schematic description of an object, relationship, or theory that accounts for its known or inferred properties and may be used for further study of its characteristics. 2) Model *for*: an example to be imitated or compared. So religion offers both a model *of* the Sacred and a model *for* living congruently with our values, connecting belief and behavior.

mother coven indicates a lineage relationship between covens. The mother coven is where the daughter coven's leaders were trained.

mystery something that cannot be fully explained in words, but must be grasped by direct experience. When capitalized, *Mystery* refers specifically to the experience of Sacred Presence, but it can also mean baking bread, listening to music, making love . . . any experience that is beyond verbal description.

myth a story that conveys the values of a culture or sub-culture, or offers a model for appropriate behavior. Myths need not be literally true; they carry meaning, not fact.

norm a standard of behavior or achievement expected of people.

oathbound lore that is restricted by oath to members of a particular group, usually a Wiccan Tradition.

Otherworld the realm of the Gods, the Dreaming, the place where the great myths happened or are continuously happening.

outer court a training group in which people prepare for Wiccan initiation. Sometimes called a "grove."

Pagan follower of a polytheistic, Earth-centered, shamanic religion.

placebo originally an inert substance given to patients in place of medication, such as sugar pills. When it was noticed that people given placebos actually did improve, the term *placebo effect* came to denote the power of expectation and the importance of attitude in healing.

polarity   used in Witchcraft to denote two principles that are both desirable, but that are understood as being opposite or reciprocal to one another. Polarities are the source of the dynamic tension that empower much of our work. Unfortunately, sometimes oversimplified as gender differences.

Procrustean   in Greek myth Procrustes stretches or shortens captives to force them to fit into his iron bed. *Procrustean* thus means whatever ruthlessly enforces conformity—for example, trying to force our experience to fit our symbolic models instead of fine-tuning our models to more accurately reflect lived experience.

psychospiritual   an adjective used to communicate the close relationship between psychological and spiritual functioning.

Rede   an archaic, Middle English term meaning "advice" or "counsel." The "Wiccan Rede" is the core ethic of Witchcraft:

> Eight words the Wiccan Rede fulfill
> An it harm none, do what ye will.

reify   to mentally convert an idea or concept into a thing. Treating our metaphors, models, and symbols as though they were objective facts is one of the most important symptoms of fundamentalism.

religion   from the Latin *ligere*, which means "to connect," activities intended to create, maintain, and strengthen the connection between spiritual experience and everyday life. A more succinct and very traditional way of saying this is, "As within, so without." Religion has also come to mean organized, institutional support for such activities and for spiritual and ethical development in general.

Another useful definition of *religion* comes from the writing of anthropologist Clifford Geertz: "A religion is a system of symbols, which acts to establish powerful, pervasive, and long-lasting moods and motivations by formulating conceptions of a general order of existence, and clothing these conceptions with such an aura of factuality that the moods and motivations seem uniquely realistic." Reading Geertz's essay "Religion as a Cultural System" is slow going, but extremely worth the work.

ritual   religious performance; enactment of the myths and symbols that convey and reinforce the core values of our community, and our understanding of and relationship with our Gods.

role model   someone we would like to emulate.

Sabbats   the eight neo-Pagan seasonal festivals at the Quarters and cross-Quarters of the year.

scrying   gazing at an object or surface using a relaxed, meditative, "soft-eyed" gaze, and observing whatever images may form. Scryers may use the stereotypical crystal ball, but many other, less expensive, objects work just as well: a black mirror, a bowl of water, the clouds.

seeker   a person who is seeking a spiritual path but not yet ready to commit to Witchcraft. A person who wants to begin serious study of Witchcraft and is seeking a coven or teacher.

Shadow   a metaphor for all of the things we do not want to know or understand about ourselves. The Shadow is often perceived as the guardian at the gateway of any spiritual growth path.

shaman   one who trances, dreams, or otherwise explores the Otherworld on behalf of the tribe or community; a "technician of the Sacred."

spirituality   conscious contact with the Sacred; activities intended to create, maintain, clarify, deepen, or increase such contact.

support group   a group whose members support each other as they work through difficult issues in their lives. It can be specific, as in a widows' support group or a twelve-step group.

symbol   something that carries associations or connotations of something else, often something invisible; a token; a visible or tangible metaphor. Symbols are usually complex and multivocal.

talisman   a physical object intentionally created as a symbol of a goal, or of energies we wish to have present in our lives.

task group   a group that comes together to work on a project; a committee or team.

thealogy   pronounced the same as *theology*, but this spelling emphasizes the Goddess. Thealogy is reflection on or discourse about the Goddess in specific.

theodicy   theological consideration of the "problem of evil"; questions about how a Deity understood to be both good and omnipotent could allow evil to exist in the world. This question does not arise in a polytheistic frame.

toolbox, the Witch's the skills and techniques associated with Witchcraft.

Tradition any one of the major subdivisions of Witchcraft, comparable to a Christian religious order.

trance an altered state of consciousness in which distraction is minimized and focus is greatly heightened. Trances can vary greatly in intensity and in level of arousal. Different types of trances are useful for different purposes.

transcendence a theology that conceives the Sacred to be Wholly Other, entirely separate from the manifest world.

Appendix B

Τhε Charge of Τhε Goddess

(As Adapted for Proteus Coven)

Listen to the words of the Great Mother who was, of old, also called among you Artemis, Astarte, Dione, Melusine, Aphrodite, Cerridwen, Diana, Bride, and by many other names. [Add or substitute names freely.]

Whenever you have need of anything, once in the month—and better it be when the Moon is full—when you shall assemble in some secret place and adore the spirit of me, who am Queen of all the witcheries.

There you shall assemble, you who fain would learn all sorcery, who have not yet won its deepest secrets, to these will I teach that which is yet unknown.

And you shall be free from slavery, and as a sign that you be truly free you shall be naked in your rites. And you shall dance, sing, feast, make music and love, all in my presence.

For mine is the ecstasy of the spirit, and mine is also joy on Earth, for my law is *love unto all beings*.

Keep pure your highest ideals. Strive ever toward them. Let none stop you or turn you aside.

For mine is the knowledge that opens the door of youth, and mine is the cup of the wine of life; and the Cauldron of Cerridwen, which is the Holy Grail of immortality.

I am the gracious Goddess, who gives joy to the human heart.

Upon Earth I give knowledge of the spirit eternal, and beyond death I give peace and freedom; and reunion with those who have gone before. Nor do I demand aught in sacrifice, for behold, *I am the Mother of all things*, and my love is poured out upon the Earth.

I am the beauty of the green Earth, and the white moon among the stars, and the mystery of the waters, and the desire of the human heart. I call to your soul, "Arise, and come unto me," for I am the soul of Nature who gives life to the universe.

From me all things proceed and unto me all things must return. Beloved in all the Worlds, your inmost divine self shall be enfolded in the raptures of the infinite.

Let my worship be in the heart that rejoices, for behold, *all acts of love and pleasure are my rituals*, and therefore let there be beauty and strength, power and compassion, honor and humility, mirth and reverence, within you.

And you who think to seek me, know that your seeking and yearning will not avail you unless you know the mystery. That if you do not find what you seek within you, you will never find it without. For behold, I have been with you since the beginning, and I shall be with you until the end of days.

Index

Alexei, 6, 47, 49, 52, 217, 220, 248
Alice, 43, 49, 52, 249, 252
Anne, 231

Baby blessing ritual, 79
Banishment, 28–29
Bear, 225
Beginning study (ritual), 167
Behavioral psychology, 162–164
Birthing a coven (ritual), 18
Blessing a partnership (ritual), 239–240
Bonewits, Isaac—Cult Danger Evaluation Frame, 54–59
Brainstorming, 184
Branch sculpture (ritual), 209
Brigantia, 31, 144, 203, 246, 259

Caitrin, 150–152
Carol, 4, 43, 196, 252, 253, 265
Children, 66–85
    child care, 71–76
    religious education, 80–82
Chuck, 46
Circle casting, 89, 239
Co-dependency, 206
Cognitive learning, stages, 158
Community, 6, 16, 24, 25, 29, 107, 259–268
Competencies, 141–142
    knowledge, 142, 147, 157–160
    perceptual, 142–143, 147
    skill, 142, 147, 160–161
Completing a project (ritual), 193
Confidentiality, 29, 37, 115–116
    limits of, 115–116

Conflict, 31–35, 172–176,
    180–181
  between partners, 211–213
  suppression of, 186–212
Confrontation, 126–128
Consecrating a project (ritual),
    190
Consensus
  shared leadership, 25–27
  inclusive decision making,
    185–188
Core group, 17, 20
Counter transference,
    205–207
Coven—word derivation, 3
Covert leadership, 21–22, 31
Covert norms, 35
Co-visioning, 238
Crowley, Vivianne, 133–134
Curriculum development,
    145–162

David, 139
Debbi, 66, 156, 172, 173, 177,
    178, 179, 182, 188, 189,
    191, 226
Deborah, 182, 192
Decision making, 185–188
  exercise, 123
Dedication ritual, 62–65
  discussion of, 21
Deference, zone of, 211–212
Degree system, 132–135, 145,
    161–162
  craft guilds stages, 161
Devyn, 47, 50, 226, 252
Divination, 33, 36, 94, 120,
    122, 179, 184, 213, 238,
    256

Dreamwork, 33, 36, 42, 94,
    120, 122, 179, 184, 213,
    256
Drop-in groups, 16
Duty to warn, 115–116

Ethics
  code, 104–107
  procedural norms, 36
  training, 149
Evening blessing (ritual), 104

Facilitation, 176–180
  basic developmental,
    177–178
  in growth/support groups,
    117
  in task groups, 179
Family of choice, 43, 44,
    196–209
Fantasy coven exercise, 59–61
Food blessing (ritual), 98
Four c's, 90–107
  creed (theology), 90–98
  cult (ritual), 98–103
  code (ethics), 104–107
  community, 107
Freud, Sigmund, 112

Gawaine, 45, 49, 52, 72, 74,
    148, 150, 152, 208, 217,
    220, 227, 229, 244, 249
Generativity, 193, 206
Geocentric training, 153–154
Goal setting
  personal, 118–119
  project, 183
  ritual for, 125
Grey Cat, 148–151

Group bonding exercises, 258
Groupthink, 174–175
Grove (outer court), 18, 20
Growth/support group, 19, 46,
   109–138
   facilitative skills for, 117
   self-disclosure in, 37
Guidance invocation (ritual),
   190

Haragano, 262
Hawk, 71, 72, 74, 76
Healing invocation (ritual),
   114
Hergest, 230
High priestess' disease, 30, 207,
   216
Hiving off, 18, 39–40, 244–258
   assessing readiness, 247
   redefining relationship,
      255–257
   screening, 254
Holly, 52, 148, 149, 150, 151,
   201, 217, 220, 228, 252,
   253

Immanence, 90–91, 164, 224
Initiations and elevations, 28,
   38, 82–82, 132–135
   self-initiation, 14, 133

Iontas, 46, 50, 52, 219, 220,
   252

Jehana, 148, 150, 182, 189,
   191, 193
Jim, 77, 151
Johari Window, 120
Hournal, 42, 146, 147, 160

Kathy, 42, 50, 149, 253, 263,
   266

Learning group, 19, 139–169
   cognitive developmental
      stages, 158
   competencies, 142
   curriculum development,
      145–157
   degrees of guild stages,
      161–162
   motivation (behaviorism),
      162–164
   teaching methods, 157–166
Lineage, 5, 13–14, 18, 35, 188,
   202, 222, 257, 261
   formal authority, 24–25

Magenta, 44, 53, 74, 76, 77,
   152, 227, 252, 264, 266
Magic
   and children, 81
   in curriculum, 150
   definition, 110
   directed to others, 136–137
   projective, 124
   receptive, 122
Margarian, 44, 50, 54, 144,
   149, 153, 218, 251, 252,
   253, 262, 263
Marjorie, 67
Maslow, Abraham, 193
   hierarchy of needs,
      112–113
Meditation, 33, 42, 120,
   122–123, 150, 151, 179,
   204, 213, 256
Mirror dance (exercise),
   238–239

Morning blessing (ritual), 100
Mutual gaze (exercise), 238

Needs, hierarchy (Maslow's),
    112–113
Norms, 34–38
    sources, 35–36
    types, 36–38

Occupational analysis, 146–147
Outer court (grove), 18, 20

Parliament of the World's
    Religions, 1993), 88
Partnership, 210–243
    becoming partners, 219–221
    blessing ritual, 239–240
    compatibility questions,
        237–238
    conflict in 211–213
    exercises for, 237–239
    and marriage, 225-234
    soul friends, 221–225
    work sharing, 213–217
Passage rituals, 129–131
Patrick, 45, 72, 74, 198, 220
Personal growth, 3, 4, 7, 9, 10,
    46, 109–138, 151
    necessary and sufficient
        conditions, 118–129
Polarity, 10–11, 93, 95, 219,
    220
Polytheism
    ethics, 106
    mythos, 91
    training, 145
Power, interpersonal
    in decision making, 187
    legitimation (authority),
        24–27

problems concerning, 30–34
    sources, 22-24
    "storming" phase, 21–34
    use of, 27–30
Power, magical
    directing to others, 136–137
    empowering projects, 190
    raising and storing, 124
Priest/ess role, analysis,
    146–147
Project sequence, 181–192

Quartered circle, 93–96
    decision making guide, 123
    evening blessing, 104
    morning blessing, 100
    partnership blessing, 239

Redmond, 230
Religion
    definition, 87
    aspect of coven life, 86–108
Rhea, 48, 50, 53, 54, 67, 71,
    73, 75, 134, 250, 254
Rhomylly, 50, 75, 149, 230
Ritual
    components of, 100–101
    definition, 99
    design criteria, 102
    of passage, 129–131
    post-ritual critique, 241–242
    teaching ritual design,
        148–149
Rogers, Carl 127
Role conflicts
    mentor/evaluator, 7–8,
        165–166
    in partnership, 220, 225
    in task group, 178–179
Ronald, 5, 8, 208

Self-dedication, 8, 41-42
     (ritual)
Self-generated coven, 14,
     16–17, 134
   emergent leadership in, 25
   ritual for birthing, 18
Self-initiation, 14, 133
Seminary-coven training,
     154–156
Seven trees exercise, 154
Shared inner journey exercise,
     242
Spirituality, 179
   definition, 87
   source of authority, 23
Stages of coven life, 14–40
Starspawn, 76
Susan, 42, 204, 208, 218, 250

Talking stick, 180, 182–183
Tarasoff, Tatiana, 115–116

Task groups, 19, 170–195
   facilitation, 176–179
Theos, 20 (w. Phoenix), 68, 73,
     80–82, 129, 197, 200
Therapy—growth/support,
     111–112
Training group, 139–169
   curriculum, 145–162
   teaching methods, 157–64
Transference, 200–205

Vesto, 53, 69–70, 205, 233,
     250

Weyland, 42, 50, 53, 250, 253
Wheel of the Year, 96–98,
     150
Wicca (definition and
     derivation), xii
Wiccan Rede, 34, 104–106, 116
Working partner, 31, 210–243